DEAN COURT DAYS

MICHAEL DUNNE

DEAN COURT DAYS

HARRY REDKNAPP

AT AFC BOURNEMOUTH

pitch

First published by Pitch Publishing, 2018

Pitch Publishing
A2 Yeoman Gate
Yeoman Way
Worthing
Sussex
BN13 3QZ
www.pitchpublishing.co.uk
info@pitchpublishing.co.uk

A CIP catalogue record is available for this book from the British Library.

ISBN 978-1-78531-384-4

Typesetting and origination by Pitch Publishing

Printed in India by Replika Press

Contents

DEDICATION

For my wife Claire, boys Owen and Ellis, and the eternal glory of the mighty Cherries

ACKNOWLEDGEMENTS

My first offering of thanks goes to Harry Redknapp himself. There have been several books by and about Harry in recent years, so he had no reason to want to cooperate with another one for no tangible reward. However, he welcomed me into his home and, a close encounter with his bulldog Bruce notwithstanding, gave freely with his time despite me testing the limits of his memory more than once.

Thanks to Stuart Morgan for putting me in contact with his long term colleague and friend and for his assistance with and interest in the writing of this book. I am also very grateful to former Bournemouth players and staff Dickie Dowsett, Ian Thompson, John Williams, Kevin Reeves, Milton Graham, Shaun Teale, Luther Blissett and the late John Harriss for making themselves available to discuss their years at Dean Court with Harry and overlooking my fanboy tendencies.

AFC Bournemouth's club secretary Neil Vacher and former Head of Media and Communications Max Fitzgerald were extremely helpful, particularly in the early and late stages of writing the book. Thanks should also be offered to the staff at Bournemouth Central Library for their tolerating my at times rapacious hogging of the microfilm reader.

Finally, I thank my family for their their love and support. My Dad, for reading my initial drafts chapter by chapter and ignoring almost all off my grammatical errors. Above all, to my beautiful wife Claire and two boys Ellis and Owen for reasons too numerous to mention, although the boys ought to be reciprocating this thanks as a result of my having gifted them a lifetime of Cherry tinted reverie.

Foreword

THE 15 years I spent at AFC Bournemouth as a player, coach and manager were amongst the happiest of my career in football. I first arrived in 1972 when my old friend John Bond was the manager and the club were on the up. Everything seemed set for promotion, but we never quite made it and when John left for Norwich things were never quite the same again. I enjoyed my playing days there, we had a great squad, but we never quite fulfilled our promise and persistent injuries limited my impact on the team in my final couple of seasons.

Despite the frustrations of those injuries, I loved every day I spent at Dean Court. My family loved the area as well. Coming from east London, we weren't used to living near the coast but it wasn't difficult to appreciate the benefits of bringing up our two boys near the seaside. That was why we kept our house in the area whilst I was playing in America. Thank goodness we did, because I was seriously considering a life outside of the game when we returned from the States for good, but the Bournemouth manager Dave Webb phoned me up out of the blue and asked me if I could help out with pre-season training as I was living just down the road. That was the start, and when Dave left and the club had no money to attract an experienced manager, they turned to me.

I didn't get off to the best of starts, and the 9-0 drubbing at Lincoln in my very first game in charge remains one of my low points in football. We improved as the weeks went on, but when the club was sold the new owners brought in Don Megson as manager and I returned to my role as coach. To be honest, I was grateful, as I was sure Don's arrival would see me out of the door.

When I finally got the manager's job on a permanent basis when Don left after just a few months in charge, I was a little more competent than the first time around. In my first season in charge we knocked Man United out of the FA Cup and won Bournemouth's first trophy since just after the Second World War. After that, it was all ups and downs as I fought to create a decent squad whilst all the while the club struggled to stay solvent. To say that was a good grounding for a career in football management would be an understatement, as every day brought different challenges both on and off the pitch, and I relished every moment of it.

There were some extreme highs and lows in my days as Bournemouth manager. Promotion to the second tier for the first time in the club's history when winning the Third Division title in 1987 was the highlight of my time at Dean Court, and still ranks among the best achievements of my career. Three years later, I was at my lowest ebb following relegation back to the old Third Division on that dreadful day we lost to Leeds, and the death of my great friend Brian Tiler following our terrible car accident in Italy a few weeks later.

Other events that stick out during those years are promotion from the Fourth Division with Dave Webb, George Best turning out at Dean Court to double the normal gate, Colin Clarke scoring at the World Cup for Northern Ireland as a Bournemouth player, the night we knocked Newcastle out of the FA Cup on penalties at St James' Park and my son Jamie making his full debut for the Cherries at my old club West Ham.

I left Bournemouth in 1992, but have always lived in the area and the Cherries are still very close to my heart. More than once I have been extremely concerned that the club was about to go to the wall, so to see it in such good health these days brings me as much joy as anything else in the game.

I am just glad I was able to play a small part in Bournemouth's history and am grateful that it is still remembered over a quarter of a century later.

Enjoy the book.

Harry Redknapp
December 2017, Sandbanks

Chapter One

Bright Lights to Pier Lights

1972/73

HARRY Redknapp had been a gifted footballer in his youth, a skilful and pacy winger whose signature was coveted by clubs across London. He played a key role in England's triumph in the 1964 UEFA European Under-19s Football Championship, playing alongside Howard Kendall and John Hollins in a 4-0 victory over Spain. Reflecting on the experience 50 years later, Kendall said:

'Harry Redknapp was a big personality even back then and was already upsetting people. Nothing has changed!'

Following four years in the Tottenham Hotspur youth team, Harry moved to West Ham United in 1962 at the age of 15. Over the next ten years at Upton Park, Redknapp became a popular member of the Hammers' squad, honing his trade at the feet of the famous academy led by manager Ron Greenwood and senior players like John Bond.

Redknapp had looked up to Bond from an early age. 'I first met him when I was ten years old,' recalls Redknapp. 'Every afternoon all the West Ham players would go to Cassettari's, the cafe next to the ground and talk football, moving salt and pepper pots around on the table, talking tactics and all that.

'I was standing outside, waiting. I had this team photograph from the Christmas party. In it, John Bond is holding a chicken leg and I wanted him to sign it. And he did. He was as good as gold with me and I just remember staring up at this big man. I then watched him walk home.'

Eventually Redknapp would get to train and play with Bond. 'One summer I think he'd fallen out with Ron Greenwood and he didn't go on the pre-season tour so he came and trained with the kids,' says Redknapp.

'I was about 16 and he was brilliant with us. He was a great player, a right-back. He could use a ball as well as anyone I've seen. He could see a pass to the striker, and he was a great striker of the ball, too. He could score goals and he had this arrogance about him.'

After finishing his playing career with a short spell at Torquay, Bond tried his hand coaching at Gillingham. It didn't last, and the now retired right-back found himself unemployed with a young family to support. Footballers' salaries were paltry compared to the million-pound contracts of the Premier League era, and even West Ham's World Cup-winning heroes Geoff Hurst and Martin Peters were forced to take run-of-the-mill jobs after hanging up their boots.

With Bond's fingers crossed in the hope that he would find another role in the professional game, Harry Redknapp stepped in to help his old friend out. 'Me and Frank Lampard senior used to do coaching in those days at Pretoria School in Canning Town,' he recalls. 'We got £2.50 a session and split the money. John was out of work so we shared our job with him. We did four afternoons a week and made our £20 between us go three ways. John came in because he was struggling.'

Bournemouth was little more than a footballing backwater at the time of Bond's unemployment, having never featured in either of the top two divisions of English football since their formation in 1899. A reputation for a pleasing style of play and rare forays into the latter stages of the cups caused no more than a ripple beyond the faithful that gathered within the leafy confines of King's Park on Saturday afternoons. After being relegated on goal average to the Fourth Division for the first time in the club's history, manager Freddie Cox, the architect of the side the press dubbed Cox's Pippins during Bournemouth's run to the quarter-finals of the FA Cup in 1957, was relieved of his duties in May 1970.

Along with the vacant manager's post, Bournemouth advertised for a new assistant manager, a role which was rarely at the time filled by the new manager's preferred choice.

'John kept applying for jobs,' recalls Redknapp. 'He applied for the coach's job at Bournemouth, not the manager. Cyril Lea, who was assistant to Bobby Robson at Ipswich, was going to get the manager's job, but he missed his train. John went in for the interview and Harold Walker, who was the chairman of Bournemouth, liked him so much he made him manager.'

A lifelong supporter of the Cherries, Walker had been a director since 1967 and succeeded to the chairman's office after a successful takeover bid in 1970. He wasted no time in making public his ambitions for the club, declaring that he saw the potential for Bournemouth to become 'the Newcastle of the South'.

With the flamboyant Bond on board and former striker Dickie Dowsett installed as commercial manager, the club made a concerted effort to shake off its low wattage reputation in the years immediately preceding Harry Redknapp's arrival.

For the 1970/71 season, the Cherries changed their colours from the red shirts and white shorts worn since before the Second World

War, to red and black stripes with black shorts, a combination which remains unique in English professional football. Bond is normally credited with being the architect of this change, the new colour scheme said to have been inspired by Italian aristocrats AC Milan, who had recently won their second European Cup. This reaching out for reflected glory is unlikely to have had much impact upon results, although the club were promoted to the Third Division in the new kit's first season on the back of Scottish striker Ted MacDougall's remarkable 42-goal haul from 46 league games.

After narrowly missing out on a second successive promotion the following season, the Cherries' name was changed by Dowsett from the traditional Bournemouth and Boscombe Athletic to AFC Bournemouth. Touted as reflecting a new, streamlined era at Dean Court, it was also a none too subtle ploy to get the club to the top of the alphabetical list.

'I said to John Bond, "If we call it AFC Bournemouth, then we will always be at the top of the list when they print the fixtures," remembers Dowsett. 'AFC stands for Athletic Football Club because before that it was Bournemouth and Boscombe Athletic Football Club, so we dropped the Boscombe part and swapped the rest around.'

Dowsett completed the modernising by contributing a new badge to replace the modified local borough council crest and erroneous monogram 'BFC' which had previously adorned the shirts. Folklore has it that Dowsett himself is the player depicted heading the ball on the now iconic badge, a theory confirmed by the man himself. 'Harold Walker had a design company,' says Dowsett. 'We were thinking of changing the badge after we had done the kit and name. I went down there, and they used an image of me heading the ball. I was always good in the air, that's how I scored at least half of my goals.'

Despite this rapid overhaul of the club's identity, Dowsett claims he received little resistance from the supporters, a notoriously conservative constituency in every sense: 'I did it in the summer when everyone was away!'

Despite the agonising finish to the previous season, optimism was still in abundance at Dean Court. As was money, or so it seemed. There was at least enough in the coffers to dissuade Bond from being tempted away to pastures new. Coventry City were reported to have offered Bond £15,000 a year in June 1972, but Harold Walker fought back a few days later with the offer of a new ten-year contract worth £7,500 a year that would make Bond, in the words of the Cherries' chairman, 'one of the best-paid managers in the game'.

Bold as ever, Bond told the local press, 'We will get promotion next time,' before adding the caveat that, 'we will still be better equipped if we can get a bit more experience in a couple of positions. For instance, I need someone who can give the team command in the middle of the park. I felt that we really struggled to find any real authority in midfield during a vital period of the season.' In Redknapp, whom Bond had already attempted to lure to Dean Court when he first took over from Freddie Cox, the Bournemouth manager saw a potential supply of quality crosses for MacDougall to fire the Cherries into the second tier.

In contrast to the paranoid and shadowy approach taken with most football transfers, Harry's courtship by Bournemouth was played out in public. Posing next to a suited Redknapp in the *Bournemouth Evening Echo* on 5 June 1972, Bond summarised the process of wooing the Londoner to the south coast: 'He will be here for a day or two for a thorough look at our set-up, and I am confident that we can persuade him to join us.'

Redknapp spent the following day looking around the area, presumably at accommodation for his expanding young family. By 7 June, Harry, still under contract to West Ham, was pictured in the *Echo* making the Cherry Bees prize draw alongside vice-chairman Clifford Pardy.

With all of this quaint preamble out of the way, the deal was sealed the next day, for a club record fee of £31,000. Jimmy Gabriel, who would go on to coach Bournemouth under Redknapp, signed for the club from Southampton on the same day. The two additions were due to commence training with their new team-mates on 17 July.

'I'm prepared to risk a little on this player,' said Bond, in a veiled reference to the persistent knee problems Harry had suffered at Upton Park. Never one to talk himself or anyone else down, the manager went on to declare Redknapp as, 'potentially the best right-winger in the country. I feel I will be able to get that little bit extra out of him.'

At just 25 years old and playing for one of the top clubs in the country, Redknapp dropping two divisions was greeted with some surprise among the footballing press and public. Did Harry feel it was a significant step down? 'No, not really,' he says. 'It was difficult, but because I'd kept in touch with John, I just thought it was a club that was going places. I could see the potential in the players Bournemouth had like Ted MacDougall, Phil Boyer, Tony Nelson and Dave Jones, who all went on to play in the First Division. And John had something about him as a manager. Also, we really liked the area.'

For John Harriss, the long-serving groundsman at Dean Court, his first impressions of Redknapp the player were positive. 'He was a cheeky chappy,' says Harriss. 'Cheeky Harry I called him. Always had a smile on his face. I liked him straight away. He was a very good crosser of the ball. Took people on down the wing. It would be unfair to call him an old-fashioned winger, but he had all the attributes, a bit of pace. That was his game.'

As pre-season training approached, ambition was not in short supply around Dean Court. Chairman Harold Walker submitted plans for a new £1 million stand to replace the Brighton Beach End terrace and promised to offer the 'finest spectator facilities anywhere in the country'.

Redknapp did not turn out for his new club in the first pre-season friendly against Tottenham. However, displaying early evidence of his charismatic touch, he starred in the only photo the *Echo* published from the match, grinning happily at the camera as Harold Walker attempts to engage him in conversation.

Despite being just a friendly, a fixture with Manchester United on 1 August drew a crowd of 16,924 to Dean Court, an attendance that was only bettered once in the season that followed. It was also the game where Cherries' fans had their first opportunity to see new winger Harry Redknapp on the pitch. Two goals from Ted MacDougall helped Bond's side to a memorable 3-1 win. In a development that foretold the tale of Redknapp's playing career at Dean Court, the 25-year-old was forced to leave the game midway through the first half.

It was an injury that saw Redknapp miss Bournemouth's first three games of the season, leading to frustrated speculation from supporters as to why the expensive acquisition was not on the team sheet. Barely hiding his impatience with the fans' tittle-tattle, Bond sought to clarify matters in the match programme:

'There have been several silly rumours as to why Harry Redknapp has not played in our first few games,' wrote Bond. 'Let me squash these right away and tell you the real reason was he came on against Manchester United, was not 100% fit, and did a silly overhead kick and trapped a nerve in his back which resulted in him being unable to play in our early games.'

Consequently, Bond was as delighted as the player himself when Redknapp was finally available for selection for the encounter with Watford at Vicarage Road on 22 August. 'This is great news for Harry and for the club,' said the manager, who retained high hopes the winger would emerge as a powerful attacking force within the team.

Despite receiving praise for his performance, Redknapp could not prevent the Cherries from losing 3-2, a defeat made all the more galling as Bournemouth had led 2-0 after 32 minutes thanks to a brace from MacDougall. With his side now languishing near the foot of the Third Division table, Bond was less than happy.

'I am the worst loser in the world and, in the circumstances, this really hurt. We must be more ruthless and cruel, in a footballing sense, when the opportunity arises.'

The Cherries were distinctly failing to live up to the pre-season hype, with just two wins in their opening eight games, including a 1-0 victory over Halifax Town in Harry's debut at Dean Court.

Like the team as a whole, Redknapp was struggling to impress, his nagging knee injury stripping him of his pace and the ability to provide the service required by MacDougall and Boyer as a result. By the time an epic League Cup tie with Blackpool came around, Harry was again sidelined by a leg injury, and although he made an appearance in the first replay at Bloomfield Road, the winger was then injured in training, missing the next two league fixtures. He had recovered in time to line up against Blackpool at Villa Park in a second replay, only to finish on the losing side as the Cherries went down to an extra-time goal from Frank Barton.

At least a dozen First Division scouts made their way to Villa Park that September night to run the rule over Ted MacDougall, whose 93 goals in the preceding two seasons had made him one of the hottest properties in the Football League. At a recent meeting of the Dean Court Football Supporters and Social Club, Bond had told members, 'We will be getting new players in the next few weeks and I might have to let one or two of the present players go. But you can rest assured, it will not be players like MacDougall.'

However, after the Scotsman scored the goal that earned the Cherries a point at Griffin Park against Brentford, Bond bowed to the inevitable and sought to ramp up any fee that might be forthcoming for his star player: 'I would not let him go for less than £200,000. He has made such great progress in the two years I have been at the club, but it may be as much progress as he can make in the Third Division.' Within nine months of being transferred, he would be the top scorer in the First Division.

Amid reports of interest from Tottenham, Manchester United, Crystal Palace and West Ham, MacDougall scored in the last game of his first spell at Dean Court in the 4-0 victory over Port Vale. With supporters hanging on every development in the transfer saga, they could be forgiven for overlooking Harry Redknapp's maiden goal for the club in the same game. Having contributed to the first two goals of the night, Redknapp rounded things off in style. Impressive play from Dave Jones and Bobby Howe released Phil Boyer on the left-hand side of the Vale half. Boyer delivered a fine cross which Harry struck low past goalkeeper Boswell into the far corner.

There was little time for the fans to enjoy the result before speculation regarding MacDougall's future was ended when the *Evening Echo*'s front page lead the following day announced: 'SUPERMAC FOR MAN UTD'.

United manager Frank O'Farrell had been a team-mate of John Bond's at West Ham. Following 'secret negotiations' between the pair, in which MacDougall had little or no involvement, the deal was struck. 'I am happy for Ted, heartbroken for the club and disappointed for myself,' said the Bournemouth manager. 'I wanted to keep him here, but understand and appreciate his feelings.'

With supporters in dismay over losing their top scorer and talisman, Bond sought to soothe the turmoil. 'Rest assured, it will not be long before the money is spent and the team, for promotion – for that is our aim – is strengthened,' he said.

These developments were observed closely by Harry Redknapp, who had been sold the vision by Bond of delivering cross after cross to MacDougall to fire goalwards. Was he surprised the marksman had moved on so quickly after his arrival? 'Yeah, I was,' says Harry. 'Obviously Ted wanted to go, he was ambitious. The opportunity came for him to move and he grabbed it. The club couldn't do anything about it really.'

As well as an almost certain loss of firepower, there was suddenly a vacancy for the role of club hero. For a brief moment, it appeared that Redknapp was in contention to assume the mantle. The Cherries' first post-MacDougall fixture was at home to Shrewsbury Town, and the winger put in a match-winning performance which saw the team given a rousing ovation at the conclusion of a 2-0 victory. Allowed space by the Shrews' defence, Harry sped down the line and delivered a series of accurate crosses which had the crowd singing 'We've got Harry, Harry, Harry Redknapp, Harry Redknapp on the wing' for the very first time.

Harry's status as Bournemouth's record signing did not last long, as John Bond splashed out £100,000 of the money he received for MacDougall on Cardiff duo Ian Gibson and Brian Clark. Keen to invest the balance in the playing squad before it disappeared down a financial black hole, Bond then signed Shrewsbury's skilful 24-year-old winger Alan Groves for £40,000 three days later.

With Gibson also a midfielder, Redknapp had every motivation to put in a performance against Bournemouth's next opponents Tranmere in order to retain his place in the starting eleven. But Harry struggled in the 1-1 draw, failing to deliver the quality crosses he had produced in the Shrewsbury triumph and being singled out as the 'biggest disappointment of the night' in the *Echo*'s match report.

Harry somehow started the following fixture at Rotherham United. With all three new signings playing together for the first time, the Cherries made hay after Millers keeper Jim McDonagh was forced to leave the game with concussion in the first half. With only one substitute permitted at the time, Carl Gilbert, who had scored to put the home team ahead after five minutes, filled in for McDonagh between the sticks. There were no unlikely heroics from the stand-in keeper, who ended up picking the ball out of his net four times before he in turn was replaced by Mick Leng, who provided little in the way of improvement as the game ended 7-2. It was Bournemouth's first away win of the season and a record away victory for the club at the time.

Emboldened by his side's lack of mercy for the luckless opposition, Bond brushed aside suggestions that circumstances had favoured the Cherries:

'No goalkeeper would have stopped these lads, the way they were playing. I have always maintained that some team would suffer once we got going and this was it. There would have been goals whatever the opposition.'

After a patchy start to the season, the Cherries found themselves 12 games unbeaten when they recorded a third successive away win at Lawrie McMenemy's newly promoted Grimsby Town. Redknapp played a key role in the 1-0 triumph, taking the corner from which fellow wingman Alan Groves back-heeled the ball into the net.

Groves had made quite an impression on Redknapp from the day he arrived at Dean Court, and the prowess of his late team-mate remains fresh in Harry's mind to this day. 'Alan was fantastic,' he said. 'I thought he was one of the most amazing talents I had ever seen. If he'd have been around now, he'd be such a superstar. So strong, such a big, powerful lad. Could run like no one I had ever seen. Dribble, shoot, hard as nails, he had everything.'

The win at Blundell Park took Bournemouth to the summit of the Third Division table and saw expectations escalate around Dean Court. On the pressure of fulfilling fans' hopes and dreams, Bond said, 'It suits me just fine. It is better than being at the other end of the table. We have the points but the others have to get them. We have been making steady progress this season after a poor start. There is still a lot to be done, of course, but the signs are very encouraging.'

The signs were less encouraging after Bond's side lost their next fixture and the lead of the division to Port Vale. Two goals from Vale's Irish striker Sam Morgan denied the Cherries the points and had Bond rapidly revising his confident attitude of a few days previously:

'There has been a lot of talk about us gaining promotion as if it were a foregone thing. If others want to talk about us being certainties in the promotion race that is fine by me. I will start talking when it happens.'

Redknapp was again on hand to provide the assist for the only goal in the next game in which Bournemouth consolidated second place in the table against Wrexham. Fulfilling the role that Bond had envisaged, the winger accurately crossed the ball for Keith Miller to head home.

With spirits high around Dean Court once again, Bond finally signed the reported £75,000 ten-year contract with the club in November, making him one of the highest-paid managers outside of the First Division. With such a sweetheart deal on the table, the Bournemouth boss unsurprisingly described his relationship with Harold Walker as the best enjoyed by a chairman and his manager in the entire Football League. 'It's a fantastic contract and a tremendous token of faith by my chairman.'

As far as Redknapp was concerned, Bond deserved every penny. 'John was a very good coach,' he remembers. 'He was flamboyant. He had his moods, but he had a great way about him – loved a team meeting, loved to talk to the players. He was excellent, popular with the players, a real character. You always knew he would go on to manage at a bigger club.'

Redknapp was still on the treatment table when Bournemouth won 2-0 at Layer Road in a replay to see off Fourth Division Colchester in the second round of the FA Cup. Bournemouth's reward for making it into the third round was a trip to St James' Park to play First Division Newcastle United. Bond was delighted with the outcome. 'What a good draw,' he said. 'This will give us the opportunity to try out our football against a big club. I believe we can go to Newcastle and put up a good performance.'

Redknapp was keen to play a part and confirmed his fitness with a run-out in the reserves five days before Christmas and returned to the first team in the 1-0 defeat at Walsall on 23 December. Harry retained his place in the side as results picked up again over the remainder of the Christmas period. He was on hand to provide two assists in the 3-0 thumping of Watford in early January which consolidated the Cherries' first place in the Third Division table going into the cup tie at St James' Park.

Around 1,200 supporters made the long journey north, half of them on a train chartered by the club. Newcastle's famous black and white stripes clashed with Bournemouth's home and away kits, requiring the club to commission a third kit, an unusual move in an era when the replica kit market was almost non-existent. The dark blue shirt featured red and white diagonal stripes and it was the only occasion it was ever worn by the Cherries.

In front of nearly 34,000 spectators Redknapp, in his first appearance in the cup for Bournemouth, joined the rest of John Bond's team in running on to the pitch holding up placards reading 'Our aim – to entertain'. Newcastle's aim, on the other hand, was to get into the fourth round and avoid another embarrassing exit following their defeat at Hereford United the previous year. As it was, the home side ran out 2-0 winners, with the Cherries living up to their pre-match promise despite the defeat. Redknapp was singled out as the most effective of Bournemouth's wingers by Newcastle manager Joe Harvey.

With the cups off the agenda for another year, the Cherries returned to league action with a 1-1 draw at Scunthorpe's Old Show Ground. Bond's frustration with his team's inability to take a return of maximum points from a fixture they dominated was soon forgotten when the team coach skidded off the road as heavy snow fell across Yorkshire. Redknapp recalls the frightening incident in which the vehicle he was travelling in was written off. 'The coach was a mess,' he says. 'We were coming down the road and suddenly the coach just took off and kept going. The road turned one way and the coach just started to skid the other way. We knew we weren't going to stop. We went straight into the wall of a garage. Kenny Brown, who was the first-team coach, got all mangled up in the wreckage and broke his thigh.'

Brown was taken to hospital in Doncaster for the night. Redknapp, who was sitting across the aisle of the coach from Brown, was fortunate to escape relatively unscathed, a happy circumstance that would not be repeated outside Rome 17 years later. The rest of the passengers were equally blessed, although captain Keith Miller lost two teeth as a result of the impact.

The front end of the coach, where Redknapp, Brown and the rest of the card school were playing, was wrecked, with not a window left intact. Despite the shock, Bond and his staff considered themselves lucky:

'I just don't know how we came out of it so lightly,' said Bond. 'There could have been five or six players badly injured considering the state of the vehicle afterwards.'

Stranded in freezing conditions, Redknapp says that little help was forthcoming for the uninjured players and staff to continue their journey south. 'We ended up getting a train home. Nowadays another coach would come and pick you up, but not back then. We had to get taxis from where the accident happened, wait in a station, catch the milk train home, change trains and we got back about four o'clock in the morning.'

Whilst the coach crash left the players thanking their lucky stars, it did little for results. Two defeats in a row, the second a 1-0 reverse at Rochdale, saw Bond stage a late-night team meeting in a Manchester hotel to thrash out the reasons for the Cherries' lack of goals. Redknapp, never one to contribute significantly to the goals tally, escaped censure as his recent form had seen him provide several opportunities per game which were then being squandered by his team-mates.

The second thrashing of Rotherham in the space of four months put such concerns to one side, as Redknapp put in a man-of-the-match performance in possibly his finest outing for the club. The frequency and accuracy of his crossing was a persistent thorn in the side of the Millers' defence and an audacious lob from a deep-lying position to set up Boyer's second goal was one of the highlights in a game full of them. The winger had found his feet at last, and continued to play an influential role in performances as the season wore on, providing the telling pass in goalscoring moves time and again.

Stuart Morgan, who played alongside Redknapp at Dean Court and had known the winger since their teenage years together at West Ham, recalls the attributes that Harry had at his disposal when fit and healthy: 'Harry was a tremendously skilful player,' says Morgan. 'He had a lot of Ryan Giggs about him. Great pace, ability with both feet, he'd drop his shoulder to the right, come back to the left. He was an absolutely tremendous crosser of the ball, probably one of the best near-post crossers of the ball that I've seen. He was a typically out-and-out winger, not strong in the tackle and defensively probably a bit weak, but on his day he was always at the hub of things in a match.'

This was the case in mid-February, when a bumper crowd of 18,374 at Dean Court saw Bond's side beat Bolton Wanderers 2-0 in a top-of-the-table clash in front of the *Match of the Day* cameras. Redknapp's pinpoint centres made both of the goals, scored by Brian Clark and Micky Cave in the second half. Bond was understandably delighted with the outcome, stating that the win was 'virtually worth four points'.

Thereafter, results stalled, and Redknapp found himself left out of the starting eleven five times in March and April as Bond reshuffled the side to accommodate new signing Paul Aimson in the hope that results would again pick up. This did not prove successful, and the Cherries' indifferent form over Easter saw Bond recall him to the side for Bournemouth's visit to Charlton, their first visit to The Valley for 38 years. Redknapp played a key role in getting the point that was secured in a 1-1 draw, crossing the ball which Brian Clark headed on for Jimmy Gabriel to score. But come the next weekend's victory at home to Oldham, Redknapp again found himself out of the squad.

There appears to have been little wrong with Harry's fitness at this stage, as he played the full 90 minutes of a testimonial match for Alan Green, a Bournemouth player who had retired due to a heart condition.

Testimonials are only played at half throttle, so if Redknapp's troublesome knee was bothering him, appearing in a friendly was significantly less risky than turning out when there were points at stake. Redknapp did enough, however, to convince Bond he was ready to return. He found himself on the bench for the game against Blackburn at Ewood Park, which pitted fifth-placed Bournemouth against third-placed Rovers. With the home side just a point ahead of the Cherries, there was no hiding the importance of the fixture, with Bond describing it as 'the big one'.

Bournemouth, without Redknapp, had beaten Rovers 3-0 at Dean Court less than a month before, but the Lancashire side got their revenge with a 2-1 win. Harry came on after an hour to replace Jim De Garis, but he could not help the Cherries to drag themselves back into the game.

With just four matches remaining of the campaign, it was a result which left Bournemouth relying on several results going their way to have any chance of promotion, and Bond knew the game was up.

'Promotion looks improbable for us now, but we will be aiming for maximum points in the remaining matches and, because football is so unpredictable, we cannot be written off yet.'

Qualification for the short-lived Watney Cup was the only realistic target Bournemouth had left to aim for. One of the first football tournaments to have a title sponsor, the competition was a pre-season affair that featured the two top scorers from each division who had failed to be promoted the previous year. Unsurprisingly, money was the main motivator for clubs to be involved, with £4,000 going to qualifiers to help pay the summer wage bill with a further potential bonus of larger pre-season crowds to watch what was advertised as competitive football.

Every little helps, and Bond called upon his troops to 'score plenty of goals' in the final fixtures as the Cherries were in contention to qualify. With an almost resigned air of inevitability, his side managed only one win and two goals before the final whistle blew to end the season. Redknapp played in three of the four matches, all of which Bournemouth failed to win. He was replaced in the starting line-up by the inexperienced David Chadwick for the home game against Swansea on Easter Saturday, which ended 2-0 in Bournemouth's favour. It was the final game at Dean Court that season and, tellingly, it was the first in which the attendance dropped below 10,000.

The campaign concluded at Halifax in a 2-0 defeat, prompting Bond to describe his team's performance as 'one of the worst I have ever seen'. Qualification for the Watney Cup was not forthcoming, with Bournemouth's 64 league goals trailing in behind Bristol Rovers' 77 and Plymouth Argyle's 74.

Bournemouth ended the game at The Shay with ten men. Defender Dave Jones injured his hip midway through the first half and was replaced by substitute Paul Aimson. Bond was forced to reshuffle his side's formation, but they had little time to settle into their new roles before Redknapp, dropping back to help out in defence, was injured and had to be stretchered off the pitch. With only one sub allowed, Halifax made hay, using the numerical advantage to take the two points which saved them from applying for re-election to the Football League.

Redknapp made 37 appearances in all competitions during a season in which confidence had ebbed out of the team once again during the business end of the campaign. Fans were restless, wondering how long a wage bill, said to be one of the highest outside of the First Division, could be sustained before the squad broke up.

Manager Bond, possibly forgetting his similar prophecy before the season kicked off, was having none of it:

'To all the pessimists I would say we did not do too badly, either last season or last year,' and he reiterated his belief that the club was on the verge of the big time. 'The club, the town and the supporters deserve Second Division football and I would not have turned down other jobs if I did not think we could achieve it.'

He didn't stop there, declaring that the team would 'set the town alight' the following season, before promising, 'If it's next year or the year after, I'll see this club on its way to the First Division.'

Chairman Harold Walker was equally bullish, stating at the season's end: 'We have got to maintain our efforts, and we are all convinced that, in the end, we can do it,' before responding to the age-old claim that the club were in fact reluctant to achieve promotion by asking the doubters, 'Why would we have spent all that money otherwise?'

In time-honoured fashion, the words of both manager and chairman were to contrast sharply with the events played out at the club in the following few years.

Chapter Two

Exodus

1973/74

DURING his spell at Dean Court as a player, Harry Redknapp and his young family lived on the newly built Riverslea estate in Stanpit, a tiny former smuggling village located between the picturesque quaysides of Christchurch and Mudeford.

In the same development, the club also found homes for team-mates Jimmy Gabriel and Bobby Howe. After sharing lifts to and from training, the three men would retire to the historic Ship in Distress pub across the road from their new homes. It was here that they created their own take on Cassettari's, the famous cafe near West Ham's Boleyn Ground, and talk long into the evening about football, skills and tactics. They are days that Harry still remembers fondly. 'Jimmy Gabriel used to call the Ship in Distress the QE2,' he says. 'One night we told Alan Groves and Micky Cave we were going for a drink at the QE2 around the corner from where we lived and they drove up and down for about an hour looking for the QE2, but of course that was not the name of the place. Finally they found it and they were not happy. The pub is still there, it's got a restaurant now, but in those days it was just a tiny little place, like someone's front room. We used to talk football all the time. Jimmy was football mad and Bobby Howe went on to become a very good coach. It was just non-stop football.'

In an extravagant move that, in hindsight, appears indicative of the limitless but naive ambition around Dean Court in the era, 17 members of the playing squad, manager Bond, youth team coach Trevor Hartley and physio John Kirk embarked upon an epic close-season tour consisting of 11 matches in Australia, New Zealand, Iran, New Caledonia and Tahiti. The 25,000-mile round trip was an unqualified success, with the Cherries losing just once and winning praise and friends wherever they seemed to land. This somewhat incongruent triumph could have been significantly different, however, after many of the party had a narrow escape from death when swimming in the South Pacific. Jimmy Gabriel takes up the story.

'It was very hot in New Caledonia, so obviously the lads went down to the beach a few times to cool off. There was all the usual horseplay and mucking about. It all seemed so natural. But we noticed while we were there each day that a couple of ladies came down with their kids, and while the youngsters were allowed to play in the sand, none of them ever set foot in the water. The ladies kept themselves to themselves, and so did we, but on the last day we started talking to them. We asked one woman why they never went for a swim, even though it was so hot. The answer took our breath away. She said, "We don't swim because there are little fish in this bay with spines. If you step on them in three seconds you will be dead." We just stood there with our mouths open. The whole team could have been wiped out.'

Whilst his globetrotting team-mates were dodging an early grave, Redknapp stayed at home because Sandra was heavily pregnant with their second child. A few weeks after the conclusion of the tour, on 25 June 1973, Mrs Redknapp gave birth to a baby boy named Jamie Frank at Barton on Sea maternity hospital in nearby Hampshire.

On the surface, all appeared well as players and staff vowed to bring the much coveted promotion to the Second Division to reality following the previous year's disappointment. However, there was thinly veiled unrest behind the scenes, with John Bond coming under fire for his dealings in the transfer market. Harold Walker's tepid public backing of his manager proved to be a portentous sign of things to come.

'I have been under pressure to sack the manager,' revealed the Bournemouth chairman. 'There have been some silly mistakes made and, in some cases, the club has overpaid for the transfer of players. There have been suggestions that other people, given the same money, would have done a better job as manager. But I am not so sure.'

Redknapp may have been one of the players Walker was referring to, although he retained the favour of the Dean Court faithful and continued to appear regularly in the first team throughout the campaign to come. For his part, Bond was honest enough to accept his share of responsibility for the discord. 'Anyone can make mistakes and I am no exception,' he admitted. 'Some of the players I have bought have not come up to expectations. I have done things wrong and spent money I should not have spent.'

Harry featured in just one pre-season friendly as the Cherries beat West Brom at the Hawthorns, with the winger providing the cross for fellow midfielder John Delaney to score the only goal of the game.

This contribution may have been a case of too little too late for Bond, and Redknapp found himself turning out for the reserves on the day of the season's opening game at Dean Court against the holders of the Watney Cup, Bristol Rovers.

A calamitous 3-0 defeat to a Rovers side led by future Bournemouth manager Don Megson brought a swift change to Bond's thinking. Harry was elevated into the starting eleven as an instant opportunity for revenge presented itself when the Cherries faced Rovers again the following Tuesday in the first round of the League Cup.

Redknapp grabbed his chance with both hands, prodding the ball past Rovers keeper Jim Eadie from close range in the second half for the only goal of the game. This strike was the catalyst for a brief purple patch in front of goal for Harry. In mid-September he scored two and made the other in a 3-0 win at home to newly promoted Aldershot in what was described as his 'most aggressive display' since joining from West Ham over a year earlier. Redknapp opened the scoring in the 43rd minute of the midweek encounter when he sent a thunderous strike off the post and into the Shots' net to end a four-game goalless streak for the Cherries. In the second half, with Bournemouth dominating possession, Redknapp confirmed the victory with his second goal four minutes from time. Exchanging passes with the ever-energetic Phil Boyer, Harry slotted home from close range, the ball coming off Aldershot's goalkeeper Tony Godfrey on its way into the net.

Redknapp's tail was up, as was his team's. Although the Cherries conceded a goal after just 17 seconds of their next match away at Walsall, they bounced back to win 2-1, with Harry returning the compliment to Boyer from the Aldershot match to send in the cross for the forward to score.

A week later, Redknapp fired in the decisive second goal in a 2-1 victory over Third Division pacesetters Tranmere Rovers, a team who had not conceded a goal in their first six league matches. After John Sainty's first-half opener finally breached Tranmere's defensive shield, Steve Buttle passed the ball to Redknapp in the 72nd minute and the winger drilled the ball from the corner of the penalty box through a posse of defenders to finish into the opposite side of goalkeeper Johnson's net.

Harry, who would never be so prolific again, found himself leading the early-season scoring charts at Dean Court, with the

Evening Echo heralding his run of goals in the following day's match report under the headline 'Harry The Hammer Now Top Scorer For The Cherries'.

Redknapp was less happy in the following game at Huddersfield. Although the Cherries maintained their unbeaten away record with a draw at Leeds Road, the winger felt ill throughout the match. His recent form and Bond's faith in his ability kept him on the pitch until the 73rd minute, when he was laid flat out after taking a blistering shot full in the face. Harry's woes delayed Bournemouth's return south as he was forced to visit a local doctor before being given the all-clear to travel.

Despite losing out in the League Cup to Sheffield Wednesday after a second replay, the Cherries' league form did not falter throughout October. John Sainty grabbed a hat-trick at the Recreation Ground in the return meeting with Aldershot, clipping in Redknapp's cross for the second goal. According to Bond, 'That cross was pure magic.'

As the clocks changed, Bournemouth were near the top of the division despite playing nine matches in all competitions during the previous month. Confidence was high going into the winter months, and following a hard-fought draw at Halifax at the beginning of November, Redknapp told the press, 'Now there is a feeling that we are not going to be beaten.'

These words were not entirely prophetic, as the Cherries lost their next match against their nemesis Blackburn Rovers 2-1 at Dean Court.

It was Bournemouth's first defeat in 12 league games, and John Bond was not impressed. 'I told them in the dressing room, "Half of you have let me and the club down today. You can think about it at the weekend." I did not name any players. I did not have to. Those I referred to know who I meant. There must be a truly professional approach to every match if the team is to get anywhere. The same discipline must apply all the time.'

Whether Redknapp was amongst those worthy of Bond's scorn is unclear, although he retained his place in the starting eleven for the next match. Soon afterwards, rumours began to circulate that Bond was considering his future. Results were holding up well, but by the time the Cherries met Charlton for the second time in ten days in a first-round FA Cup tie, Bond was being strongly linked with the vacant manager's job at Norwich City. He did little to distance himself from the speculation, saying only, 'I am flattered.'

Bond had grown frustrated at the inability of Bournemouth to make the leap into the Second Division and knew that the precarious financial situation at the club was a significant obstacle in him building a squad that could last the distance in the Third Division promotion race. In the week leading up to his departure, the club announced an annual profit of £132,000. In isolation, this appears a healthy return for the era, but it was only a headline figure.

Attendances were down, salaries and expenses had gone up and the bill for the Walker Stand was rising a good deal faster than the building itself. In fact, the club would have already been in serious debt if it were not for a £185,000 injection from subsidiary building firm B & B of which Harold Walker was also a director. With the wolf once again at the door, the Bournemouth chairman would only say, 'We hope the completion of the stand and the playing results achieved will, in the future, produce compelling reasons for more supporters to attend our games.'

This was hoping against hope, as Walker already knew he was on the verge of losing the key figure in the club's transformation from also-rans to promotion contenders. Bond refused to comment on reports naming him as one of the leading candidates to replace Norwich's Manchester City-bound manager Ron Saunders, although he did concede that he 'needed inspiring, and this has not always happened at Bournemouth. I am not referring to the chairman, but to other aspects of the club.'

What those aspects were remained unclear, but fans suspected a rift with Walker regardless of Bond's denials. After seeing the Cherries safely through the Charlton tie, Bond travelled to Norfolk to accept the Norwich job, stating that he was 'a bit upset and slightly disillusioned' about the situation at Dean Court.

His disillusionment increased when Walker attempted to block the move by holding Bond to his recently signed contract. 'I have been told I can't go,' said Bond. 'I had agreed terms with Norwich subject to them negotiating my release from Bournemouth. The chairman has decided, at the last moment, that I had to honour my contract here and that he would not release me from it. Therefore I have no alternative but to stay at Bournemouth.'

Much to the relief of the players and fans, Walker putting his foot down appeared to have worked. Redknapp, who was a close ally of Bond's, summed up the mood of the squad: 'John Bond has done a lot for this club and it would be a sad day to see him go. All the first-team squad are delighted he is staying.'

Unfortunately for the Cherries, Walker's apparent determination regarding the contract in his attempt to retain Bond at Dean Court was little more than a show of public resolve before the inevitable exit of his star employee. It is possible that this posturing was intended to soften the fans up for Bond's ensuing departure and ensure the supporters' finger of blame would point at their club's soon-to-be ex-manager.

The following day, 28 November, the saga drew to a close. Walker, again being careful to paint Bond as the villain, admitted defeat. 'How can you keep somebody who plays this sort of game?' he said. 'I had no alternative but to say that the manager could go. I am sick and flabbergasted and feel I have been kicked in the stomach.'

This was the defining moment of the decade for Bournemouth, and one they would not recover from until Redknapp himself assumed the reins at Dean Court some ten years later. It came as no surprise to Harry that Bond moved on. 'I always knew that John was going to have big clubs interested in him,' he says. 'He was hitting the headlines, he was a flamboyant young manager. When the opportunity came for John to go to a bigger club he took it. But I don't know why he moved on really, as he had everything going for him at Bournemouth. I'm sure that he would have got us promoted that year. But he decided to move on and once he went, they all went.'

In a move which aped the so-called 'continental' approach Walker clearly admired, he promoted 26-year-old Trevor Hartley from running the youth team to first-team coach, announcing, 'There is no vacancy. We are not going to appoint a manager at all. We have enough experienced administrators on the staff to keep the club running smoothly on the same course. Nothing will be changed. The club will continue to play to the same pattern as before.'

Trevor Hartley's youth made it difficult for him to establish firm authority in the dressing room, and he was unable to fall back on any kudos from his playing career. A contemporary of Redknapp's at West Ham, the Yorkshireman made just five appearances for the east London club before accepting ex-team-mate Bond's offer to move to Bournemouth. He played 42 times for the Cherries as his promising coaching ability saw him be given charge of the youth team. With reports linking the likes of Bobby Moore with the 'non-vacancy' he was filling, Hartley soon struggled in his new role after a propitious beginning.

His first game at the helm on 1 December saw the Cherries take on a Wrexham side that was unbeaten at the Recreation Ground all season. Redknapp retained his place under the new boss, who sought to give his players his full confidence before kick-off, telling them, 'I have no doubts about the way you will approach this match. I know your attitude is right as good professionals and you will not let recent happenings bother you.'

As often as not, teams going through periods of adversity find deeper reserves of motivation, and this proved to be the case for Bournemouth. Redknapp had a hand in the only goal of the game, releasing Micky Cave from a throw-in to rifle the ball across the goalmouth where a defender's lunge saw it loop perfectly to Phil Boyer, who calmly headed home.

Hartley's elevation to the Dean Court hot seat suddenly looked inspired as the Cherries went on to win their next four matches, a run which included victory over Watford in the second round of the FA Cup. However, although results were promising, prospects for the second half of the season began to look increasingly bleak as Bond returned to Dean Court time and again to tempt his old charges to join him at Carrow Road.

Leading the exodus were defenders Mel Machin and John Benson, as well as goalkeeper Fred Davies, who headed to East Anglia in exchange for £50,000. Harold Walker could not believe the squad was being dismantled before his eyes by the very man he had built it with. He took to the pitch to address the angry and bewildered Bournemouth supporters before kick-off in Hartley's first home game against Cambridge United.

'I did everything I could to keep them,' said the chairman, who had offered Benson and Machin coaching roles in an attempt to convince them to remain on the south coast. 'It is no use holding anyone unless they are 100% with us. I hope this is not the thin end of the wedge and we are determined to keep the rest of our players.'

With disbelief turning to resignation, no sooner had Machin headed east than the Bournemouth faithful were wondering, 'Who's next?' As it turned out, the answer was Harry Redknapp. Bond was keen to bring his old pal along for the ride, and dangled City striker Peter Silvester in front of Bournemouth as bait. Once more, the Dean Court board stated they were not interested, but by now it was unlikely even they believed that.

Bond may have been keen to sign Redknapp for a second time, but the winger's long-term knee injury was hampering his attempts to even break into a run. The prospect of a return to a higher division was certainly enough to turn Harry's head, and he admits that he would have gone to Norwich had the Canaries offered him terms. The reality was that his body was no longer up to it, and the deal never materialised.

Redknapp's prospects of recovering from his injury were hampered by the rudimentary level of medical care afforded to the players at the time. As he turned out week after week in the Third Division, pre-match preparations were minimal to say the least. 'People don't realise. We didn't even warm up before a game,' Harry remembers. 'We didn't stretch. In those days, we didn't go on the pitch, have a warm-up and come off. We sat in the dressing room and three minutes before kick-off the bell would go and we would all run on to the pitch. We'd have one ball, maybe two balls if you were lucky, and the captain would go straight to the middle and toss up. While he was tossing up you might be kicking the ball to one another or just standing around, and then just start the game. All this going on the pitch, having a warm-up and coming off; when I came back from America was the first time I saw that and that was about 1980. We used to just sit in the dressing room when I was playing. Some players would still have their clothes on at a quarter to three. Even in the week, we'd just come out for training in the middle of winter and start straight away. We didn't stretch. We didn't know what it was to stretch. And the medical treatment was the same. The physios weren't qualified. It was impossible to get an injury like mine treated properly back then.'

Redknapp took his frustration out on Watford defender Duncan Welbourne in the match that followed the aborted transfer to Norwich at the end of October. Harry drove the ball straight at Welbourne when the Hornets' player had refused to retreat the full ten yards at a free kick, and then squared up to his opponent in a move which guaranteed that the referee showed the Bournemouth winger the yellow card.

Despite occasional flashes of temper, Harry was perennially popular at Dean Court with both supporters and team-mates. His acumen for leadership was never in doubt, although during his playing days he sometimes used this skill set in a way he would later frown upon as a manager. 'He was a character in the dressing room,' remembers Stuart Morgan. 'He was always doing something crazy. It makes me laugh every year when I hear Harry has cancelled the Christmas party at whatever club he is managing because Harry used to organise them when he was a player. He was the life and soul.'

Hartley's honeymoon came to an end when Bournemouth lost 2-1 away to Chesterfield in their final game of 1973. Redknapp, who had been joined in midfield by long-term absentee Ian Gibson, scored the Cherries' goal when he equalised Arthur Bellamy's effort for the home team a minute after half-time. It was to be his last as a professional footballer, discounting the own goal he scored at Old Trafford nine years later.

The new year brought little respite for the Cherries and their supporters. Hartley's side won just once in five games in the first month of 1974, with goalscoring a significant problem. Despite the poor run, the Bournemouth manager remained optimistic. 'I am certain that we have the ability to go on from here and gain a promotion place,' he said. 'We want the lads to stick together and, if they continue to work for each other as they have been doing, I reckon we'll make it.'

Unfortunately, Hartley reckoned without John Bond reappearing to further demolish what he himself had built. Rumours circulated throughout January that Phil Boyer was about to take the now well-worn path to Carrow Road. Bond made little attempt to hide his interest, going so far as to criticise the intransigence of opposing managers in hampering his attempts at team-building. 'I have made more than 20 approaches this week,' he said in mid-January, 'but managers aren't interested in selling. I keep running into a solid wall of refusal.'

Managers may have appeared impenetrable when it came to selling their players, but as Bond himself had proved only a few weeks earlier, they were no different to players when it came to fulfilling ambitions and improving their salary. Harold Walker, who by this point must have been at the very end of his tether, again attempted to stem the tide, stating firmly, 'Phil Boyer will not be sold to Norwich.'

But John Bond was not to be put off and continued to persistently haunt the club, even going so far as to bring his Norwich squad to Bournemouth for a mid-season break following their League Cup semi-final defeat to Wolves. The ill feeling that had erupted since Bond's departure was threatening to hamper the progress and reputation of both clubs, a fact that was confirmed when Norwich chairman Arthur South extended an invitation to Harold Walker to take a few days' holiday at his home to smooth things over.

This peace offering proved duplicitous. Soon after, Phil Boyer left Dean Court for East Anglia. With the player determined to move on and his form dipping drastically since he made his request to leave, the board reluctantly placed Boyer on the transfer list following their monthly meeting. An initial bid from the Canaries of £145,000 was rejected, but the Carrow Road side were merely testing the water and came back the following day with another of £150,000 which the Cherries accepted. Having paid just £20,000 for Boyer from York City, it represented a healthy profit for Bournemouth, but as a result the gloom that had settled around Dean Court grew darker still.

A 3-0 defeat in a top-of-the-table clash with leaders Bristol Rovers brought stinging words from Hartley for his squad. 'We cannot let this happen again,' he said post-match. 'The players who do not want to do the job will not stay in the side. Everyone must give 100%, otherwise he is letting down his team-mates and the supporters.'

Hartley did not go so far as to name names, so it is not clear if Redknapp was among those he surely criticised more directly in the dressing room. The public rebuke, however, was enough to suggest that Hartley was struggling to stamp his authority on the squad, and the situation would only get worse as the year went on.

Hartley's biggest challenge was to control the mercurial Alan Groves. Described by Redknapp as 'the best I have ever seen', Groves was a free spirit who was no stranger to brushes with authority. Despite not being injured, the winger had been limited to just two starts and a handful of substitute appearances since the beginning of the season. He was then surprisingly recalled to the first-team squad for the encounter with Oldham Athletic in early February.

Groves, who had been described as 'possibly the best winger outside the First Division' by John Bond when signing him from Shrewsbury, replaced Jimmy Gabriel at half-time after the crowd had chanted his name throughout the first half. It is unlikely that his mood improved much, however, as the Cherries lost 3-0 for their third straight defeat. Hartley, who had seen his side concede three goals in each of those reverses, again laid into his players in public. 'Those who wanted to play were affected by the others,' he said. 'The fans could see for themselves those that were prepared to put some work into it. Some of the players let their club down with their approach to the game.'

Groves' 45 minutes were impressive enough for Oldham, who soon made an offer for his services which was rapidly accepted by the Cherries' board. The winger soon established himself as a crowd favourite at Boundary Park, scoring in each of his first three matches for his new club.

When Bournemouth visited Oldham the following month, a determined Groves scored twice in a 4-2 win for the Latics, but the tempestuous winger was not satisfied to leave it at that. Redknapp, who was facing his old team-mate on the Bournemouth right, was reduced to shocked sniggers by what happened next. 'Alan was fantastic,' he says. 'I just thought he was one of the most amazing talents I had ever seen. If he had been around now, he would be such a star. He was so strong, a big, powerful lad, could run like no one I had ever seen, dribble, shoot, hard as nails, just an amazing player. He had everything. Anyway, we sold him to Oldham, and when we went there to play, Grovesy absolutely ran us ragged. With about five minutes to go he dribbled the ball along the halfway line. We all thought, "Where's he going?" He got in front of the dugouts, stopped, and he smashed the ball straight at Trevor Hartley. The ball was ricocheting around Trevor's head. After the game, Trevor barricaded himself in the away dressing room and refused to come out until he was sure Groves had left the ground.'

Hartley may have wished he had stayed there because abuse grew louder from the Dean Court terraces as results continued to disappoint. Redknapp was on hand to provide John Sainty with the cross for the Cherries' third goal at Ewood Park, but Bournemouth still managed to lose 4-3 to Blackburn Rovers in their next match.

Harry dropped out of the Bournemouth team for the match against struggling Southport at Haig Avenue in late February. Painkilling injections, which had been keeping the winger available for selection, this time failed to have the desired effect, and Keith Miller stepped in to make his first appearance since November.

Redknapp's lay-off only lasted a single game, and he returned to play his part in the 3-2 win over Hereford at Dean Court the following Saturday. The Dean Court faithful hoped the win would be the catalyst for the Cherries to rediscover the form of the first half of the campaign and contend for a place in the Second Division. Instead, they would see their team win just one of their remaining 13 fixtures.

Hartley dropped Redknapp again for the draw at Southend on April Fools' Day. Having held on to his place throughout the

Cherries' period of plummeting form since Bond's departure, the winger then only appeared in three of the final eight matches of the season.

Redknapp's absence did not go down well with Bournemouth's supporters, who made their appreciation of his reappearance in the number seven shirt in the goalless draw at Charlton loudly heard at The Valley. With Brian Greenhalgh missing a penalty for the away side midway through the second half, Redknapp was one of the few bright spots in an otherwise drab 90 minutes, tormenting the Charlton defence with his skilful runs and dangerous crosses.

Selection for the forthcoming clash with Plymouth Argyle on Good Friday was virtually guaranteed until Harry then fell ill and was unable to appear. He recovered to reclaim his place in the starting eleven for the draw with Grimsby and made his final appearance of the season as the Cherries played Plymouth for the second time in four days on Easter Monday, adding an unwelcome defeat to the point gained at Dean Court.

Hartley now cut a desperate figure, reaching for platitudes of the 'we still have to go all out to try and gain as many points as possible' variety as his team staggered towards the end of the season.

As Redknapp saw out the campaign in the reserves, there was a glimmer of hope for the future of the club as 16-year-old Howard Goddard impressed in Bournemouth's final three games. It is symbolic of how demoralised the side had become that the youngster was given the responsibility of taking a penalty in the defeat at already relegated Cambridge United, a chance he missed as his far more experienced team-mates watched on irresolutely. The youthful striker soon bounced back, however, scoring his first goal for the club as the Cherries drew the rearranged game with now recovered Halifax 1-1.

The season ended with a 1-0 defeat at Dean Court to Wrexham, who stole into the final promotion spot as a result. A chipped own goal from Clive Payne in the 80th minute gave the Welsh side the victory and summed up the second half of Bournemouth's season. In his programme notes, Harold Walker referred to the 'alarm and despondency in the town' as a result of the Cherries' difficulties, but promised 'we will get there in the end'.

This promise seemed wildly optimistic when, as well as the departures to Carrow Road, first-team stalwarts John Sainty, Micky Cave and David Jones all moved on during the close season. With his squad paper-thin, Hartley saw an opportunity to expel doubts about his position in the shape of the talented youth programme overseen by assistant manager Reg Tyrell. Mark Nightingale, Steve Gritt and Kevin Reeves all followed Goddard into the senior squad and would make significant contributions in the seasons that followed.

Reeves, who went on to play twice for England, remembers meeting Redknapp whilst still a schoolboy prospect at Dean Court. 'Now and again we would train with the first-team players,' says Reeves. 'I always remember Harry being fantastic with the youngsters. He always had a great rapport with players and a great way about him, Harry. He'd do anything for you and he would help you. I remember doing a little training session where you had to do a jinking run and pass forward between cones. It was difficult, but Harry had made better angles than anybody else and it made it easier for him to pass the ball, so I just copied what he did. I can remember him coming up to me afterwards and patting me on the head and saying, "Well done. You are trying to learn."'

Regardless of Redknapp's popularity within the club, he was told that he too could leave Bournemouth when the campaign drew to a close, despite being selected for 39 Third Division matches and starting all seven of the cup ties the Cherries had played that season. The word coming out of Dean Court was that the board were looking to recoup all of the £30,000 fee they had paid to secure his services two years previously.

Chapter Three

Falling Down

1974/75

WHILE Hartley tried to turn the tide by signing five new players over the close season, off-field problems showed no signs of abating. Harold Walker was determined to press on with construction of the new stand at the Brighton Beach End, but a combination of building regulations and affordability were dogging the project.

As a result, the necessary planning permission was only granted for phase one of the project. Walker, for his part, pointed towards the downfall in the UK economy when defending the club's financial position. 'I don't think the country's finances have ever been in a worse state,' said the Bournemouth chairman. 'We must view the future with apprehension, not just us but other football clubs. I can finish the stand, although I may have difficulty.'

With Redknapp sidelined for the foreseeable future with his persistent knee injury, the rest of the Bournemouth squad returned for pre-season training. It was Trevor Hartley's first taste of leading this crucial preparation period, and he did not intend to allow the opportunity to pass him by. The players, who had been used to training for a couple of hours in the morning before having the rest of the day off, found themselves working unusually long hours as the novice manager looked to build up their stamina for the demands that lay ahead. Many of the squad grumbled that it was the toughest pre-season they had ever faced. 'We have been doing the usual toning work,' said Hartley. 'The lads have been getting down to it well and there has been the usual crop of bruises and blisters. It's got to be hard, because there is a long season ahead and we have got to be ready for it.'

Following a pre-season tour of the West Country, the team returned south to reports that Redknapp was about to join John Bond and the ex-Bournemouth cadre at Norwich City. A fee of £10,000 was reportedly agreed between the clubs, subject to a medical and the approval of the League Management Committee.

The Canaries' medical staff cannot have failed to pick up on Redknapp's injured knee, which may have been the reason the proposed permanent transfer was downgraded to a loan. This caution on the part of the Carrow Road club proved prescient, as Redknapp never made an appearance in Bond's new team. 'I had a few months there,' says Harry, 'but I just couldn't get my knee right. John came down to buy me when the first team were away on a trip somewhere. He came down to do the deal with Trevor Hartley, but he didn't know I was injured. I said "John, I can't play." He said, "What do you mean you can't play?" I said, "I've got big problems with my knee at the moment." In those days, you didn't have medicals. Even if you were moving to Liverpool the medical took about a minute. You had an old doctor who would ask things like, "Have you had a cough or a cold or anything lately?" There were no scans or X-rays or anything like that. So John came down to buy me, but no one had actually told him that I had a dodgy knee. I think our board were looking forward to stitching John up by selling him a crocked player as he wasn't very popular around Bournemouth any more.'

Meanwhile, the season started surprisingly well at Dean Court, the resentment brewing among the senior players towards Hartley notwithstanding. One defeat in the opening six league games included a goalless draw with table-topping Southend United. The Essex side had failed to drop a single point in the league before the game at Dean Court, which Hartley described as 'our best of the season'.

Indicative of a wider disquiet behind the scenes was the sacking of striker John O'Rourke in mid-October. Signed for £45,000 from QPR at the start of 1974, O'Rourke was fined for a breach of club discipline shortly after arriving at the club, and had yet to appear in the first team since the start of the new season. After giving the forward his cards, Hartley said, 'The player's contract has been terminated for alleged misconduct and on disciplinary grounds.'

Taking such a step on the strength of what the manager himself had stated were allegations seemed somewhat premature. This proved to be the case, as O'Rourke's appeal to the League Management Committee was upheld, causing Hartley to reveal that the striker had refused to play in a 4-0 win over Crystal Palace. O'Rourke, through his father, refuted this allegation. Hartley initially said if the player turned up at Dean Court he would be suspended pending the outcome of an appeal of the club's own against the decision, although someone must have drawn the Bournemouth manager's attention to the realities of employment law and O'Rourke was subsequently permitted to train alone at the club in the late afternoon. Redknapp remembers these events well. 'What happened was that Trevor Hartley called John O'Rourke into the club for a meeting,' he recalls. 'He told John he was going to play him in the next match but John said, "I wouldn't ever play for you. I told you I'm not playing for you ever again after the way you have treated me." Harold Walker was in the next room and heard all this, and he came in and said, "Right, that's it. You have refused to play so you are sacked."'

Soon after, the club dropped its counter-appeal altogether, presumably following the realisation that success was unlikely. Meanwhile, John Bond was still keen to make Harry Redknapp the eighth man to follow him from Dean Court to Carrow Road. Doubt over the winger's recovery from torn knee tendons was delaying the deal, and a fitness test in the form of a reserve match took place on 9 November. With the knee holding up well, Redknapp's injury curse struck again, and he was forced to go off with a sprained ankle. Hartley, who was considering recalling Redknapp to the Cherries' team as results continued to nosedive and injuries mounted, commented, 'He will be out for a few weeks, but once his injury clears up he will be ready to play for Bournemouth again.'

The rudimentary facilities available to injured players during the mid-1970s hampered Harry's return to full fitness. Redknapp's description of the treatment provided by unqualified 'physios' could easily be mistaken as the script for a poorly written sitcom. 'I was struggling badly with my knee back then; I just could not get it right,' he says. 'I had tendonitis on my patella, so I went to see a specialist in London called Dr Roper. He said, "You will have to be nine months in plaster." I said, "I haven't got nine months." It was difficult trying to get fit. I'd play, and then my knee would go again. But you had no real medical treatment in those days. No disrespect, but the physios weren't physios, they were just ex-players. Our physio was Arthur Cunliffe who had twice played for England. He hung up his boots and became reserve team coach, then he was assistant manager, then groundsman or something and eventually he became physio. I remember we got a new machine down there one day, an ultrasound machine, and Arthur was rubbing it on my leg. We'd only had it for a few days, and after the third day I said, "It's cold this machine, Arthur. We had one at West Ham and it was warm." I looked down and it wasn't plugged in! It had a green light that was supposed to come on when it was ready and obviously that had never come on. That's just how it was in those days.'

A 2-0 defeat at Walsall in early November was the Cherries' fifth in a row, a period in which they had scored just two goals. So desperate was Hartley becoming, that he was forced to swallow his pride and restore John O'Rourke to the side to partner teenager Howard Goddard up front in the next match at home to Bury. O'Rourke seized his chance to return from the wilderness, ending the Cherries' barren run by scoring the winning goal 13 minutes from time. A very pleased O'Rourke praised the endeavours of his team-mates post-match, but made no mention of the manager who had attempted to sack him weeks earlier. 'It was great to see that one go in,' he said. 'I was pleased for the lads who had worked really hard. Now we want a few more goals and a few more wins.'

O'Rourke's wish was granted as results briefly stabilised, with two wins and a draw in the next three games. The Cherries then found themselves drawn against non-league Wycombe Wanderers in the second round of the FA Cup. In the week leading up to the game, the players took a relaxed approach to the tie, attending a club dance at Maison Royale while Wycombe warmed up with a friendly against Basingstoke. Despite his side's casual preparations, Hartley was eager to do well in the competition, saying, 'We would love a run in the cup because it would provide everyone with a bit of excitement.'

Excitement was in short supply come the day of the game. The Cherries' fans that made the trip to Loakes Park had little to cheer in a goalless draw. Hartley reflected, 'We knew it would be a difficult match and that's the way it went. But we are still in the competition and that's the important thing. Now it is up to us to make the most of our second chance of beating Wycombe.'

Before the replay, the draw for the fourth round paired the winners at home to Jack Charlton's high-flying Middlesbrough. Hartley described his players as 'excited' at the prospect of facing the previous season's Second Division champions.

Unfortunately, the excitement was misplaced, as Wycombe produced an incredible display to knock Bournemouth out of the competition with a 2-1 win in the replay at Dean Court. The Cherries had taken the lead through Howard Goddard, but when goalkeeper Kevin Charlton was unable to return after half-time due to a shoulder injury, the tide turned in the Isthmian League side's favour. After seeing his team go out of the cup as a result of conceding two second-half goals, Hartley was apoplectic at the final whistle. 'Diabolical,' he raged. 'The greatest surprise to me is that some of the players were not ashamed of losing this game. They went out to a nightclub afterwards when I thought they would have wanted to hide away somewhere. Their approach to the game was all wrong.'

With the prospect of a money-spinning tie against Middlesbrough now lost, Harold Walker had little to cheer shareholders at the annual general meeting the evening after the FA Cup defeat. 'I feel almost like an estate agent trying to sell a house the day after the roof has blown off,' he said.

Further defeats followed over Christmas, and after a controversial reverse at Swindon Town on 28 December, Hartley was relieved of his duties. Asked about his decision, Harold Walker left little to the imagination, commenting that Hartley was given his cards 'to relieve the frustration and unrest within the club'.

Hartley, for his part, helped fill any gaps in Walker's brief but enlightening statement. 'This morning the chairman said that there was too much pressure on him so I had to go,' he revealed. 'I did not promise miracles, but I did not have much time to reorganise in the way I wanted. After all, you cannot achieve a lot in five months. There was no money to get the extra players I wanted to strengthen the side.'

For months, the squad had been growing restless, with a number of seasoned professionals challenging the manager's authority by questioning his limited playing experience. John Harriss,

Bournemouth's long-serving groundsman, suggests Redknapp was among the mutinous players in the Dean Court dressing room, although his recollection of events may be inaccurate. Harry was on loan at Norwich during the final three months of Hartley's tenure. 'What was amazing about Trevor's sacking,' says Redknapp, 'is that I came back from my loan at Norwich, and the day I came back the players were staging a meeting that night at the Grange Hotel in Southbourne to have a vote of no confidence in the manager. John O'Rourke was there, a fellow called Alan Greenall, Brian Walsh, it was a big group of players. Trevor had fallen out with almost all of them. Anyway, they had the vote and then phoned up Harold Walker who came down to the hotel. Mr Walker said, "OK, fine. I'll sack him in the morning," which was unbelievable. The next morning we all came in and were sitting in the dressing room and I said to them, "All those who had a lot to say last night, Mr Walker is going to sack all of you. There is no way he's going to sack the manager." But sure enough, I was completely wrong. He walked in that morning and said, "I've sacked the manager. Carry on lads," and that was it.'

Whilst Brian Clough and legendary former Tottenham manager Bill Nicholson were being linked with the vacancy, chief scout and former centre-back Tony Nelson briefly took charge of team affairs, assisted by goalkeeper Fred Davies. 'Lovely man, Tony Nelson,' says Redknapp. 'A very quiet man. He was a centre-half who became an estate agent in Bournemouth and was involved scouting with John Bond. Tony was an absolute gentleman.'

While Nelson was spending as much time as possible with his newly inherited squad, Redknapp was on the comeback trail in the reserves, playing the full 90 minutes in a 1-0 victory over their counterparts from Southampton. 'It was difficult playing in the reserves,' says Harry. 'John Kirk was the reserve team manager and he had the hardest job in the world. You've got players out of the first team that don't want to play, and kids who are trying to find their way up the ladder. It was very, very difficult and poor old John had to suffer it. There were a lot of players around at the time who weren't in the team who had the needle. The reserve team manager's job was certainly the most difficult job at the football club.'

The partnership of Nelson and Davies largely failed to inspire the squad, with a 7-3 hammering by Plymouth at Dean Court symbolising the malaise within the club. Terrorised by strikers Paul Mariner and future Cherry Billy Rafferty, Bournemouth somehow managed three goals in 16 second-half minutes, but the final scoreline looked anything but respectable. 'They are a good side and they punished us for our defensive lapses,' commented Nelson with almost whimsical restraint.

Redknapp missed that game, instead picking up a foot injury whilst playing for the reserves at Oxford United. Despite this latest knock, the calamitous performance of the first team in Devon saw Harry make his first Third Division appearance of the season in a meeting with Aldershot the following weekend.

Redknapp did his share at the Recreation Ground to ensure Nelson's tenure would not end winless. On a poor pitch that initially threatened a postponement, the winger tested the Shots' defence several times with his accurate crossing from the right before his floated free kick from a wide position gifted Trevor Howard the opportunity to head the Cherries into the lead at the far post. A second-half goal from Howard Goddard gave Bournemouth the win, lifting them out of the relegation zone.

Prior to the next fixture against Walsall, John Benson, whose departure to Carrow Road two years earlier still rankled with the fans, returned from Norwich to take over as player-manager. Harold Walker knew the appointment of the 32-year-old Benson, who still had a home in Christchurch, would be unpopular, admitting, 'Some of the supporters are not going to be very pleased about it.'

Redknapp, on the other hand, was delighted. The arrival of his old team-mate heralded a run in the side that did not end until the final two matches of the season. So keen was Harry to retain his place in the first team that he made himself available for selection in midweek Combination League fixtures in an attempt to enhance his fitness. This dedication produced mixed results, as the heavy pitches of the mid-1970s winter took their toll on his always suspect knee. 'I was pleased to see Benno back,' says Harry, 'but it was a difficult time when he came in as manager. The club disbanded the youth team and we only had a squad of 16 players to save money. It had been going seriously downhill ever since Bondy left.'

Back in the relegation zone by the end of February, optimism was in short supply at Dean Court. Benson was unable to maintain his hitherto buoyant demeanour. 'I do not want the team to go down any more than anyone else,' he said, 'but what we need here is a more positive attitude about the real chance of staying up, rather than the too frequent references to the Fourth Division. The situation is complex, the problems numerous. It will take time to sort things out. That is why it is difficult to plan for the long term when considering, as we must, the short-term factor.'

Benson continued to pick Redknapp regardless of results, but they both knew the situation at the club was grave. Despite the omnipresent financial chaos, the manager moved to reinforce his squad by signing John Rudge from Bristol Rovers for £6,000 and splashed out a further £3,000 on Welsh centre-half Stuart Morgan on transfer deadline day in late March. Morgan, who had been a close friend of Redknapp's since their days together as teenagers at West Ham, cites his move to the south coast from Colchester as an early example of Harry dealing in the transfer market. 'Colchester played Bournemouth at the start of March, but I was sub,' says Morgan. 'Harry knew I wasn't happy, so he said to Benno, "Look, we're desperate for a centre-half. Stuart captained Colchester to promotion last season and he wants away, go and get him," and that's how it came about.'

Benson's luck finally came good in his seventh game in charge as the Cherries ran out 1-0 winners over Preston at Dean Court thanks to a first goal in almost 600 minutes of football from Les Parodi. The manager, who had retained himself at right-back, slumped to his knees with arms aloft at the final whistle. Preston still had their own player-manager in Bobby Charlton and in a move that would seem unthinkable today, were able to field a second World Cup winner in the shape of Nobby Stiles. The gap-toothed enforcer had lost some of his bite by the mid-seventies, and was no match for Redknapp, who ran the former Manchester United midfielder ragged throughout.

The Cherries had stopped the rot, but not for long. Goalscoring continued to be a problem, with just two recorded in the next five games and no more wins to celebrate. The slide down the table appeared unstoppable. 'We are not giving up,' said Benson. 'We are still aiming for the final total of 40 points and, although it is getting more difficult all the time, there is still a chance for us.'

Unfortunately, a surprise 3-2 win at soon to be promoted Charlton proved to be a false dawn. Although Redknapp hit the post with an inswinging corner in a midweek game at Peterborough in April, Bournemouth still went down 3-0 at London Road. After a 4-1 thrashing by Malcolm Allison's Crystal Palace in the next game, the pressure began to tell. Benson took the unusual step of pleading with the opposition to reciprocate the generosity of the Cherries' defence, saying, 'Nobody is creating goals against us. All of a sudden we are giving them away. I wish somebody would give us something for a change.'

Bournemouth visited Gillingham for their final away fixture of the season. Five years previously, the Gills had pipped Bournemouth on goal average in another relegation dogfight when the final game of the season saw the two clubs fight out a goalless draw. This time around, the Priestfield side, who sat comfortably in mid-table, went one better and claimed all the points thanks to a 35-yard screamer from Dick Tydeman ten minutes from time. Redknapp was replaced by Neil Merrick three minutes later, but Bournemouth were unable to find a goal and, barring unlikely mathematical circumstances, would be spending the next season in the Fourth Division. This time, even Benson didn't bother trying to make the best of it. 'We can't get out of trouble now, it seems. It's very disappointing for everybody.' Everybody included Harry Redknapp, whose withdrawal at the tail end of the game turned out to be his final act of the season.

Only an unlikely return of six goals from the Cherries in the last game of the campaign against their recent conquerors Peterborough would keep them in the Third Division. Benson put himself back in the side and gave future England striker Kevin Reeves his professional debut at 17 years of age. Bournemouth managed to win the game, but only by two goals to one, and the agony was finally over. Relegated for the second time in five years on goal average, the heady days and boundless optimism at the zenith of the Bond era seemed light years away.

'You simply cannot afford to lose so many games on your own ground,' said Benson at the final whistle, 'but it is no good looking back – we are going forward. If we all combine as one unit, work hard and roll our sleeves up, we can put this club on the road to success.'

Benson was aware that the club was not in the best of financial health, but it is unlikely he knew just how penurious circumstances were. Prior to the Peterborough match, seven players, including first-team stalwarts John Wingate and Alan Welsh, were released. To add insult to injury, less than a week after Fourth Division football became a certainty, the board announced that admission prices were to rise the following season by an average of 30%.

Supporters were no doubt delighted to see the relegated players and austerity-peddling chairman boarding a plane for Tunisia a week after the season ended. A tournament was staged in Sousse against Swansea, Charlton and Millwall whom Bournemouth, despite their poor season, managed to beat in the final. Harry Redknapp collected the trophy, a large silver platter, from Yorkshire comedian and former Doncaster Rovers centre-half Charlie Williams.

That somewhat incongruous final act in Redknapp and Bournemouth's season did little to paper over the cracks and by the time the new Fourth Division season kicked off in mid-August, both had good reason to be worried about what the future had in store.

Chapter Four

Desperate Times

1975/76

HARRY Redknapp would prove to be a bit-part player in his final season at Dean Court, making just seven starts and coming on four times as substitute. With Harry's knees about to give out and a non-existent transfer kitty, Benson increasingly relied on talented youngsters Mark Nightingale, Howard Goddard and Kevin Reeves. Despite being only 28 years old when the season kicked off, the knee injury meant that Redknapp was no longer a match for the youth team products, who all justified their selection by scoring regularly in the opening weeks of the season.

Over the summer, Benson, who had to cut short his stay in Tunisia when his wife fell ill, did what he could to prepare for a crack at an immediate return to the Third Division. Fred Davies, whose transfer to Norwich had been one of the most controversial of all, returned to replace Tony Nelson as coach. Davies' former Cardiff City team-mate John Impey joined on a three-month trial.

Benson did manage a break in Greece, declaring upon his return, 'This is one of the quietest close seasons I can remember.

There is no movement and no money. We won't be signing players for the sake of it.'

As the demands of pre-season rose with the new campaign approaching, Redknapp tore a calf muscle which ruled him out of contention for what was described as a 'secret' friendly with Chelsea. It was no more than a training exercise behind closed doors, but when the Cherries ran out surprise 3-2 winners, Benson wasted little time in contacting the *Evening Echo* to ensure they and the town learnt about this triumph. 'Naturally I was pleased that we won,' he said modestly, 'but what impressed me was the fitness of the players – they were much quicker than Chelsea. The work rate was excellent and so was the shooting.'

Benson was confident that preparations were going well as the first public friendly approached against Aldershot. Redknapp was put through what was described as a 'rigorous' fitness test, and, after coming through unscathed, made the bench for the match at the Recreation Ground. He played the entire second half, but ended up wishing that it had been another 'secret' encounter as the Shots ran out 3-0 victors. Benson, with commendable one-eyed vision, said after the match, 'Aldershot are not a good side, but on the day they were better than us.' What this said about his own team, the Bournemouth support shuddered to think.

Redknapp made another appearance in a defeat to Yeovil, which Benson described as 'terrible stuff'. Soon after, a recurrence of the old knee injury saw Harry miss the rest of pre-season and he remained on the treatment table for the opening games of the Fourth Division campaign. Desperate to bring his injury curse to an end, Harry turned to an unorthodox method of recovery. 'When I was trying to get fit,' he recalls, 'my father-in-law made me a boot, with a normal shoe and a bar through the bottom where I could screw two weights on the end so I could do leg lifts. And that boot, everybody at the football club used it. It was just a normal black shoe, size nine. Anyone who was injured who could get their foot in it would use it. That was there for years and years. People don't realise how basic it was. We didn't have any machinery, we had no gym equipment and no one went to the gym.'

Before the league campaign kicked off at Hartlepool, it emerged that work was soon to recommence on the ill-fated Walker Stand. The new headline figure for completing the project was £750,000, way beyond the reach of the football club who were holding out for a £50,000 grant from the Sports Council to get building work going.

The 700-mile round trip to Victoria Park ended in a 1-1 draw after Howard Goddard headed Bournemouth into the lead after just 35 seconds of the second half. Meanwhile, Redknapp was again striving to return to full fitness as he starred for the reserve team in a defeat to Swindon Town's reserves. Time and again the winger sent in his trademark dangerous crosses from the right, but none of the inexperienced Bournemouth forwards were able to take advantage.

Redknapp remained in the second string for the Combination League match against Fulham when the first team took on Darlington in the opening home game of the season. Benson was understandably eager to get off to a winning start at Dean Court, saying before kick-off, 'It will be good for the team and the supporters. If we approach it the right way, and take nothing for granted, then we should get the right result. This is bread and butter stuff.'

Just 4,298 of the faithful bothered to turn up for the match, hoping the three years the Cherries had spent in a higher division would be enough to see them home against the Yorkshire side. Howard Goddard scored again, but two goals from the Quakers meant Bournemouth remained winless. Trevor Howard, who was donning the number seven shirt often worn by Redknapp on the right wing, literally threw it away when being substituted for Ian Cunningham in the second half, a fit of pique which did not impress his manager. 'The player has been suspended and heavily fined,' said Benson. 'He was frustrated, but it is not right to do that sort of thing.'

Redknapp may have had to suppress a wry smile when he saw Howard's shirt flying towards the dugout, as he knew it would soon be landing on his own back. Fit again, at least for the time being, he was immediately recalled to the starting eleven for the second leg of the first round League Cup tie against Plymouth.

Benson's hope that Redknapp's supply of quality crosses into the penalty area would be strongly in evidence proved groundless as Harry had a quiet night and saw little of the ball. Bournemouth took the lead through Derek Rickard with their first meaningful attack, but goals from Phil Burrows and future England forward Paul Mariner sent the Cherries out of the competition at the first hurdle.

Harry's anonymity on the night was unusual, but even in a below-par performance he was not afraid to voice his opinions to try and influence the outcome of the game. 'He was very vocal on the pitch,' says Stuart Morgan. 'If you didn't do your job he'd let you know about it whether he was playing well or not. He'd come in at half-time and sometimes he'd take over from the manager. He'd point things out to a lot of players, and he used to point the finger at everyone. Looking back now, there was always a manager in him then. I'm not sure when he first thought about it, but it must have been a long time before he finished playing.'

Redknapp does not deny that he was a vociferous presence on the field of play, claiming youthful exuberance was in part responsible for his outspoken approach. 'I was probably a bit cocky,' he says. 'I'd normally end up having a bit of verbal with somebody on the other team. I always had that type of personality I suppose, especially as a youngster.'

Fortunately for Harry, his peripheral role in the League Cup defeat did not cost him his place in the midfield for the following

Saturday's Fourth Division match at Bradford as Howard was still serving the suspension imposed by Benson.

The leaden skies and torrential rain that enveloped Valley Parade in late August did not bode well for the Cherries to break their duck for the season at the fifth time of asking. Referee Morris Baker was forced to call for the floodlights to be switched on after just half an hour as the two teams struggled to see through the downpour. By then, Redknapp had gone in Baker's book for deliberate handball and the always pugnacious Stuart Morgan had been stretchered off after clashing with one of the City strikers.

Conditions continued to deteriorate and both teams laboured unsuccessfully. With John Benson making his customary appearance at right-back, Fred Davies was charged with making the substitutions and in the 83rd minute he instructed 17-year-old Kevin Reeves to do what he could to warm up. Just as Davies was rifling through the subs' boards for Howard Goddard's number, Bournemouth's other teenage striker rose to meet Redknapp's cross and head in the goal that would give the Cherries their first win of the season.

Redknapp had come to life in the second half, teasing the Bradford defence with his trickery and precise crossing, and Goddard had no hesitation in praising his team-mate. 'It's great when Harry lays them on like that. That cross was pure magic, and all I had to do was put it away.'

This may have been years before Redknapp's fame and public persona took on a life of its own, but he wasn't found wanting when it came to a soundbite. 'Didn't he do well?' commented the winger when asked about Goddard's goal, combining just the right mix of flattery and impudence in exactly the way that would endear him to the wider football world two decades later.

Trevor Howard returned to the first-team squad for the next fixture against Doncaster at Dean Court, but Redknapp retained his place on the right wing courtesy of his fine performance in the monsoon at Bradford. To accommodate both midfielders, Benson, possibly concerned about Fred Davies' ability to take charge from the touchline, dropped himself.

The Bournemouth manager was eager for his side to begin picking up points at home. 'We have got a couple of good results from our away matches, but now we have got to make sure that we do the same at home. It's no use picking up these away points if we let them slip away on our own ground.'

But let them slip away the Cherries did. After pummelling Rovers' goal for the majority of the match, the home side ran out of steam as the second half wore on and conceded what proved to be Doncaster's winning goal in the 79th minute. Redknapp joined his team-mates in surging past the opposition's concrete-booted defence from the first whistle, but a series of wasted opportunities saw the Yorkshire side's goalkeeper Peacock remain unbeaten. As the prospect of another home defeat loomed after the goal, the Dean Court faithful began to vent their frustration on Benson and the players.

It was at this time that Redknapp's former West Ham team-mate and good friend Bobby Howe left Dean Court. Since Trevor Hartley's departure, Howe had been coaching the youth team after injury had curtailed his playing career. With the youth set-up on the verge of being broken up as a cost-cutting measure, Howe jumped ship for a similar position at Plymouth Argyle. He and Redknapp were to remain in touch, however, and would soon be seeing each other again in unlikely circumstances on the other side of the Atlantic.

Howe's departure also meant that there was a temporary vacancy managing the youth team. Harold Walker and the board of directors were not about to attempt to hire someone new for this role because youth development at the club would soon be a thing of the past. Instead, they charged John Benson with the role, and the beleaguered Bournemouth manager was quite happy to pass that responsibility on to anyone who showed a flicker of interest. It was these circumstances that led to Harry Redknapp dipping his toe into management for the very first time, as he and Stuart Morgan teamed up to put the youngsters through their paces. 'At certain times John Benson would let Harry get on with things,' says Morgan. 'Harry and I went off and took the youth team after Bobby Howe left. They were more or less scrapping the youth system at that time. We took them when they were playing in the South West and Wales Youth League. We did several games together.'

Supporters were cheered by the inclusion of youth product Kevin Reeves in the starting eleven for the next match at Stockport County. The closest Bournemouth came to scoring in a goalless draw was when Redknapp hit the woodwork after Reeves had generously laid the ball into his path. In the event, the winger was flagged offside anyway. It proved to be a frustrating evening for Harry, who was substituted for Derek Rickard in the second half, a seemingly innocuous event which turned out to be the beginning of the end of the future manager's time at Dean Court as a player.

Towards the end of September, Benson's team recorded a long overdue first home win against Fourth Division pacesetters Newport County with goals from Stuart Morgan and Kevin Reeves. The delighted Bournemouth manager, who described the victory as 'great for morale', confirmed after the match that he would not consider reinstating himself despite his return to full fitness, saying, 'I cannot come into the side after that fine performance. What would be the point of changing it anyway?'

After trudging off the pitch at Portman Road following a last-minute defeat in a reserve match against Ipswich on the same day, Benson's words would not have been music to Redknapp's ears. After holding on to his shirt for the large part of the previous season's doomed battle against relegation, Harry had now lost his place in the first team just as results were beginning to pick up.

One defeat in the next six games saw the Cherries climb the table and threaten to make good on their publicly voiced aim of an immediate return to the Third Division. If Redknapp were in any doubt that his own demotion to the netherworld of reserve team football would not be prolonged, Benson was on hand to clear matters up. 'The kids are staying,' announced the manager after Kevin Reeves and Howard Goddard had both scored in an impressive 3-0 victory over high-flying Brentford in the next match. 'I am building up a side, and that means I intend to keep my players, not get rid of them.' The Bournemouth boss knew transfer activity was not entirely in his control, but the message to Redknapp was clear: while the kids stay at the club, they stay in the team.

For once, it was not Harry's knee that was keeping him out of the first team. He was turning out regularly in the Football Combination and wins over Leicester and Chelsea saw the reserves climb their table. Although Redknapp was proving a key figure in this success, it was little consolation for him and others such as Les Parodi and John Rudge who had grown used to first-team football at Dean Court.

In the decades since Redknapp hung up his boots, there has been the occasional suggestion that following his transfer from the cultured environs of West Ham, he was unable to cope with the physical intimidation he experienced in the Third and Fourth Divisions. The accusation that a lack of courage was instrumental in Harry's lengthy spells out of the team towards the end of his playing days at Dean Court is most forcefully levelled in John Crace's book *Harry's Games: Inside the Mind of Harry Redknapp*. Crace asserts that having suffered from serious injuries more than once, it would only make sense if Redknapp felt intimidated by the defenders in the lower leagues. It's a theory that Crace proffers over more than two pages, but he is only able to produce an unnamed 'Bournemouth old-timer' to confirm that Harry was a 'fancy dan' who shied away from the rough stuff.

Redknapp has not forgotten the physical nature of the Football League's bottom two divisions, laughing at the memory of the battle that formed a significant part of each match. 'Everybody got the same treatment from the opposition's defenders,' says Harry. 'That's what full-backs were; they were cloggers and their job was to stop you playing. Their motto was: "The ball might go past, the man might go past, but the ball and the man won't go past." They could get away with anything. It didn't worry me. Most of them were slow in the Third Division compared to the First. It was just the standard of football was nowhere near what I had been used to. A lot of teams would come here and just look to stop us playing, look for a draw. It was quite difficult at times.'

Harry puts forward an alternative, tactical reason that his playing career began to wane at a relatively early age. 'From the early seventies, the full-backs started to get tighter to the wingers. They would almost stand next to you. So it became very, very hard to get the ball when you were stuck out there. You had to rely on people to give you the ball if you played out wide and it became a position that was almost null and void.'

Kevin Reeves, who played many times with Redknapp at Dean Court as a teenager, does not remember his team-mate appearing nervous at the prospect of facing the opposition's hard men. 'The full-backs were absolute brutes,' Reeves recalls, 'but Harry wasn't frightened of anybody in terms of him playing. He had fantastic ability; great feet. I suppose when you lose that little bit of pace, that little bit of zip, it becomes difficult when you are playing in the lower leagues. It is easier to play at a higher level than down the divisions because you are playing with better players. But Harry didn't have any fear and I'm surprised it has been suggested.'

Stuart Morgan, who was a battle-hardened lower league defender himself, remembers Harry taking a good deal of punishment when they played together for the Cherries. 'Harry was obviously never the strongest of players,' says Morgan. 'He looked like someone from Belsen when he was 18 he was so thin and skinny. He didn't get a great deal of protection. Full-backs were coached and encouraged to get tight to wingers. Harry used to get an awful lot of rough treatment when he was at Bournemouth, but he could deal with it. He'd lay the ball off and get in behind defenders. He used to have a few little rucks with other players. Everyone knew what he was like so he got that treatment because he had a bit of pace. He was always getting whacked around his ankles and that sort of thing. The attitude of the opposing managers was, "Stop Redknapp and you stop Bournemouth."'

Redknapp's disappointment at being confined to the Combination League did not impact upon his performances. The day after the first team's victory at Southport he put in an impressive performance as the reserves drew with QPR. The winger was a constant thorn in the side of the Rangers defence and was unlucky not to score when his rasping effort hit the post in the first few minutes of the match.

It was the same again for Redknapp in the following weekend's reserve outing against a less than popular Norwich City. Harry's trademark crossing accuracy was praised at the conclusion of the match by onlookers, but he was unable to claim any assists as the game ended goalless.

At the end of October, John Benson himself conceded the penalty which gave Fourth Division leaders Lincoln, led by 31-year-old future England manager Graham Taylor, all three points at Sincil Bank. On the same day, the 692 enthusiasts who turned up at Dean Court to watch Redknapp and the rest of the reserves play Arsenal in the Football Combination were cursing the home team's lack of potency as they laboured to their eighth draw in 15 games.

This lack of success may have driven those present to distraction, with many of the crowd heading for the exit long before the final whistle, but that was of little concern to John Benson, whose only aim was to see the Cherries climb further up the Fourth Division table. Unwilling to play himself again in the next match against fellow mid-table hopefuls Cambridge United, the Bournemouth manager installed Ian Cunningham in the starting eleven and called Harry Redknapp up from the reserves to take the number 12 shirt.

The delighted Redknapp came on for Steve Buttle in the 70th minute, by which time Bournemouth were already 2-0 up. Five minutes later he was reminded how it felt to be on the pitch to celebrate a goal with his team-mates when Kevin Reeves coolly steered the ball past United keeper Graham Smith to assure the Cherries of victory.

Unfortunately for Harry, Benson paid little heed to the time-honoured practice of not making any changes to a winning team once star striker Goddard passed a late fitness test prior to the midweek fixture against Crewe at Gresty Road. The results of the test may not have been entirely conclusive, however, as Benson chose to cover his selection by handing the substitute's spot to striker Derek Rickard with Redknapp dropping out.

Harry was once again confined to the purgatory of the Combination League. His mood at returning to the reserves so quickly may not have been sunny, and it would have darkened further when they blew a two-goal lead to draw 3-3 at Reading. Even a return to his old manor, the Boleyn Ground, was unable to provide a boost for Redknapp's now flagging playing career. With old friends and colleagues watching on, Harry found deeper reserves of motivation than any of the other 21 players who plodded through 90 rain-soaked minutes in east London. Redknapp was Bournemouth's best player going forward and in defence that afternoon, overcoming the conditions to orchestrate the Cherries' rare attacks and frequently chasing back to frustrate the unrelenting Hammers. Second only to Redknapp for the majority of the match was goalkeeper Steve Chalk, who dealt well with the slippery ball until the 76th minute when he let a quickly taken Geoff Pike free kick slip through his hands to give the home team a 1-0 victory.

Throughout the painful decline in his playing career, Harry continued to develop his skills as a coach, taking his coaching badges at Lilleshall and picking up ad hoc experience during Bournemouth's training sessions. 'John Benson was looking for some help,' recalls Stuart Morgan. 'Harry was so confident in his coaching ability, even as a player, that he would step in during training and say, "I think we should be doing it this way. I think we should be getting the ball a little bit earlier to the other wing. We should be getting the ball in quicker to the strikers." Harry was always like that. Always positive and he always spoke well. A lot of players respected him and thought, "Well, he was right that time." He was always that way inclined.'

With Redknapp's unofficial input, the first team continued to put together decent results and going into the winter months were well placed to make a push for promotion. Optimism grew following a goalless draw with top-of-the-table Northampton Town at the end of November, with the Cherries being the first side to take as much as a point off the rampant Cobblers in eight games. Benson joined the murmurs of satisfaction around Dean Court after the final whistle. 'We matched them well and might have won,' he beamed. 'If we are prepared to work the same way in future games, then we can maintain our challenge in the league.'

And maintained it was, with three wins and just one defeat in the Fourth Division in December. With the pitches growing heavier and the toll of a lengthy spell in the first team and playing for England Youth beginning to take its toll, Benson took the decision to rest Kevin Reeves at the start of the month.

'He needs a break,' said the Bournemouth manager of Reeves, a circumstance which opened the door for Harry Redknapp to return to the line-up for the long trip to Workington. The Cumbrian side were struggling near the foot of the table, and Redknapp made light of his spell in the reserves to feature prominently in a 3-1 victory. He looked fresh and full of running throughout, and played the key pass in the build-up to substitute Derek Rickard scoring Bournemouth's third goal.

Despite the result putting his team in fifth place in the Fourth Division, Benson was unimpressed with the performance. 'We did enough to win it, without playing all that well. But the players know they can do better and that's the main thing.'

They would have their chance in the second round of the FA Cup. In an era when the competition was still the grandest prize in English football, it was unheard of for a manager to field a weakened side to concentrate on the league. Such had been the case in the first round when Benson had sent out his strongest eleven to face non-league Sutton United.

Even at full strength, Bournemouth struggled to overcome the part-timers as they drew 1-1 at Gander Green Lane and then squeezed through with a 1-0 victory in the replay at Dean Court. The draw for the second round paired Benson's team with Hereford United, whose January 1972 win over Newcastle United went down for ever in FA Cup folklore.

In the days leading up to the tie, Redknapp was pictured in the *Evening Echo* trailing Keith Miller as the squad ran up St Catherine's Hill in Christchurch as part of the 'hard day' in their weekly training routine.

His fitness seemingly not in doubt, Redknapp retained his place in the side. Hereford were riding high in the Third Division, and as a result the game was viewed as the most attractive of the season to date at Dean Court. A crowd of 6,181, Bournemouth's highest attendance of the campaign, paid at the turnstiles, a figure which pleased chairman Harold Walker, who was still fighting financial fires off the pitch.

Prior to the cup tie, Walker outlined 'streamlined' plans for the stand bearing his name, conceding the original scheme was too expensive. The framework of the stand had remained untouched for over 18 months, leading to growing complaints from residents about the 'ugly skeleton' looming over King's Park.

Bournemouth came out of the match against Hereford with their heads held high. A 2-2 draw meant a replay would be required at Edgar Street in midweek, another useful payday for the club. Redknapp was involved in both of the Cherries' goals at Dean Court, taking the throw-in that led to Phil Ashworth's opener and the corner from which Howard Goddard equalised in the 86th minute. Benson again cut a frustrated figure at the final whistle, dissatisfied with both his players and the prospect of a visit to York City's Bootham Crescent should his team win the replay. 'I specifically told the players not to be satisfied with holding on to that one-goal lead. I urged them to keep attacking. Of course it's a bad draw, but we want to get through.'

Unfortunately for Bournemouth, hopes of a surprise win at Hereford faded when Neil Hague and Stuart Morgan were ruled out through injury. Benson was forced to play himself for the first time in months. Although his team put in a spirited display, they went out of the competition after two quick goals from the Bulls in the second half ended the contest. Redknapp again showed himself in a good light, being at the centre of most things the Cherries did going forward.

Benson was happy to return to the dugout when Stuart Morgan was declared fit for the Fourth Division match against Huddersfield Town. Redknapp was named on the bench with a refreshed Kevin Reeves drafted back into the attack. Harry was not given the chance to enter the field of play as Howard Goddard, who was himself only declared fit minutes before kick-off, scored the only goal of the game to give the Cherries another valuable two points.

Redknapp was on the bench again for the post-Christmas encounter with Swansea City, coming on for Howard Goddard in a 2-0 win which put the Cherries in the top six going into 1976. The game was goalless at half-time, and Benson read the riot act in the dressing room after a first-half performance that had him tearing his hair out. Suitably chastised, his players upped their game in the second half, but it was only through the introduction of Redknapp that they managed to avoid another earbashing at full time.

Entering the contest in the 73rd minute, Harry swung in one of his trademark pinpoint crosses ten minutes later from which Steve Buttle gave the Cherries the lead with his first goal of the season. Three minutes later, Phil Ashworth clipped in a second and the victory was secure.

After the match, Benson revealed that the two points gained meant his players were on target to reach the 28 points he had set them to achieve by New Year and a draw in the next fixture at Torquay would suffice. Redknapp kept his place on the bench for the match at Plainmoor, and it would have come as some surprise to him that he was not called into action despite a poor display by the Cherries leading to a 2-1 defeat against Benson's former club.

A quick opportunity to bounce back presented itself as Bournemouth visited Torquay's Devon rivals Exeter City for their first match of 1976. With Clive Payne and John Impey unavailable, Benson was forced to don his boots once again in a match wrecked as a spectacle by howling 80mph gales. With Bournemouth a goal behind at half-time, Benson replaced himself with Redknapp in order that the Cherries might attack the Grecians' goal at every opportunity. Unfortunately, this move came too late, as Bournemouth were against the wind in the second half and failed to muster a single shot on target in the 45 minutes before the game came to an end.

Perhaps Benson saw the error of his ways because he handed Redknapp a starting slot for the next game against Bradford City. The match took place eight days after the defeat at St James Park, a period in which Benson had been forced to confront the reality of the minuscule transfer kitty available to him as he searched for a striker to bolster the push for promotion in the second half of the season. A £2,000 bid for Southport's Bobby Gough failed and attempts to bring in forwards from clubs in higher divisions on loan were equally unsuccessful. It was not an experience Benson enjoyed. 'It has not been a good week,' said a frustrated Bournemouth boss. 'You don't get any favours.'

To make matters worse, Benson was then forced to suspend his star striker Howard Goddard for two weeks when the teenager, full of bravado following his outstanding start to life in the first team, decided he couldn't be bothered to turn up for training. 'That's all I needed,' complained Benson, before conceding, 'I had to do it. No one player is bigger than the club and I will not put up with this sort of attitude. This sort of thing can be taken too far. In fairness to the other players, I could not let it pass without taking action.'

After months of frustration in the reserves and bench warming, Goddard's youthful conceit suddenly provided an opportunity for Redknapp to stake a claim for a longer run in the first team. Yet again, he did not allow his chance to go to waste. Against Bradford, Harry cleverly swept past the onrushing City defence midway through the second half and slipped the ball inside for Kevin Reeves who finished well from a tight angle. Redknapp then won the free kick that led to what proved to be Bournemouth's winning goal. Mark Nightingale took the set piece, finding Steve Buttle, who finished with the aid of the inside of the post.

Unfortunately for Redknapp, his opportunity was short-lived. Benson finally managed to bring some new blood to the squad when midfielder Billy Steele arrived on a month's loan from Norwich. After such an arduous and frustrating search for a player, there was no chance Benson was not going to find a place in the starting eleven for Steele and Redknapp, despite performing well whenever he had been on the pitch, was back in the number 12 shirt.

Steele's debut came at Newport County, where the home side benefited from an early Stuart Morgan own goal. Redknapp replaced the beleaguered Welsh defender in the 65th minute and again delivered his customary assist, this time for Clive Payne to grab Bournemouth's consolation goal in a 3-1 defeat.

Steele's arrival coincided with a testimonial for Cherries physio Arthur Cunliffe. The former England winger made use of his contacts at Carrow Road to invite John Bond to bring Norwich City to Dean Court for the occasion, a fixture that he hoped would attract a decent crowd with Ted MacDougall and Phil Boyer spearheading the Canaries' attack.

Through no fault of Cunliffe's, the game became the focus of vitriol and protests from many Bournemouth supporters who remained bitter about Bond's ransacking of their team once he had departed for Norfolk. A boycott of the match was organised, although the stay-away fans made a point of contributing what would have been their entrance fee to Cunliffe's fund. Many among the 4,720 who did attend took the opportunity to hurl abuse and missiles at Bond and the City players throughout the match.

Redknapp lined up alongside former team-mates Alan Groves and Micky Cave, who were making guest appearances in red and black on the night. Mel Machin was another old boy in the Norwich team and he joined MacDougall and Boyer on the scoresheet to remind the Bournemouth fans exactly why they were so furious with Bond. Redknapp had retained a good relationship with the Norwich manager, but was left to regret turning out in Cunliffe's honour when he sustained a groin injury which rendered him unavailable for selection in the upcoming game against Stockport County. Although he wasn't to know it at the time, this latest niggle would put an end to his playing days at Dean Court save for a brief but eventful return to the line-up in the role of player-coach six years later.

Redknapp's struggle to be fit for selection was boosted when severe winter weather led to Bournemouth's game at Rochdale being called off twice, resulting in a gameless fortnight for Benson's side as January turned to February. When thawing conditions on the south coast allowed the Dean Court ground staff to get the next scheduled game on against Crewe, Redknapp's injury had not healed and he was unable to even make an appearance for the reserves. From there, events moved apace, and with the first team continuing to put the results together, the winger knew he would have to endure another season on the periphery were he to be retained by Benson.

'Absolutely I was worried about the future,' says Harry. 'I thought, "Where do I go from here?" At that time, I looked at buying a Bournemouth taxi but didn't really have the money. I would have had to have taken out a loan to buy it. There was no money in the game. When you finished playing, you came out of it with nothing. Even the top players didn't earn serious money. The boys who won the World Cup in 1966 had to get jobs after they finished playing. Geoff Hurst worked in insurance!'

Fortunately for Harry, friendships forged during his days in the Cherries' squad were to prove useful for more than just a few pints at the Ship in Distress. As he and Sandra wondered where the next pay packet would come from when the season ended, a long-distance call from his old pal Jimmy Gabriel couldn't have arrived at a better time.

Tired of mooching around the lower leagues playing for managers he didn't respect, Gabriel had left Britain for the nascent North American Soccer League. Appointed player-coach of the Seattle Sounders, the Scot had not forgotten his old team-mate and car-sharing pal from their days together on the south coast. When the Washington State club's manager John Best announced he was on the lookout for a winger, Gabriel called Redknapp, who did not require a great deal of persuasion. Harry remembers how the transfer came about. 'Jimmy Gabriel went out to Seattle and played. He was player-coach and then assistant coach. That's when he phoned up and asked me to go out there. He had the house opposite me and when he came back he said, "Look, do you fancy coming over?" and I said "Yeah, I'd love to Jim," so that was it.'

In mid-February Gabriel flew back to Britain to seal the transfer, and received little in the way of objection from John Benson. 'It's a good opportunity for Harry,' said the Bournemouth boss, who in all likelihood was preparing to release Redknapp at the end of the campaign to further trim the wage bill. Despite his obvious talent for coaching, there was little chance of him remaining at Dean Court in any capacity. As long-serving groundsman John Harriss says, 'Harry had this problem with his knee and it slowed him down. Hampered him really. From what he was good at he struggled through fitness to achieve his high standards. In those days the backroom staff was much smaller, so when your playing days were up or your contract was up that was it. The club didn't retain you.'

With the NASL season running through the summer months, the Redknapps were due to fly to the US in April before the conclusion of the Fourth Division campaign. With his injury record and always suspect knee, it would have seemed reasonable that the winger would not have exposed himself to the risk of further setbacks. Miraculously, Harry recovered soon after signing for Seattle to turn out for the Cherries' reserve team against a West Ham side packed with his old friends from east London. Foremost among these was Billy Bonds, returning from a three-month lay-off himself. Bonds, whose close friendship with Redknapp ended years later in disputed circumstances surrounding Harry's elevation to the manager's role at Upton Park, showed the handful of onlookers why he had such a long and distinguished career in claret and blue, scoring twice in a 3-0 win for the Hammers.

Whilst the Redknapps were packing their bags in preparation for the move to the US, Benson struggled to keep the first team in contention for a return to the Third Division. A 3-3 draw with Southport was notable, not only for the six goals scored, but for a bomb scare in the 76th minute which led to the 4,433 in attendance making an unscheduled Dean Court pitch invasion whilst the game was held up for 20 minutes before the all-clear was given by the police.

Another six goals were scored in bizarre circumstances when the Cherries visited table-topping Northampton a week later. A goal down in the 37th minute, Bournemouth somehow managed to concede a further five times before the players trudged off at half-time to pay their last respects to their hopes of promotion. Benson then reminded his players of their responsibilities in no uncertain terms, and the second half did not produce another goal. On the prospect of making an immediate return to the third tier, Benson commented, 'We have to be realistic. We are now left in a position where we cannot afford to drop more than two or three points in our last ten matches.'

As it transpired, Bournemouth would win only three of those matches, and finish in a disappointing sixth position. Harry Redknapp did not hang around to watch this morale-sapping run-in to the end of the season. Having been advised by medical experts to bring down the curtain on his playing career, he had subjected his knee to a series of injections in the hope that the treatment would allow him to have a future in the Football League upon his return from the USA. Sadly, the knee was damaged beyond the repair of mid-1970s medical science, and he was all but finished as a player in English football before turning 30. On Thursday 29 April, Harry, Sandra, Mark and Jamie flew out to the Pacific coast of the United States to join up with Jimmy Gabriel and the Seattle Sounders. 'Bournemouth didn't stand in my way,' he recalls. 'Back then when the club was in the Fourth Division, it was a pretty desperate time.'

Chapter Five

Hiatus

1976 to 1981

SINCE its inception in 1968, the North American Soccer League had succeeded in establishing itself in a very American way. To build its brand in the highly competitive US sports market, the league used a combination of signing star players from South America and Europe and riding roughshod over the sacred traditions of the game. Pele, Johan Cruyff, Franz Beckenbauer and George Best were among the globally recognised names whose presence at the likes of the Los Angeles Aztecs and the New York Cosmos saw the league boom in the mid-1970s. By introducing initiatives such as domed stadiums, artificial pitches and overtime to do away with 'ties', the NASL brought enough colour to the game to ensure it was growing rapidly at the time the Redknapps crossed the Atlantic.

No sooner had they unpacked than Redknapp found himself sharing a pitch with Pele as the Seattle Sounders welcomed the Brazilian's New York Cosmos for a friendly to celebrate the Washington State team's relocation from the 12,000-seat Memorial Stadium to the new King County Domed Stadium, known locally as the Kingdome. For Harry, life must have suddenly seemed very sweet indeed as he swapped the icy conditions of Somerton Park in Newport, where he had played his last competitive game in front of 1,473 hardy souls in January, for a 58,128 sell-out crowd in a $56 million development, the like of which would not be seen in English football for at least another two decades.

Harry's knee remained delicate, even in the gentler confines of the NASL, and after appearing in the victory over the Cosmos, he was unable to turn out in any of the Sounders' first three fixtures in the Western Division of the Pacific Conference. Redknapp finally made his competitive debut for his new club on 7 May 1976 in a win over San Diego and then assisted in all three of the Sounders' goals in a 4-3 defeat to the George Best-inspired Los Angeles Aztecs. When his team met the Aztecs again later in the season, Harry was instrumental in the Sounders gaining their revenge, scoring his first 'goal' in the NASL when calmly finishing the decisive penalty in a shoot-out which concluded any match that remained level after extra time.

In all, Harry played some part in 15 of the Sounders' 24 regular season matches in his debut season in the US, although rarely did he complete a full 90 minutes. A second-place finish saw Seattle qualify for the end-of-season play-offs, where they reached the quarter-final before being knocked out by the Minnesota Kicks in a 3-0 defeat in Bloomington.

At the season's end, John Best left Seattle to take the head coach's position at the Vancouver Whitecaps. It was a decision which led to Jimmy Gabriel being promoted to the top job at the Kingdome, and the Scot wasted no time in promoting his former Ship in Distress drinking partners Harry Redknapp and Bobby Howe to be his assistants. Thus Redknapp's first official coaching role would soon begin.

First, however, Harry would have to find a way to tide himself and his family over during the winter months. The NASL season ended in late August and pre-season training did not begin again until March the following year. The Redknapps returned to England, and with his options limited, Harry attempted to extend his playing career in the Fourth Division by signing on a month-long trial for Brentford. The Bees had finished 17th in manager John Docherty's first season in charge, and the prospect of signing a 29-year-old with Redknapp's pedigree for no transfer fee appeared too good to refuse.

The west London side had made a poor start to the 1976/77 season. Knocked out of the League Cup by Watford before the league campaign had even kicked off, they picked up a solitary point from their first four matches and found themselves joint bottom of the table going into their next game against an unbeaten Aldershot.

With his job on the line, Docherty decided to take a look at Redknapp in a reserve match three days before the meeting with the Shots. With his team trailing at half-time, Docherty was farcically relieved of his duties, entering the dressing room to tell his players that he had been sacked and wishing them good luck in the second half.

His head still reeling from this turn of events, Redknapp found himself in the first team for the match at the Recreation Ground on 10 September. If there were any lingering hopes that he could still stand the rigours of the English game, they were dashed when his brief comeback was aborted after 38 minutes of what turned out to be his only appearance for the Bees when he suffered three broken ribs after coming off worse in a challenge with an Aldershot defender.

When Harry recovered from his injuries he rejected opportunities to try out for a handful of Football League clubs and instead signed for AP Leamington, a side at the foot of the Southern League Premier Division. Unlike the professional clubs he had flirted with since his time at Brentford came to an end, Leamington did not require Redknapp to turn up for midweek evening training sessions. As a result, Harry was able to remain in Christchurch with his family whilst maintaining his level of fitness by training with John Benson's squad and his old team-mates at Bournemouth.

Upon returning to Dean Court, Harry found the Cherries in an even more beleaguered state than when he departed. With the club struggling in the Fourth Division, the remnants of what was John Bond's squad were long gone and the half-built Walker Stand stood rusting and abandoned behind the Brighton Beach End. Even the match programme, which had broken new ground with its innovative design and content, had reverted back to a plain and functional document.

Merely to ensure he would have a full squad to select from at the start of the 1976/77 season, John Benson was forced to sell Howard Goddard to Swindon. This was a decision which infuriated the faithful who had watched on as the striker made his debut whilst still at school in April 1973 and played with maturity which belied his tender years in the seasons that followed. Although Benson brought in experienced players like Hughen Riley and Geoff Butler with the fee he received for Goddard, the playing staff, like everything else at the club, remained threadbare.

Eight points in the first five games, at a time when two points were awarded for a win, threatened to lift the gloom that engulfed Dean Court, but not for long. The Cherries failed to win away from home again for the rest of the season and only managed a total of 15 goals on the road in the entire campaign. The team were knocked out of both cups at the first hurdle and to make matters worse star striker Kevin Reeves was sold to Norwich for a paltry £50,000. Once again, the Cherries were left to regret their profligacy at their leisure, as Reeves went on to represent England and command a £1 million fee when he moved on to Manchester City.

A 13th place finish was well below expectations around Dean Court. With no money to spend and a pile of debts that were threatening to become a mountain, the following season promised little but more of the same.

Redknapp's time at AP Leamington's Windmill Ground was brief and inevitably disrupted by injury. He made a handful of appearances, laying on plenty of chances for his team-mates with his trademark crossing, but missed more games than he played. Such was Harry's regret at having to withdraw from so many fixtures that he began to refuse to draw whatever wages he was due from the club.

It was with some relief that after muddling through the British winter the Redknapps returned to Washington State on the last day of February 1977. He was joined in Seattle by his old friend Bobby Moore, who would play seven times for the Sounders during the coming season. The former West Ham defender had already tasted the NASL with San Antonio Thunder, but appears to have taken little persuading to leave Texas and head to the Pacific North West.

Although still registered as a player, with coaching now his main responsibility, Redknapp was not expected to feature a great deal on the pitch during the season. Despite this, Harry was able to find the resolve to travel to Hawaii to play in a pre-season friendly against the former San Diego Thunder who had left California for Honolulu during the close season. With the NASL season proper kicking off before the English season had finished, Harry was also required to turn out in the first four Sounders games. After three defeats, the 2-1 victory over the San Jose Earthquakes on 21 May was Harry's last appearance of the season as the contingent from the Football League, which included former Cherries team-mates Mel Machin and Micky Cave, arrived to bolster Gabriel's squad.

Redknapp was not idle during the remaining months of the season as he cut his teeth in management. To begin, he oversaw the Sounders reserves, but it wasn't long before he was having regular input into the first team. In what appears with hindsight to be a sign of what was to come, he tasted success from the touchline almost immediately.

The Sounders' second string recorded 12 wins and just three defeats in their first season under the Londoner's guidance, with defender Jim McAlister breaking into the first team at the end of the season. Harry's comments in a Sounders programme from that year demonstrate an early commitment to blooding youthful talent. 'When you get the boys coming in and playing in the first team, it's very satisfying,' he said. 'It's a boost for me to see them coming in after working with them for a year or so.'

Gabriel's team showed patchy form throughout the campaign, finishing third in the four-team Pacific Conference Western Division with a record of 14 wins and 12 defeats. Sneaking into the end-of-season play-offs by the skin of their teeth, the Sounders hit form at the perfect time, seeing off the Vancouver Whitecaps, Minnesota Kicks and Los Angeles Aztecs to progress to the 1977 Soccer Bowl against Pele's New York Cosmos in Portland's Civic Stadium.

With Redknapp assisting Gabriel on the touchline, a crowd of 35,548 saw the Cosmos' Steve Hunt steal the ball off Sounders' goalkeeper Tony Chursky in the 19th minute to score the game's opening goal. Seattle managed to equalise through Tommy Ord four minutes later, but Italian Giorgio Chinaglia scored a header in the second half to give Pele victory in the final game of his professional career. Harry's protege Jim McAlister was as disappointed as the rest of his Sounders team-mates at not collecting the trophy, although he did manage to claim Pele's shirt for his endeavours.

Back in Dorset, meanwhile, the glamour Redknapp and the other exiles from England were tasting in America was distinctly absent. As the 1977/78 season approached, promising youngster Steve Gritt was sold to Charlton Athletic in a further attempt to balance the books. Following a 1-0 defeat to Northampton in

October, Bournemouth found themselves second bottom of the entire Football League and the portentous prospect of applying for re-election hung over Dean Court. Fortunately, a bargain £5,000 signing of Roger Brown from Redknapp's old employers AP Leamington just about did enough to shore things up. A 17th place finish told its own tale of another poor season in the Fourth Division with the league's lowest tally of 41 goals scored in 46 games. Further poor showings in the cups, a shoestring budget and tumbling attendances added to the bleak mood around Dean Court.

With his coaching credentials in the ascendancy and a permanent role in Seattle's backroom staff, Redknapp was able to make ends meet over the winter back in England by scouting for the Sounders. His immediate money troubles had eased, although Harry knew that the future remained uncertain. 'I was pleased about going to play in Seattle,' he says, 'but even then, although we were really enjoying it, it wasn't long term. I was always wondering what I was going to do next. It was a very difficult time in those days as a footballer. None of us had any real money to talk of and it was always going to be a struggle.'

Putting these concerns to one side, Redknapp featured in three regular season matches in central midfield for the Sounders during April, the first month of the NASL season. The second of these appearances saw the now veteran winger play a starring role in a shoot-out tiebreaker victory over the Toronto Metros. In order to succeed in the tiebreaker, Harry was required to start 35 yards from the goal and beat the Toronto keeper within five seconds of his first touch of the ball. Described in the match report as one of the 'big guns' that the Seattle line-up rallied around, Harry did not don his boots for the remainder of the season, concentrating instead on developing his reserve team players and coaching skills. He maintained, however, that his playing days were not yet over, telling reporters, 'I'd still like to play for this club, but I also enjoy coaching as well. I'm happy coaching, but I still think I could play in this league, no problem.'

Despite this understandable desire to prolong his playing career, Redknapp's coaching style was already developing, with boosting his players' egos high on the agenda. 'If they don't feel confident, then they're never going to be there,' he told the Seattle media. 'They're always going to feel second best. And if you feel that way in life, you are never going to be the best, are you?'

Harry also provided Sounders' fans with a glimpse of his working relationship with Howe and Gabriel. 'I've got the greatest respect in the world for Jimmy and Bobby,' he said. 'We're real mates anyway, and we've got a really great relationship between the three of us. It's great to work with people like that.'

The harmonious coaching trio led the Sounders into the play-offs as a 15-15 regular season record saw the club finish third in the Western Division of the Pacific Conference. With such an average record, it was no surprise when Gabriel's team fell at the first hurdle of the knockout stage to a Franz Beckenbauer-inspired New York Cosmos.

As Redknapp returned to England once again to continue his scouting role, John Benson was doing his best to make the small transfer kitty he had been given by the Bournemouth board of directors go as far as possible. Six new players were signed, including goalkeeper Kenny Allen from the Southern League following the departure of long-serving custodian Kieron Baker to Bobby Robson's Ipswich Town for £20,000.

The Cherries once again flattered to deceive and, after a victory over south coast rivals Portsmouth saw them well placed in the promotion places, another poor run of form in the autumn saw them slip out of the top six into mid-table. Spirits were raised when the prodigal Ted MacDougall returned on a free transfer from Southampton. By coincidence, on the day MacDougall returned, Bournemouth were awarded over £20,000 by the High Court following a legal wrangle over his initial transfer to Manchester United five years previously.

A run of four straight defeats in December was only halted when a spell of atrocious winter weather saw a rash of postponements at the beginning of 1979. The Cherries only played one match in the whole of January, but a 1-0 defeat at home to Crewe Alexandra was enough for John Benson to tender his resignation, citing the pressure the job was putting on his family. Following a brief search in which Bobby Moore and Rodney Marsh were both touted as candidates, the board at Dean Court appointed the experienced Alec Stock.

Stock must have been as surprised as everyone else around the club when, in his first game in charge, the Cherries thrashed Doncaster Rovers 7-1. This best league win for 22 years featured a brace from Ted MacDougall, his first goals in the Fourth Division since his much-heralded return.

MacDougall was on target again as the Cherries beat Port Vale 3-1 the following Tuesday and supporters were suddenly dreaming of a dramatic surge up the table. Once again, this proved to be a false dawn as Bournemouth won only five more games in the second half of the year. A final position of 18th somehow managed to outdo the previous campaign's failure as the Cherries recorded the unenviable record of failing to score in 21 of their league fixtures.

Redknapp's faith in his ability to combine playing with his coaching role had diminished completely come the start of the 1979 NASL season. Harry was not registered in Seattle's 21-man playing roster but was forced to make an appearance alongside Bobby Howe and Jimmy Gabriel when a labour dispute between the NASL players' union and the league saw the majority of the squad withdraw their services for the defeat at the Dallas Tornado in Texas. Although the playing squad was back to full strength the following week, it was not to be the only reverse Seattle suffered that season. A total of 13 wins and 17 defeats saw the Sounders record their first losing season in their short history despite some high-scoring victories, including a 9-0 win over the Edmonton Drillers.

Little consolation came Redknapp, Gabriel and Howe's way when their team ended the season with a 5-1 victory over local rivals the Portland Timbers to claim the annually contested Mountain Bar Cup. Attendances at the Kingdome had fallen to an average of 18,997, and the team was sold at the end of the season to local businessman, Vince Coluccio.

Coluccio's first act as the Sounders' owner was to remove Jimmy Gabriel from his head coaching role, replacing the Scot with former Derby County winger Alan Hinton. Redknapp followed Gabriel out of the door, and once again he was left to ponder the future with some trepidation.

As Harry, Gabriel and Howe were overseeing their final fixtures at Seattle in the summer of 1979, the Cherries were engaged in what amounted to a squad rebuilding programme in an attempt to address their woeful form of the previous two seasons on the bottom rung of the Football League. The sale of Roger Brown, inevitably to Norwich, for £85,000 financed the acquisition of six new players, including the bubble-permed Irish midfielder Tommy Heffernan from Spurs.

By the end of Stock's first full season in charge, Bournemouth found themselves in 11th place. Not a cause for celebration, but an improvement on the previous two years in the bottom tier. Fans hoped that this chink of light would prove to be a starting point for an upturn in the club's fortunes. One of the few highlights of the campaign came in March when the Dean Court faithful bore witness to the league debut of one Ian Botham. England's leading cricketer came off the bench for Scunthorpe United to help the Yorkshire side to a valuable away point in a 3-3 draw.

After vacating the manager's seat in Seattle, Jimmy Gabriel had accepted the head coach's position at the newly formed Phoenix

Fire of the American Soccer League. The ASL was by far the oldest professional league in the United States, having started life in the 1930s, but had been usurped by the NASL in the late 1960s. In an attempt to compete, in 1976 the ASL tried to broaden its reach from its traditional north-eastern strongholds, awarding expansion franchises in the western states.

In 1980, insurance executive Leonard E. Lesser formed Phoenix Professional Sports Incorporated with a view to establishing a professional soccer franchise in Arizona. Following a failed bid to move the Memphis Rogues of the NASL to Phoenix, Lesser applied for and was awarded an ASL expansion franchise.

Gabriel set about building the Fire's playing squad, with Redknapp high on his wanted list, as much for his coaching ability as his increasingly rare forays on to the field of play. Soon enough, the duo were reunited in the Sonoran Desert and Harry set about luring several of the players he had previously scouted for the Sounders to Arizona. With their squad populated, the Fire played several exhibition matches in preparation for their ASL opener on 22 March against another expansion club, the Golden Gate Gales of San Francisco. It was a game that would never take place.

The squad received their first pay cheque on 1 March 1980, but when Phoenix Professional Sports missed the next payroll, the players and employees knew something was amiss. With the *Arizona Republic* newspaper reporting the club was on the brink of folding, the ASL postponed the match against the Gales. Instead, the Fire played an exhibition match in an attempt to raise funds to pay the players, but by 27 March the club officially went to the wall after failing to meet the ASL's deadline to find new investors.

The first Redknapp knew of any of this was when he went to withdraw some dollars to celebrate his birthday on 2 March only to discover that his bank account had been closed and what little money he had had been reclaimed to service the Phoenix Fire's debts. Harry eventually managed to convince the bank manager that around £5,000 of the money was his and not the club's, but it was all he had left in the world.

In January 1981, a grand jury indicted Lesser on 14 charges related to his doomed venture with the Phoenix Fire, including conducting fraud, theft and falsification of corporate records. Prosecutors alleged that Lesser misrepresented the financial resources of the team to attract investors, diverted corporate funds for his own use, and then falsified the team's balance sheets and cheque books to prevent his investors from learning the true state of the team's finances. In December 1981, Lesser was sentenced to serve one year in the Maricopa County Jail in Phoenix. None of this was much consolation to the Redknapp family, who were eventually forced to return to England with less to their name than when they had left five years earlier.

Meanwhile, more mundane but by no means less significant events were taking place at Dean Court in the summer of 1980. Dave Webb, an uncompromising 34-year-old defender who had scored the winning goal for Chelsea in the 1970 FA Cup Final, joined Bournemouth from Derby County and was appointed player-coach by Alec Stock. Stock had managed Webb at Leyton Orient and QPR, and told the *Evening Echo* succinctly, 'Dave has a lot to offer.'

Whatever it was Webb had to offer, it wasn't immediately apparent on the pitch. With supporters' hopes rising, results at the start of the season failed to live up to expectations. Just one goal in the opening four matches and patchy form throughout the autumn months, including five defeats in seven games before Christmas, saw Stock moved upstairs to the directors' box and Webb elevated to the manager's position. 'It's one of those things we said would happen when Dave came here,' said Stock, although it appears to have happened somewhat sooner than originally planned.

Once in the hot seat, Webb's fighting spirit and capacious personality galvanised the squad. At the turn of the year the rejuvenated Cherries embarked on a 14-match unbeaten run which saw them climb the table as the town once again began to dream of promotion. Webb was named the Bell's Fourth Division Manager of the Month for February and Bournemouth did not taste defeat again until they lost to Southend at Roots Hall on 17 April.

Sadly, that was the first of a run of four straight reverses as the team's impressive form in the second half of the season deserted them. They finished in 13th place on 45 points, with just 47 league goals scored. As Webb took the players away on an end-of-season holiday, the *Echo* was scathing in its summary of their campaign, describing the late run of defeats as a 'complete anticlimax'.

Redknapp's return to England after his American adventure went sour must have felt similarly anticlimactic and the 33-year-old was desperate to find a way to make ends meet and support Sandra and their two young boys. Harry's popularity in the game has rarely been in question, and after a spell of unemployment when Sandra's hairdressing skills were keeping the Redknapps afloat, his friendship with the great and the good of the English game came to the rescue.

They didn't come much bigger than Bobby Moore, England's World Cup-winning captain and a friend of Redknapp's since the West Ham days in the 1960s. Moore's management career had never threatened to approach the heights he achieved as a player. By the time Harry found himself kicking around back in Christchurch considering his employment options, his old pal from the East End was in charge at Oxford City of the Isthmian League, the eighth tier of English football.

The club clearly had ambition, but to see a man whose greatest achievement remains unique in English football patrolling the touchline at the tiny White House ground was incongruous to say the least. According to Redknapp, there was no shortage of opposition players and fans who were willing to remind Moore how far he had fallen.

Looking for an ally who could help improve the playing squad, Moore turned to Redknapp. Although it was a daily four-hour round trip and he appears to have spent the majority of his time rattling around in a Portakabin whilst his players were doing their day jobs, Redknapp wasn't in a position to be choosy and the opportunity to draw a wage and get back into English football was not to be sniffed at. 'It was meant to be part-time but I had to be there all day,' remembers Harry. 'They gave me a little Ford Fiesta to drive but the money was nothing really very much. I was driving backwards and forwards, Sandra was doing a little bit of hairdressing locally, running around the streets with her big hairdryer doing the old ladies' hair. £1.50 I think she charged. The boys were young and it was difficult.'

Neither Redknapp nor Moore had any experience at Oxford City's level and although Harry's contacts book was already bulging, it did not extend down as far as the Isthmian League. Without any knowledge of the teams they were facing or what players were available to sign, it was no real surprise that results nosedived and the club were relegated at the end of the season. Bobby Moore resigned almost immediately, and, once again, Harry was without a job.

Chapter Six

In Return

1981/82

DESPITE the disappointing end to the previous season, the summer of 1981 brought renewed hope to Dean Court as the unbeaten run between January and April demonstrated that a corner had been turned and at last it appeared that the Cherries were on the up.

Over the summer, Redknapp had been kicking his heels at home waiting for the phone to ring. With little to occupy him save the worries about life outside the game and putting food on the table, it was a difficult period for a man who had only ever known football.

Once again, Harry's network of contacts saved him from the wage slavery of ordinary working life. Before going on to make his name at Chelsea and elsewhere, Dave Webb had been on the playing staff at West Ham in the early 1960s. A year older than Redknapp, Webb was in the Irons' reserves whilst Harry was in the youth team and the pair barely spoke before Webb left for Leyton Orient in 1963. The defender did, however, become friendly with Stuart Morgan during that time, and consulted the Welshman years later as he considered offering Redknapp a coaching role at

Dean Court. 'Dave Webb asked me what I thought of Harry,' says Morgan. 'I knew Dave quite well and he phoned me up and he asked me about Harry as a coach. I couldn't speak more highly of him. I told Dave it would be a lot more difficult getting anyone else and Harry was on the doorstep living in Christchurch. He knew the club inside out, knew a lot of the players. After that, Dave didn't hesitate. I think he made Harry coach the next day.'

As Redknapp recalls, Webb contacted him in late June with an invite to lend a hand at pre-season training. 'Dave Webb rang me up and asked me if I wanted to come in and work with him,' says Harry. 'I didn't know Webby very well, but he was looking for a coach and he asked me if I would fancy it. Obviously it was a great opportunity for me to come back to work at Bournemouth. I enjoyed working with Webby, he was a real character.'

Once appointed, Redknapp made his presence felt quickly. 'Every day I was just in there with Dave,' says Harry. 'I did a lot of the coaching, took the training. It was just me and Dave with John Kirk. We had a great time. It was a great season. I liked Dave. He was larger than life. He knew what he wanted. He made some good signings. He took people out of non-league and had a good eye for players to play in the Football League.'

A hooligan-blighted pre-season friendly at Andover saw a group of so-called Bournemouth fans attack the home supporters with an intensity that took police by surprise. Despite this unseemly distraction, Webb was able to focus for long enough during the match to spot the potential of a player who would go on to win the First Division title with Liverpool seven years later. 'Dave bought Nigel Spackman from Andover after he came on at half-time in a friendly against us,' recalls Redknapp. 'The people at Andover couldn't believe they were going to get £1,000 for him because he couldn't get in their team. Credit to Dave, he spotted something and he was dead right. Nigel went on to have a great career.'

The remainder of pre-season was mercifully less eventful than the visit to Andover. Bournemouth participated briefly in the inaugural Football League Group Cup in mid-August. A forerunner to the Football League Trophy, a competition that was to give Redknapp one of his best moments as a young manager, the Group Cup was introduced to create another revenue stream for lower league clubs following the demise of the Anglo-Scottish Cup.

The Group Cup was also the first opportunity English clubs had to gain three points for winning a match. This alteration was the brainchild of Jimmy Hill, football's own renaissance man, who was concerned that the two points for a win system was leading to a defend at all costs approach in too many league matches. Hill proposed the idea to encourage more entertaining football which in turn might persuade the thousands who were turning their back on the game in the early eighties to return to the terraces. After due consideration, Dave Webb gave only mild approval to the change, opining, 'I don't think it will make that much difference until perhaps the last third of the season when the situation is sorting itself out a bit. But it is worth a try.'

The Cherries' contribution to the nascent competition was less than glorious. They entered and exited the cup in the space of a week, drawing all three matches they played and scoring just one goal.

By the time Webb and Redknapp had guided their side to nine Fourth Division games without defeat at the start of the league campaign, any disappointment over the performance in the Group Cup was long forgotten. But Webb's confrontational personality meant that he was never far away from another spat. In the days when managers and clubs still had significant power over player movement and contracts, Webb was able to let rip at his players without fear of much of a backlash. Redknapp remembers Webb's style having a positive impact on performances. 'He was good at motivating the players,' says Harry. 'I think there was a bit of fear there with Dave.'

Redknapp's assessment of Webb's powers of inspiration are confirmed by Milton Graham, a 19-year-old midfielder who was beginning to make his way in the game at Dean Court. 'Scary Dave Webb we called him,' says Graham. 'He had a presence about him. He was a big guy and if you saw him coming down the corridor you would find somewhere to hide.'

Bournemouth's early-season form saw the club featured on *Football Focus* on BBC1 in mid-September. Bournemouth fans' delight at this recognition was somewhat thrown into confusion as they struggled to get to grips with the incongruous sight of comedian Jim Davidson appearing alongside Dave Webb and Alec Stock in the feature.

Despite being a lifelong Charlton fan, Davidson had started watching Bournemouth when he spent his summers entertaining holidaymakers at the Pier Theatre. He struck up a friendship with Dave Webb, and before long he was persuaded to join the board. The directors were keen to appoint anyone who appeared to be a potential investor and if, like Davidson, they could bring valuable publicity to the club, then better still.

'Jim Davidson got involved,' Harry remembers. 'I played in a charity game up at Wimborne and Jim played. He was down here doing a summer season. He said, "I must come to a game," and he did. Dave got quite friendly with Jim and I got to know him well. The next thing I knew he was on the board.'

After being starved of success for the best part of a decade, the board was prepared to cede some of its power to Webb, and Davidson was the most potent symbol in this shift. As if to rubber-stamp what he saw as his growing authority at Dean Court, Webb was moved to make a statement on behalf of the 27-year-old Davidson which only served to confuse supporters further as to the comedian's intentions. 'There is no question of him putting money into the club,' said Webb. 'There's nobody breathing that could come up with the sort of money that we need at the moment. But he will be good for the club.'

Harold Walker was not a fan of Webb's rambunctious style, but having, in his own words, 'found it impossible to get out of the Fourth Division despite having four chances every season', he held off from challenging his most important employee.

Webb's ego and ambition would not be checked for ever, but for now he was riding high and encouraged the town to get behind the team. 'The players could not have done better to take the leadership of this division,' he said ahead of a 1-0 victory over Rochdale. 'In return, they would appreciate a good turnout of supporters.'

Trevor Morgan grabbed his third goal of the season in a 1-1 draw with Northampton in October which kept the Cherries top of the Fourth Division table. It was Bournemouth's best start to a league campaign for 30 years when Bill McGarry's side did not taste defeat until the 15th game of the season.

Webb and Redknapp were enjoying themselves, so much so that they decided to make a return to the field of play in a reserve match in mid-October against Exeter. With the reserves away at Aston Villa in the Southern Junior Floodlit Cup the following night, manager and coach decided to rest some of the younger players and didn't hesitate to install themselves as replacements.

It was a successful return to the fray. Webb curled the ball in off the far post for Bournemouth's opening goal, and Redknapp ran riot all evening on the right-hand side of the pitch. 'It was the best wing play I have seen for seasons,' said the onlooking Alec Stock. A delighted Harry Redknapp was quick to seek to profit from his man-of-the-match performance, joking to Webb, 'After that, I think I should be in the first team on Saturday.'

Within the space of a few days, however, older Cherries fans began to wonder if the excellent start to the season was to be yet another false dawn. Goalkeeper Kenny Allen broke his wrist in training in the days leading up to a defeat at Peterborough, forcing Webb to give 20-year-old reserve team keeper Ian Leigh his senior debut. 'Kenny's injury came as a shock,' said Webb. 'These things happen in football and you must get over them. Ian has waited for a chance and now it has come.'

Regardless of that less than ringing endorsement from his manager, Leigh impressed on his debut at London Road. Bournemouth captain Brian Smith was shown the red card just before half-time, inviting Peterborough to go all out for the win in the second half, an invitation they were happy to accept.

Four days later, the Cherries tasted defeat again, going down 2-0 at Aldershot. Ian Leigh parried a fierce free kick from the Shots' Les Briley, but his failure to hold on to the ball gifted Colin Garwood the opening goal. Furious at his side's performance at the Recreation Ground, and frustrated by their goalless return in the last two outings, Webb elected to make changes to the team for the crucial match against Bury, who were now one point above Bournemouth in fifth place. Giving 19-year-old Milton Graham his league debut in place of Trevor Morgan in such a game was a bold move, but the Londoner did not disappoint.

Two goals in a 3-2 victory had a delighted Graham telling reporters, 'I can hardly believe it,' and there was little doubt that he could after he claimed his second goal when a Brian Smith cross hit his legs as he was running into the six-yard box and cannoned past a helpless John Platt in the Shakers' goal.

Graham remembers Redknapp as a key figure in the early years of his playing career. 'Harry was just a fantastic motivator,' he says. 'He had a great understanding of football. He taught me a lot of what I think are basics now but I didn't know about at the time. There's an art to how to manage people and I took a lot of what he taught me into jobs I had after football, like how to treat people. He could be a bit fiery, and I saw him lose his temper a few times, but he was a great coach.'

Doubts about the side's ability to maintain a serious promotion challenge were wiped away when they went undefeated in the league for the next three months. It was far from plain sailing off the pitch, however. On the night of Sunday 8 November a gas boiler caught fire in a kitchen next to the boardroom in the wooden main stand at Dean Court. A member of the supporters' club raised the alarm, and over 20 firefighters were soon on hand to tackle the blaze.

Windows were shattered and the boardroom was saturated having been hosed with several inches of water as the firefighters fought to get the fire under control. Part of the stand was damaged and all that was left of the kitchen was its charred remains. Club secretary Graham Mackrell, who was set to leave Dean Court for a similar position at Luton the following day, said, 'It could have been infinitely worse. If it had been an hour later, people would not have been turning out of the supporters' club to spot the flames and we could have lost the lot.'

With the bill for repairs set to run into thousands of pounds and the club pleading poverty on a regular basis, it came as quite a surprise to the Cherries' faithful when days after the fire, Webb bolstered his striking options by signing his old Derby County team-mate Andy Crawford for an eye-watering £40,000.

Crawford repaid some of the fee by scoring with a thundering left-foot volley on his debut at Blackpool. Bournemouth won the match at Bloomfield Road 3-0, leading a thrilled Webb to comment, 'That must have been our best all-round display of the season. I thought Blackpool would cause us a few problems but we outplayed them and did not have a weakness in the side.'

After the Blackpool win, Webb and Redknapp's thoughts turned to the FA Cup. The draw for the first round had paired Bournemouth with southern rivals Reading. Webb again urged supporters to turn up in their numbers, taking the opinion that each of the goals at Bloomfield Road were worth an extra 1,000 on the gate at Dean Court for the tie. 'The lads can hardly wait for that game. We just hope supporters will turn out, get behind the team and help us into the next round.'

Webb, who had scored the Cherries' last goal in the FA Cup at Charlton the previous season, then dispatched his trusted player-coach to run the rule over the Third Division high-flyers. It is not clear if Redknapp produced a scouting dossier in the style of Don Revie after watching the game, but he would have noted future England internationals Neil Webb and Kerry Dixon in the Berkshire side's ranks. Whatever observations Harry returned to Dean Court with were invaluable as Bournemouth went on to beat the Biscuitmen 1-0 thanks to a goal from top scorer Tony Funnell.

A growing belief around King's Park that this was at last going to be the Cherries' year was strengthened in December when Dave Webb managed to tempt striker Howard Goddard back to Bournemouth. Goddard, who had starred alongside Kevin Reeves in a teenage forward line at Dean Court five years previously, had spent most of the intervening period at Newport County, but had fallen out of favour despite scoring 42 goals in 105 appearances for the Welsh side.

Goddard returned to Bournemouth on a free transfer and promptly scored against opponents Colchester to earn his side a point. It was a game that Bournemouth should have won, and Webb did not hide his feelings of disappointment in the dressing room after the final whistle. The festive spirit was rekindled somewhat when the Cherries won at Torquay in atrocious conditions two days later to put them within a point of the top of the table going into 1982.

The new year did not start well, however, and it wasn't until the second game of February that Bournemouth returned to winning ways. January began with the visit of Third Division Oxford United in the FA Cup. As in the previous rounds, Redknapp was dispatched to the Manor Ground to spy on the Cherries' next opponents, but this time his report to Webb and the players did not do the trick as Oxford, led by the Third Division's top scorer Keith Cassells, left Dean Court with a 2-0 victory.

Although Bournemouth weren't at their best, little criticism was aimed at the Cherries or Webb following the exit from the cup, despite it being the 22nd consecutive year the club had failed to reach the fourth round. The Bournemouth manager, however, was battling frustration of another kind, and it came from within.

Days after the cup match, reports emerged that Webb had threatened to resign as manager. With his ego swollen further by the success his side were having in the league, Webb, who had regularly refused to speak to the press throughout the season, did not hesitate on this occasion to make his position public. 'It will be a matter of if I stay or if I go unless we can resolve a few things,' he explained. 'We have got to plan well ahead if we are aiming for Third Division football and beyond to the Second or even the First Division. It might mean spending £100,000. We have got to consider these things and, if we get promotion, it might even mean an all-seater stadium.'

The state of Dean Court was certainly among the 'few things' that Webb was seeking reassurance about before he committed his future to the club. During the defeat to Oxford, a section of the perimeter fencing had given way, leading to a delay in the match. Webb and Jim Davidson had also found it difficult to gain entry to the stadium due to crowds of supporters forming outside the ground because turnstiles were unable to operate fast enough. 'Jim Davidson and I experienced a similar frustration to the fans on Saturday and we now know how they feel,' empathised Webb. 'The supporters come back when they see you are having a go. This is reflected in the big improvement in the gates here. I feel the wrong attitude is creeping in somewhere and I stress there is still a lot of hard work to be done. We are not in the Third Division yet.'

Webb's personal ambition and self-belief were never less than sky high, and he did not shy away from letting the Bournemouth directors know who he thought should be calling the shots ahead of a meeting to discuss his grievances. 'There is the opportunity to create a great future for AFC Bournemouth,' he said. 'It is pointless to mark time. If I am not confident in the directors' attitude, there is no point in me staying.'

For now, Webb held all the cards, a circumstance of which he was well aware. Harold Walker was desperate to see the club regain Third Division status and despite serious misgivings about his manager's bullish conduct, he gave in to his demands.

Webb had been in charge of team affairs for over a year but was still on a player's contract. When he emerged from a four-hour meeting, he had a new three-year manager's contract in place and appeared to have eroded more of the directors' power. In the photo that accompanied the report of the meeting in the *Evening Echo* from 6 January, a proud and smirking Webb towers over Harold Walker, who is wearing a smile similar to an old wound reopening. 'Now we all know where we are going, and that is forward,' said Webb, satisfied with his afternoon's endeavours. 'There was some blunt talking, but in the end the board were brilliant. They felt that we have started to achieve something here at Dean Court, and now they have given me the reins and are allowing me to get on with it. Now I have full management control of the club with the new contract, I can get on with the job and, I hope, build a better club for the directors and the town.'

With the sideshow drawing to a conclusion, the Cherries' supporters had to wait another three weeks for the next league match as heavy snow across the country saw most games postponed for two weekends in a row. A thaw of sorts had begun in the south when Bournemouth's fixture at Hull was called off on the second weekend, and the ever-resourceful Webb and Redknapp hastily arranged a friendly against neighbours Southampton. In time-honoured fashion, Dean Court ground staff and volunteers cleared the remaining snow from the playing surface and over 6,500 football-starved supporters braved the cold, a higher attendance than any of the Third Division games that survived on the day.

Redknapp's influence on proceedings was not difficult to spot. With the match ending 1-1 after 90 minutes, the game was decided by an NASL-style shoot-out of the type that Harry had participated in himself in his days in Seattle. Starting out 35 yards from goal, the outfield player was given a time limit of 30 seconds to try and score.

Although still reeling from his clash with Webb, Harold Walker was pleased that the friendly had been such a success. 'The aim is to maintain our progress,' he conceded. 'Attendances have shot up and although they are still below the break-even level, the response is most encouraging. This is the sort of backing we need.'

As temperatures rose and the run of postponements came to an end, Bournemouth fans looked ahead to the springtime with a rare sense of optimism. The manager, who could never be accused of negative thinking, was the unlikely advocate of keeping feet firmly on the ground. 'If people start believing we have already got a promotion place they are wrong,' he cautioned. 'We are not halfway through the season and the toughest part is to come. I want to take this club to where it has never been before, beyond the Third Division and into the Second. The town wants this sort of success and deserves it. That applies to the board of directors as well and if everyone is in that mood there is a chance to achieve something. It is a great challenge but there are untold possibilities at this club. I think the public are appreciative of everything we are trying to do.'

And indeed they were. Webb knew he was in a strong position since the signing of the new contract but was already planning to seize greater control whilst his stock among the Bournemouth supporters was high. After his side returned to action in a drab goalless draw with Crewe, it emerged at the club's annual general meeting that the manager had become a major shareholder.

'I am giving David 40,000 shares, about 10% of the club, because I believe he has an involvement and an interest that are second to no other manager,' said Walker, sounding as if he was reading from a script composed by Webb himself. 'The manager is to be congratulated on what he has achieved with very little. I'm hoping he will stay with us for ever.'

Harry Redknapp watched these events develop with a keen eye, and noted the impact of personality over officialdom. 'Dave knew he had a lot of power at the football club,' says Redknapp. 'He'd have been too strong a character and too powerful for the board, for sure. Too big a character almost.'

Webb didn't need much encouragement to think big, and Walker's words acted as a catalyst for his boldest remarks yet. 'This club could be the greatest thing for the 1980s,' he declared. 'The place is now full of life and ambition. People are talking about the club again and we are the envy of the Fourth Division. But we can only make progress with help from all quarters and we've got to do our bit to make sure the club grows in the right way. We are trying to build a team to represent what we are doing at this club. We are trying to entertain.'

A run of draws which extended the Cherries' unbeaten run into early February came to an end when Bradford recorded their first-ever victory at Dean Court with a 2-0 win. That defeat saw Bournemouth drop out of the promotion places. Fortunately for all concerned, each of their next five matches ended in victory, a decent run at any time but somewhat remarkable given the continuing turmoil regarding Webb's position.

A thumping 5-1 triumph over York City in mid-February wiped away the disappointments of the Cherries' home form over the winter months, but the 4,373 supporters were not allowed to enjoy the result for long as reports emerged the following day that the inevitable blowout between Webb and Harold Walker had occurred before the match and the manager had gone through with his previous threat to resign. Webb was keen to sign a new striker in the push for promotion and he and Redknapp had been searching for the right player. Walker, faced with the bleak reality of the club's accounts, was unable to provide funds and complained to the press after the York match that the club could not survive for long whilst attendances were so low.

'It's disgraceful and idiotic that he should say things like that,' said Webb prior to setting off on a five-mile run in an attempt to temper his anger at Walker's comments. 'The public deserves better than they are getting. At the moment we are serving up the sort of football I don't particularly wish to see myself. You can't blame the public for not turning up. You will not get 10,000 people coming through the gates until you provide them with what they want to see. I want to improve things, but all the directors can talk about is surviving until the end of the month. We had everybody in this morning and I said my piece. The town desperately wants a good football club and the chairman can only talk about the club not being in business by the end of February.'

Walker, who was being forced to take the role of the patient parent of a recalcitrant teenager in order to placate Webb, said, 'I think he is a bit upset today and what he said about resigning may not mean anything.'

After emphasising that there were no funds available for new players, Walker called an emergency board meeting for the following morning. Webb's main ally on the board was Jim Davidson, who highlighted the different approaches to running the club by flamboyantly arriving in a helicopter which he landed on the Dean Court pitch.

It is unlikely his ostentatious character found much favour with Walker, but Davidson was a source of potential finance that the board could not afford to turn away. After another four-hour meeting, Webb again announced he would be staying on as manager after 'one or two' directors, presumably meaning the resident comedian, had pledged to make funds available to strengthen the squad. Davidson, who was appearing in Watford at the time, said, 'I only had two hours' sleep last night, but the outcome of the meeting makes it worthwhile. I'm delighted Dave is staying. A lot of things have been sorted out. He was going to leave because of things he didn't like, but those things have now been resolved.'

Redknapp, who was permanently in the wings during these encounters between manager and chairman, remembers Davidson as a somewhat unorthodox member of the Dean Court board. 'He was a right boy, Jim,' recalls Harry. 'We ended up winning one day at Stockport or somewhere to go top of the league, and on the way back we passed the Torquay United coach on the motorway. When our coach got alongside the Torquay coach, we were next to it for about ten minutes. Torquay had been beaten, we'd won and gone top. Jim, who, remember, was a director of the football club, pulled a moony out of the window. What Harold Walker thought of that God only knows.'

Buoyed by this latest triumph over Walker, Webb did his best to be magnanimous. 'I understand the chairman's problems and I just wanted him to understand mine. I know I have cried wolf before and you cannot keep doing that, but I just wanted to show how strongly I felt.'

His chairman, who by now must have been biting his tongue so hard he could taste the blood in his mouth, again chose his words very carefully. 'Dave had the interests of the club at heart in saying what he did. The meeting cleared the air.'

The football was almost relegated to a sideshow by the off-the-pitch drama, but successive 1-0 victories over Stockport, Rochdale and Mansfield saw the Cherries go top of the Fourth Division. 'It's a nice feeling,' said Webb. 'It's what we have been working for. Now we have got to the top we have to keep things going and make sure we stay there. It's encouraging having the points in the bag, and I would like another 11 wins before the end of the season.'

With just three defeats in the 28 league games to date, this did not seem out of the question. Next opponents were bottom of the table Northampton, and the Cherries went into the match confident that they could gain their ninth away win of the season. With almost parodic inevitability, Northampton ran out 1-0 winners, their first victory at home since November. 'We need to bounce back,' commented Webb after the game, adding, with the spring still in his step after winning the latest round in the power struggle, 'Luckily, we haven't got far to bounce.'

Webb's response to this surprise setback was to bring in former Arsenal starlet Charlie George. The pair had played together at Derby County and after a spell playing for Bulova in Hong Kong came to a premature end, George was keen to find a way back into the Football League, even if it meant dropping into the Fourth Division.

George turned out for the Cherries in consecutive draws with Peterborough and Aldershot, but torrential rain and strong winds at the Recreation Ground dragged him into the mire of a lower league battle. This was clearly enough for George, who swiftly departed Dean Court, his spell having effectively lasted just four days.

With four wins and a draw in April, Dave Webb picked up the Manager of the Month award before the 1-0 win over Hull City, but much to the relief of the Dean Court faithful, the associated curse was not working its dark magic on this occasion. Three crucial away games in the north were to follow, as the Cherries sneaked into the final promotion berth. A midweek trip to second-placed Wigan resulted in a 0-0 draw as Bournemouth's defence again proved its worth. Webb's side then travelled across the Pennines to leaders Bradford City. Avoiding defeat would be a huge step towards promotion, but Redknapp was having none of it. 'We are going to Bradford to play our football again and we will be looking for a win.'

As always, Harry was as true as his word. Andy Crawford gave Bournemouth the lead as early as the fourth minute and, after an error from Ian Leigh allowed City to equalise, the recalled Howard Goddard put the Cherries ahead until late in the game when the Bantams again found a way back to share the spoils. The disappointment did not last long, however, as it soon emerged following the final whistle that Sheffield United had thrashed fifth-placed Peterborough 4-0, meaning the side the *Evening Echo* had dubbed Webb's Wonders had achieved promotion with two games to spare.

As his players celebrated with the supporters who had made the trip, Webb had eyes only for his and the club's future. 'This is just the first step in a new career,' he said. 'It would be the biggest step in the club's history if it were to reach the Second Division.'

Bournemouth ended their campaign in joyous mood in front of their success-starved supporters at Dean Court against Hereford United. A season-high attendance of 9,925 joined the party as Tony Funnell, whose wife had given birth to a baby boy the previous night, made it a double celebration when he equalised for Bournemouth after former striker Derek Showers had put the Bulls ahead.

Bournemouth had lost just four times since the start of the campaign and an unbeaten run of 17 matches to the end of the season had seen them pull away from the chasing pack to claim the final promotion spot.

'I think we have shown that you can rely on good football and still get results,' said Redknapp at the time. It was a mantra that would be repeated time and again in his career in management.

It appeared the perilous financial situation at Dean Court was all but forgotten in the revelry that followed promotion. Once the party had died down, Webb, Redknapp and the squad, all resplendent in new team tracksuits, boarded a plane at Heathrow for a summer tour of New Zealand.

Chapter Seven

Stage Manager

1982/83

ONCE they had finished celebrating promotion and recovered from the jet lag induced by the trip to the Antipodes, Redknapp and Webb returned to Dean Court to plan for the Third Division.

After taking training and dealing with the various administrative tasks required in their position, the management duo then joined several of their playing squad in coaching at a summer soccer school run by the club for local youngsters on the area of King's Park adjacent to Dean Court. With money tight, Redknapp had long supplemented his income with stints at such courses and appeared happy to do so anytime he was invited.

Upon learning over the summer that attendances at Dean Court had risen 75% on the previous campaign as the Cherries successfully chased promotion, he was more than happy to take the credit. 'We entertained,' he said. 'That's why they kept coming to Dean Court. It was not simply a case of following a winning team because we drew several of our home matches. But what we did give the fans were two wingers and excitement. We were adventurous.'

In what had become a depressing ritual, the excitement on the eve of the new campaign was dampened by off-the-pitch issues. Three days before the opening fixture of the season against Walsall, the club announced it was launching an appeal for £50,000 to stay in business. The growth in attendances the previous season may have looked impressive, but an average crowd of 7,000 was required to make ends meet.

Delight at the Cherries seeing off Walsall with three unanswered goals was somewhat diluted for Harold Walker and the board of directors upon learning that only 5,330 turned up to watch. The win extended Bournemouth's unbeaten run to 18 matches, a record that still stands today despite all of the club's recent success.

Unfortunately, the run of positive results came to an end at Plymouth in the newly named Milk Cup. After dominating the game for the first 84 minutes, Webb's side conceded two late goals to leave themselves with something of a mountain to climb in the second leg a fortnight later.

Two more defeats in the following league fixtures against Oxford and Millwall moved Webb to sign experienced midfielder John Beck on a month's loan from Fulham. In doing so, the Bournemouth manager shed some light on the difficulties he was facing in attracting new players and keeping his squad together. Facing questions from Cherries fans attending a launch event for the 'Bournemouth Supports The Cherries' appeal, Webb went on to detail what he claimed were the demands of a player he had recently attempted to keep at the club, although he did not name names. 'He asked for a £30,000 signing-on fee. I can't compete with that,' said the Bournemouth manager. To very little surprise, Webb also revealed that keeping the wage bill at the club under control was another major headache.

A morsel of relief came in the shape of a 0-0 draw against highly fancied Sheffield United in the next match. The previous season's corresponding fixture had attracted almost 10,000 to Dean

Court but only 6,424 paid their entrance fee this time. It was as if the success of just a few months before was all but forgotten. The attendance may have been affected by the appearance of television cameras, always a bad omen for the Cherries, with some supporters suggesting that they should be barred from Dean Court permanently, such was Bournemouth's record when their games were televised.

On the back of four goalless outings, it was no surprise to anyone that another 3,000 fans stayed away for the second leg of the League Cup tie against Plymouth. Trailing 2-0 from the first leg, Webb's side took to the field for the return at Dean Court with their manager's words ringing in their ears. 'We've got to stick the ball in the net from the openings we create,' he told them. This elementary but sound direction was for once followed to the letter by the team, who won 3-0 on the night with Trevor Morgan's effort in the 21st minute of extra time sending Argyle out of the competition.

The Pilgrims' three-hour journey back to Devon would have seemed much longer when the draw for the second round gave Bournemouth a lucrative glamour tie against Manchester United. Ron Atkinson's side were not the powerhouse they had been under Matt Busby or would go on to become after the arrival of Alex Ferguson, but for Cherries' fans, starved of a genuinely big match since meeting Aston Villa in 1972, it was a plum draw.

Supporters hoped the bounty from the United tie would herald the beginning of the end of the Cherries' hand-to-mouth existence, but when asked about the possibility of using some of the gate money to strengthen the squad, Webb's answer did little to suggest these hopes would be met. 'That money has already been spent,' he said, 'and it was not to buy players.'

Patchy league form in the games leading up to the visit to Old Trafford was not aided by an injury crisis which would lead to a brief but notable swansong for Redknapp's playing career. After John Beck had limped off in the first half of a 1-0 reverse at Wrexham and winger Steve Carter hobbled out of training with a thigh strain in the days leading up to the first leg at Old Trafford, Dave Webb was left with just 12 fit players to choose from. 'We've got to find a replacement for John Beck and I can see Harry playing,' said the Bournemouth manager, before ruling himself out of contention despite still being a registered member of the squad. 'I can't see me playing,' he said. 'I'm not even fit enough for reserve team football in the position I play, but with Harry being a winger, it would be a different matter. It's an indictment on the club to leave themselves so short. I don't want to play myself. I would enjoy playing, but I'm not sure everyone else would enjoy it.'

And so it was that Harry found himself packing his boots as he prepared to leave for Manchester. When Carter failed a late fitness test, 34-year-old Redknapp replaced him on Webb's team sheet for his first appearance in English football for five years.

What promised to be a memorable evening for Harry proved to be just that, but for all the wrong reasons. With the Cherries holding their own against a United eleven featuring Bryan Robson, Norman Whiteside and Ray Wilkins, Redknapp inadvertently diverted a weak Ashley Grimes shot past the stricken Kenny Allen in the 28th minute. It was an aberration that had wider implications for Manchester United than were initially apparent. Waiting just behind Redknapp to tap the ball in was 21-year-old Peter Beardsley, making what would turn out to be his only first-team appearance at Old Trafford. Beardsley would go on to win 59 caps for England and star for Liverpool at the end of the 1980s under Kenny Dalglish, winning the league title twice. On the night in question, however, his luck was not in. In his 1988 autobiography, the former Newcastle and Everton winger explained, 'I was unmarked at the far post and was perfectly placed to touch home a cross as it came across the Bournemouth goal, but Harry Redknapp just got a touch before me to put it into his own net and was credited with an own goal. I often wonder what would have happened if Harry had missed the ball and I had scored. My career could have taken a completely different turn. I might have stayed on for the rest of the game, made another couple of appearances, and established myself in the United team. I was bitterly disappointed.'

Despite the own goal, Redknapp demonstrated that he could still cross the ball with pinpoint precision and gave a creditable performance against top-class opposition. Bournemouth conceded just once more, a fine Frank Stapleton effort giving the home side a little breathing space before the second leg at Dean Court.

'I enjoyed it,' said Redknapp in the days after the defeat. 'Apart from the unfortunate own goal. I lunged for it, and it hit me on the end of my toe and was diverted into the near post.'

With the treatment room still packed, Redknapp retained his place in the starting line-up for the following Saturday's Third Division encounter with Cardiff City. It was Harry's first appearance at Dean Court since January 1976 and although it is unlikely he knew it at the time, it was also his last game as a professional footballer.

With Cardiff pushing for promotion, the game looked a tricky one as the Cherries sought to cling on to their mid-table status following a patchy run of results. Buoyed by the praise they received for their performance in the Milk Cup, Bournemouth ran out 3-1 winners. As at Old Trafford, Redknapp again demonstrated that he had not lost his ability to use the ball with timing and accuracy and even came close to scoring at the right end early in the second half. Two goals from Milton Graham either side of Trevor Morgan's effort from a counter-attack secured the points. The second of Graham's goals saw the winger glide past two Cardiff defenders and fire into the corner of the goal, having ignored the unmarked Redknapp's calls to provide the assist for what would have been a certain goal.

Redknapp was included in the squad which entertained Gillingham a fortnight later, with Webb even considering picking himself after waiting in vain for good news regarding the injury situation. Come the kick-off at Dean Court, neither man was on the team sheet, nor would Redknapp ever be again. Webb did make an appearance in the home defeat to Huddersfield Town at the start of November, although his performance was such that he ended up substituting himself.

The return leg against Manchester United was the biggest game at Dean Court in a decade. A total of 13,226 tickets sold out quickly as talk turned to an unlikely victory for the Cherries.

'There are not many teams who can score three times against United. It's going to be a battle, but it's not over yet; we can still cause a few problems,' stated Webb, before bullishly adding with a flagrant disregard for football history, 'but we will have a go and, if we pull it off, it will be the biggest coup of the lot.'

Webb was not engaging in hyperbole when he predicted a battle. In the 11th minute of the game a clash between Cherries defender Phil Brignull and Ray Wilkins saw the United midfielder stretchered off before being taken to Poole Hospital where he was diagnosed with a broken jaw. It was an injury that saw Wilkins lose the England captaincy to Bryan Robson, never to be regained on a permanent basis.

Brignull also conceded a penalty a minute before half-time which gave United a 2-1 lead on the night after fit-again Paul Compton's powerful header had cancelled out Arnold Mühren's 26th minute opener. Trevor Morgan levelled again as the Cherries had the better of the second half, but the final score of 2-2 was deemed a fair result by both managers.

United went on to lose in the final to Liverpool whilst the Cherries returned to life in the Third Division. Bournemouth's battling performance over the two legs had raised Dave Webb's stock among the wider footballing world, despite a very ordinary run of results in the league. In private, however, all was not well, and in late October the *Evening Echo* took the unusual step of reporting the break-up of Webb's marriage in some detail in an era when journalists' knowledge of the personal lives of public figures was largely kept out of the newspapers.

There were rumours amongst supporters that someone inside the club had alerted the *Echo* to the story in an attempt to undermine the Bournemouth manager. Whether this was true or not, Webb's fiery relationship with Harold Walker and the rest of the board cannot have been helped by his domestic arrangements becoming the stuff of salacious reportage.

With Webb's history of confrontation, faux resignations and links to other clubs, it was inevitable that something was going to give. Power struggles at football clubs rarely end with the chairman tendering their resignation, and Harold Walker wasn't inclined to disrupt this tradition. After recording just one win in nine Third Division games, Webb was duly relieved of his duties after a 0-0 draw away at Chesterfield on 4 December. Supporters were dismayed and demanded an explanation, but Walker was unmoved. 'That is all there is going to be,' he said firmly after making a brief statement explaining that he had informed Webb of the board's decision, adding, 'We are not going to give a reason.'

When asked to comment on why he had been relieved of his duties, Webb was characteristically forthright. 'Ask the chairman,' he advised. 'It's very political; a clash of personalities. He's stubborn and so am I. Things have been brewing up in the last few days. I'm very sad about it and feel sorry for the supporters. I felt my future was here at Bournemouth. But I will sit back, take a deep breath and see what happens. I don't give up that easily – I'll get another job.'

Webb's closest ally on the board by some distance was Jim Davidson, and with Webb gone, he resigned his position at the club, but claimed his decision was not linked to his friend's departure. 'It's not because of my friendship with Dave,' he said. 'I don't want to be associated with a club that will not go forward. I think the chairman, whom I respect, has panicked. The club is in a mess financially.

Dave's way of putting the club back on its feet has frightened the chairman to death. I think the board's decision to sack Dave will show in the gates. They have got rid of the best man they have ever had. It could be the end of the club, although I hope not.'

In the days following his exit, it was confirmed by Walker that Webb was attempting to buy AFC Bournemouth with the backing of former World Speedway Champion Barry Briggs. Webb revealed that Walker had challenged him to come up with the money, which led to a dispute over the appointment of new directors and their potential investment in the club. Walker himself was scathing in his assessment of Webb's ability to run a football club. 'Dave Webb has been saying that the directors don't know how to run a football club and that he is the Messiah who would do it properly,' said Walker, sounding relieved to have finally shown Webb the door despite the club's financial woes. 'All I can see is the club getting deeper and deeper into trouble. It was up to Dave to raise the money and he was not able to do so.'

A first-round exit from the FA Cup at the hands of Webb's old club Southend meant the Cherries did not have another game for two weeks, buying the board time to find a new manager. Aside from Weymouth boss and Harry Redknapp ally Stuart Morgan publicly throwing his hat into the ring, there appears to have been a distinct lack of interest in the Dean Court hot seat.

Finance was another obstacle, and the club had very little by the way of salary to attract an experienced manager. Much like the appointment of Eddie Howe over a quarter of a century later, Harry Redknapp's occupation of the manager's office at Dean Court began as a result of desperation by a club whose main concern on both occasions was to stay in business. Harold Walker confirmed this on the day Redknapp was appointed. 'The club is at the end of its tether financially,' said Walker. 'The name of the game as far as we are concerned is survival. I have gone as far as I can. I cannot put any more money into the club.'

After a three-and-a-half-hour board meeting on 13 December, Walker emerged to announce to waiting reporters that Harry had been put in temporary charge of the team and would be supported by Webb's predecessor and mentor Alec Stock. He continued, 'We will not be appointing from the outside. We are looking to Harry to blossom as a manager. We think he will make a very good job of it.'

Although contemporary reports show that there was a gap of four days between Redknapp's appointment and his first match in charge, Harry recalls a much swifter turn of events. 'I only came in as caretaker,' he says. 'Dave left on the Friday and I took over and took the first game the next day.'

Showing an early ability to handle the press, Redknapp spoke of his regret at how he had come into his new role, whilst expressing a determination to succeed. 'I'm going to have a go at it and I know I have the full backing of the players who wanted me to take over when they knew that Dave was going. It means I can slip into the job without too much disruption.' Of his relationship with Webb, Redknapp said, 'We did not agree on everything, of course, but I learnt a lot from Dave and I think that will help me now.'

Whatever pearls of wisdom Harry had gleaned from his predecessor were soon required. Just one of a number of problems facing the caretaker manager as he prepared to make his debut on the touchline at Lincoln City was a squad decimated by injury. Nine players, including mainstays of the side Tommy Heffernan, Tony Funnell and Keith Williams, were on the treatment table as Redknapp began his tenure. 'I don't know where I can raise a full squad at the moment,' he said. 'I will be glad to get the game out of the way after what has happened at the club recently.'

If that wasn't bad enough, Lincoln City topped the Third Division table, and the Imps had won all nine of their home games in the season to date. Bournemouth travelled to the East Midlands hoping to put the past week at the club behind them with a respectable result. Instead, by the time the final whistle blew, they had been beaten 9-0, the worst league result in the club's history. It was also by far the worst day of Redknapp's career in football to date. 'It was sickening,' he said after the match. 'I cannot remember another day like it.'

Lincoln's overwhelming dominance was aided by the conditions. On a frozen pitch, which put the game in jeopardy in the hours leading up to kick-off, the City players wore plimsolls akin to the AstroTurf boots popular today. The Cherries had no option but to don their ordinary studded boots, which led to countless pratfalls from the Bournemouth players and, after keeping the score down to 2-0 in the first half, a total collapse in the second 45 minutes. Redknapp was furious at the lack of basic preparation. 'The boots made a big difference,' he raged. 'We must get the right gear for frozen pitches. This cannot happen again. It has been a hard job during the past week, taking on a new role at a difficult time. Lots of things have been happening, and they have had an unsettling effect.'

Over 30 years later the pain of that morale-sapping defeat has not entirely evaporated. 'Lincoln were a good team at the time,' remembers Redknapp. 'It was a disastrous start.'

Harry was at least able to look forward to the backing of the home support when he made his managerial bow at Dean Court against local rivals Reading two days after Christmas. Instead, he was the innocent victim of an angry protest by supporters demanding the reinstatement of Webb as manager and Walker's resignation. Walker wisely stayed away, reportedly because he had caught a 'heavy cold'. Webb, who had moved on to claiming unpaid wages and an overdue promotion bonus, was more than happy to attend the match alongside Barry Briggs, and lap up the variations on 'We want Webb' which rang out for the duration of the match.

At the final whistle, several hundred fans invaded the pitch, only to be chased off by police dogs. They then staged a sit-in at the South End terrace for 20 minutes, and upon being dispersed, they continued their protest outside the ground. Redknapp was not impressed. 'Disgraceful,' he fumed. 'Do they want this football club closed down? The supporters who want to help the team will get behind the players and give them their full backing. I was very disappointed with some of the things that happened at the ground today.'

One of those things was conceding an 85th minute equaliser after Trevor Lee, recently signed by Webb from Gillingham, had given the Cherries the lead in the 21st minute. Redknapp had no time to recover before things went from bad to worse. The following day, the Cherries travelled to Brisbane Road to face Orient, where they promptly lost 5-0. There was no frozen pitch and inadequate footwear to blame this time, and Redknapp knew it. 'Some of those goals were a disgrace,' he said, after staging a 30-minute inquest in the dressing room after the match. 'I'm very upset about this performance and I told them so. There were a few strong words but we have all got to keep battling away to put things right again. The players have lost confidence and that is something any team must have to do well.'

On New Year's Day, Brentford, the club where Redknapp had forlornly tried to continue his playing career a few years earlier, were to be the visitors to Dean Court. As 1982 drew to a close, Harry looked to rally the faithful to help the Cherries avoid another demoralising result. 'The only chance we have is for the crowd to get behind the team and help them,' said Redknapp. 'They can give them some stick, but I don't want them to crucify the players. With all the things that are happening behind the scenes it has been a very difficult period for the players. The slide started some time ago and whoever took over would have encountered the same problems.'

Fortunately for all concerned, Bournemouth managed to win for the first time in 13 games with a 4-3 victory. It was Redknapp's first-ever win in management. Although the rot had been stopped, Harry was far from happy with the strength of his squad and was keen to bring in new blood. 'I need to strengthen the squad and I have got the go-ahead from the directors,' he explained, before going on to describe a transfer policy which would become his caricature in future years. 'With a bit of wheeling and dealing I could have three or four players lined up in the next week or two.'

Such positivity would become a familiar aspect of Redknapp's vocabulary as his fame grew, but, on this occasion, it proved to be misplaced. Despite strengthening his playing resources with month-long loan signings of old Seattle Sounders team-mate Jimmy Neighbour and young midfielder Dave Madden from Southampton, the Cherries suffered a 3-1 defeat to Walsall after taking an early lead. Bournemouth surrendered the initiative to the Midlands side in the space of six first-half minutes after a mistake by Kenny Allen and an ill-judged challenge by John Impey on Walsall player-manager Alan Buckley in the penalty area gave the Saddlers the lead. 'Scandalous,' said a fuming Redknapp. 'They were schoolboy errors, the sort of thing you might expect to see in a local park. We have got to go out and battle.'

With Bournemouth slipping down the table and teetering perilously close to the relegation places, Redknapp wielded the axe for the crucial fixture against George Graham's Millwall. Kenny Allen was replaced in goal by Ian Leigh and captain John Impey dropped out due to what was described, somewhat vaguely, as 'back trouble'.

With the Lions also struggling, Redknapp was frank in his assessment of his team's plight. 'The team have only won twice in the last 17 league and cup games,' he observed. 'That's not good enough of course, and it's time we did something about it.'

With Impey out, the Bournemouth manager did do something about it, moving Tommy Heffernan to centre-back and bringing in Yugoslav Ivan Golac at full-back. Taking himself and everyone else by surprise, Heffernan obliged by hitting a hat-trick as the

Cherries won 3-0. Harry, whose relationship with Impey was at best lukewarm, could not conceal his delight. 'We certainly need that win and Tom provided the finishing power in great style. Three goals from a centre-back must be something of a record.'

After earning the first away point of his managerial career in the following game at Sheffield United, Redknapp hoped to haul Bournemouth into the security of mid-table before the relegation jitters began to set in.

Unfortunately, the Cherries' patchy form continued. Victory over table-topping Oxford United and a 5-2 drubbing of Gillingham at Priestfield sat alongside a 4-2 defeat at bottom-of-the-table Exeter City and a 2-0 defeat to Portsmouth in what was described, with scant regard for the two meetings with Manchester United, as 'the match of the season' in the *Evening Echo*.

'Everyone is afraid we'll go down, and so am I,' said a worried Redknapp. 'If I can't keep Bournemouth in the Third Division then I'll expect to be let go and let someone else have a chance. I'm not a miracle worker and I can only get the best out of what I've got, and I feel I'm doing that.'

These words suggested that Harry was already aware of manoeuvres off the pitch that would see him ousted as manager within days of the triumph over Gillingham, the best result of his first spell in the hot seat. On Wednesday 9 March it emerged that a mystery cartel of London businessmen had bought the club from Harold Walker, a sale that supposedly put a large dent in the club's reported million-pound debt.

The upshot for Redknapp was that after 14 games he was replaced by former Bristol Rovers boss Don Megson with immediate effect. Harry returned to his role as assistant coach, despite making it clear that he wanted the manager's job on a permanent basis. He was rumoured to be frustrated at not being given until the end of the season to show what he could do, but with his family to support and the riches that landed him in Sandbanks years later nowhere in sight, he had little choice but to accept the assistant manager's post and take his chances.

'We won at Gillingham who were up near the top and then Mr Walker sold the club,' recalls Harry. 'The new owners brought Don Megson in as manager. They asked me to stay on as first-team coach, as Don's assistant. So I did, I stayed on and worked with Don for a while.'

The day after Megson's appointment, the club issued the following statement: 'The board of directors of AFC Bournemouth and the consortium wish to thank Harry Redknapp for the manner in which he handled the team during what has been a difficult time for the club and its supporters.'

Like Redknapp, Megson, who had made over 500 appearances for Sheffield Wednesday, had recently returned from a spell in the United States. More significantly for the years that lay ahead, the day-to-day running of the club was put in the hands of former Aston Villa defender Brian Tiler. Tiler, who turned 40 the week he arrived at Dean Court, was full of enthusiasm and ambition. 'One of my first priorities will be giving Bournemouth fans the best. The best football and the best comfort,' promised the giddily optimistic new managing director. 'A new super stadium will be getting every consideration. We will be looking to provide family entertainment and give the fans the best facilities. And too often there is a tendency to forget arriving at the product: providing something people want to watch. So perhaps the first priority is to have a winning team – and that is Don and Harry's department.'

This was the first recorded statement where the word 'product' was used to describe anything associated with AFC Bournemouth. Tiler's arrival in King's Park would be a key moment in bringing the club into the 1980s, albeit three years into the decade. The 1970s had belonged to Harold Walker, and his departure after 13 years at the helm brought to an end an era which had begun in similarly optimistic and modernising fashion during the John Bond years.

At 68 years old, Walker could not be criticised for selling up, although he may have held on to his shares had it not been for the perennial threat of debt crippling the club. 'Although I was sad to give up the chairmanship and I shall miss it terribly, it was also a great relief,' he said the day after stepping down. 'I did it in the interests of the club, because it ensures the future of league football at Dean Court for some time to come. I had reached the stage where I could no longer guarantee the club would still be in existence at the end of the season.'

Both Tiler and Walker refused to reveal the identity of the consortium that had removed Redknapp from the manager's seat, and it would be months before the unsavoury details came to light. When they did, it emerged that Walker had sold his majority shareholding to Guernsey-based company Wigbourne Holdings. Although the sale helped wipe £500,000 off the club's mountain of debt, it ushered in a new period of mismanagement.

Wigbourne Holdings was a smokescreen for a takeover by the self-styled football entrepreneur Anton Johnson. Johnson, dubbed the 'King of Clubs' by the papers, had negotiated similar deals at two other Football League clubs, in direct contravention of Football Association rules. Walker soon regretted the sale and his gullibility in allowing himself to believe that Johnson was not purchasing the club. He certainly should have smelt a rat when Johnson confirmed to him that he was acting as guarantor for the deal and requested Walker keep his identity a secret.

Redknapp, who was not inexperienced in dealing with dubious characters in and around football, was unperturbed by Johnson's arrival. 'Anton was all right,' he says. 'He was a bit of a lad. He bought the club off Mr Walker who must have just had enough and decided he wanted to sell. He owned Rotherham at the time and he came in and bought Bournemouth. Then he bought Southend after that.'

For his first game in charge at home to struggling Preston, Megson wisely stuck with the side that won so handsomely at

Gillingham, saying before the match, 'I would not have been displeased with a 5-2 away win so why would I change things? Harry Redknapp has developed a good team spirit.'

It is difficult to imagine what was going through Redknapp's mind as the team he had just begun to turn around coasted to a thumping 4-0 win. As assistant manager he can only have been pleased with the outcome, but part of him must have pondered what might have been had he not been replaced by Megson.

By the time the midweek game against Plymouth rolled around a few days later, subtle changes were in evidence courtesy of the new regime off the pitch. The Bournemouth players took to the field amid a firework display and wearing red jockey caps which they duly gave to young fans. After a 1-0 victory made it a hat-trick of wins and an ideal start for Megson, the players gathered in the centre circle to salute the crowd. Mark Nightingale's strike two minutes before half-time secured the points and talk of relegation began to subside. A goalless draw at high-flying Huddersfield extended the unbeaten run to four games, a sequence that had the Dean Court faithful setting their sights on mid-table respectability and a quiet end to a depressingly dramatic season.

Instead, they were faced with Anton Johnson acting as the ringmaster in a circus that was refusing to leave town. Following the match at Leeds Road, reports began to emerge that Bournemouth were about to sign George Best, still considered by many to be the greatest British footballer of all time. At 36 and in the grip of alcoholism, Best was a shadow of the player who had put fear into the hearts of defences across Europe in the 1960s, but his fading skills and box office appeal were enough to briefly bring the crowds back to Dean Court.

After stating on television whilst in Southampton that he 'could be signing for a club just a bus ride away from here', Best was unveiled to a stunned local press at Dean Court on transfer deadline day at the end of March. Bournemouth had officially bought Best from the San Jose Earthquakes, then known as the Golden Bay Earthquakes, of the NASL, although the Ulsterman had not played for the Californian club in almost two years.

'Brian Tiler and Don Megson have done me a favour,' said Best after penning an agreement to play until the end of the season. 'I have had problems with the American club who have not made it easy for me because they wanted payment for my registration.'

As the football world digested this incongruous marriage of convenience, Best went straight into the Bournemouth side to face Newport County at Dean Court, replacing top scorer Trevor Morgan who was unceremoniously dropped.

How much the Johnson consortium paid to secure Best's registration was never revealed, although when Best's girlfriend and former Miss World Mary Stavin joined a crowd of 9,121 to watch him make his debut for the Cherries, the gate money from an attendance double the average at Dean Court would have helped offset some of the fee.

Redknapp, who occasionally accompanied Best on trips to Salisbury Racecourse after training, remembers the financial boost Best's presence brought to the entire Third Division. 'George Best came when Anton was there and Don was the manager,' he says. 'They brought George in and paid him by the game. If I remember correctly, even the away teams paid him. If we were playing away from home, the club we were playing paid George appearance money because he put a few thousand on the gate.'

With a young John Aldridge spearheading their attack, Newport were chasing promotion to the Second Division and were not cowed by the presence of Best and the media frenzy that greeted his arrival. A 1-0 victory for the Welsh side suggested that the new Bournemouth owners' pursuit of hyperbole outstripped their desire to create a successful team. Best showed flashes of his genius, but the frightening pace of his glory days at Old Trafford had all but evaporated. After the match, Bournemouth's new signing complained about being played out of position in attack. 'It's not my favourite role,' complained Best. 'I prefer to be in midfield and go looking for the ball, but I was asked to stay in attack and I am just part of the side now.'

The Irishman's dissatisfaction with his role on the pitch may or may not have contributed to his absence from his new club's Easter fixtures. Megson granted Best a leave of absence prior to the match against Orient on Easter Saturday after his former landlady from his early years at Manchester United passed away. He was expected to return in time to feature in the Cherries' line-up. On the morning of the match, however, it became clear that Best was not going to appear. Brian Tiler was prompted to take the unusual step of producing a poster saying 'George Best won't be playing today' which was put up outside Dean Court in order to ensure fans looking forward to seeing the former European Footballer of the Year were informed of his absence before paying their money at the turnstile.

Tiler could not have been accused of giving Best licence to do as he pleased, as his widow Hazel explained many years later. 'I remember Brian going up to London to fetch George Best back to play for the Cherries,' said Mrs Tiler. 'When he got to the Barbican, where George was living at the time, there was no sign of him. So Brian was driving round with Mary Stavin looking for him. They tracked him down to one of his favourite pubs, but George escaped through a toilet window. Then Brian caught up with him at another pub, but by this time it was obvious George was in no fit state to play the following day.'

Trevor Morgan returned to the side and made his point by scoring in the win over Orient and in the two matches that followed. Bournemouth lost to lowly Reading on Easter Monday and again Best was nowhere to be found, prompting Megson to vent his frustrations with the wayward star's actions. 'George was not satisfied with his fitness, and neither were we,' he began, in what it is safe to assume was a thinly veiled reference to Best's drinking habits. 'I will feel let down and the club will feel let down if he does not show up next time. He must get match fit and earn his position in the team on merit.'

Best did reappear in time for the next match at home to Chesterfield, and disputed talk that he had taken leave from Dean Court without permission. 'I lost someone close to me and I could not concentrate properly on training,' he explained. 'If it had happened to any other footballer there would have been no fuss. I did not go missing. Bournemouth were kept in contact and now I'm keen to get cracking again and help the club pick up some more points.'

He was as good as his word in the Chesterfield match, playing for 67 minutes as the Cherries beat the division's bottom team 2-1. The official reason for Best's substitution for Kevin Dawtry was that he was suffering from blisters on his feet. However, there were suggestions that the Ulsterman was keen to remove himself from the field of play so that he could tune into that afternoon's Grand National. Improbable as this may appear, Best went some way to confirming the rumour's veracity when, following Corbiere's triumph at Aintree, he stated in a radio interview that if he had not been substituted he would have had to 'chin the ref' in order to get sent off in time to see the race.

Despite his drink-fuelled absences, Redknapp does not recall any problems with Best when he did join up with the squad. 'George was great,' says Harry. 'He came to training; he was just fantastic. I still don't think I've seen a better player in this country. He was one of the lads. Came in, trained every day. The lads couldn't believe they had got him here to play. I think he absolutely loved it here.'

Best's only away game in a Bournemouth shirt came at Southend, where the Cherries maintained their good form in a 0-0 draw. Next up were Lincoln City, in the return match from that in which Redknapp made his inauspicious managerial debut in a 9-0 defeat.

Revenge was in the air, and Trevor Morgan bagged another goal to give the Cherries a redemptive 1-0 win. Yet despite Best's presence and Bournemouth having only lost twice since Megson assumed the reins, attendances were again returning to their pre-George Best levels, with 5,010 cheering the team on against the Imps.

Best was contributing positively to events on the pitch and Megson, who could not have hoped for a much better start to his tenure, was now keen to praise the Irishman's contribution. 'He's part of our side,' said the Bournemouth manager. 'There's a buzz of excitement when he gets the ball and that's what I want. George has been no trouble at all and he looks fully involved now.'

This brief period of harmony saw Best also appear in a testimonial at Salisbury City for long-serving trainer Cyril Smith and player Paul Christopher. The 1,700 crowd that turned out for the occasion may have looked tiny compared to even the Cherries' paltry Third Division attendances, but it was City's biggest crowd in ten years and Smith could hardly believe his luck.

This kindness on Best's part was never reported beyond the local press, with the national papers preferring to focus on the more scandalous aspects of his behaviour. Redknapp saw him at close quarters during these months, and remains positive about the Ulsterman's contribution. 'George was enjoying his life, still playing,' remembers Harry. 'Obviously he'd lost that pace and everything that he had which was a shame. He was nowhere near the George that we knew in his prime, but it was great just to have him around for that spell. I think any way the club could make a few quid at the time they would do it. George came in, gates went up home and away so I think commercially it was quite a good move for the club.'

Best was absent from the team sheet for the next two matches as Bournemouth beat Bradford City 3-2 at Valley Parade and then drew 2-2 with Doncaster Rovers at Dean Court to put any lingering relegation fears to rest. The Irishman was in attendance at the Doncaster draw, described as 'suffering from a heavy chill'. Megson's patience was again being tested, but he was able to take a more relaxed line with safety assured. 'The ideal would be to see George Best fit and sharp and producing the goods in a great team performance. That would send the supporters away happy and round off the season. He'll be here for the rest of the week and in contention for the Wigan game and I just hope we can all finish on a high note.'

The match against Wigan was the Cherries' final fixture at Dean Court of a somewhat chaotic season. By serendipitous coincidence, Wigan's caretaker manager was Best's former Manchester United team-mate Bobby Charlton, who, along with Denis Law, formed the Holy Trinity at Old Trafford in the 1960s under Matt Busby. Despite their success together on the pitch, the relationship between Best and Charlton has been described as frosty, with the older Charlton taking a dim view of Best's off-the-pitch activities.

Whether the two exchanged pleasantries at Dean Court is not recorded, but the 2-2 draw would prove to be both men's last game in any capacity in English football. Best departed on reasonably good terms with the Cherries, making all the right noises as he headed for the exit. 'There is obviously great potential at this club. With a little bit of strengthening in the squad they must have a good chance of promotion next season,' he predicted. As for the future, it appeared his wanderlust since leaving Old Trafford nine years previously was set to continue. 'I really don't know what will happen. I've had a couple of offers to go coaching abroad but there is a lot to discuss before any decision is made.' What did happen was that Best played briefly in Australia before finding himself doing a three-month stretch in Ford Open Prison a year later for drink-driving.

With the circus finally leaving town, the season wound down in traditionally low-key fashion. A 2-1 defeat to Brentford at Griffin Park was the first that the Cherries had suffered in six matches and

Megson was keen to praise his players' commitment since he took over from Redknapp two months previously. 'I have been thrilled with the way the players have responded since I took over the team. They have done well, and that's why we are taking them on a club holiday next weekend.'

The trip saw the Cherries fly out to Portugal's Algarve on the same day George Best's former club Manchester United were drawing 2-2 with Brighton in the FA Cup Final. By contrast to United's riches, Bournemouth struggled to fund the holiday despite it being sponsored by John Plank World Travel, and failed in their attempts to arrange a money-spinning friendly with Southampton to cover costs.

This quiet end to the season could not have been in greater contrast to the turmoil that had characterised much of it, and there was little sign of light at the end of the tunnel. Star performers Nigel Spackman and Tommy Heffernan were sold to Chelsea and Sheffield United respectively for a paltry £55,000, although £16,000 of that money was used to buy Ian Thompson from Salisbury City. Thompson, a qualified schoolteacher, had almost signed for Manchester City, but when the deal fell through Megson pounced, and within six months the striker would write himself, and Harry Redknapp, into Cherries' folklore.

Chapter Eight

Into The Spotlight

1983/84

DESPITE returning to his role of assistant manager, Redknapp was very much the hands-on coach during pre-season in 1983, taking care of the tactical aspects of the Cherries' approach whilst Don Megson dealt with fitness and scouting. A decent warm-up campaign saw Stoke and Southampton beaten and Tottenham held to a draw. It was a sequence of results that convinced Megson his side didn't need much in the way of new blood, a decision which undoubtedly came as a relief to the club's bank manager.

Meanwhile, Rodney Barton, who was managing director of Poole-based company Macbar Construction, assumed the chairmanship at Dean Court after Harold Walker severed all official ties with the club at the end of the previous season.

Hopes were rising among supporters that the season ahead would at last see the Cherries mount a sustained assault on promotion to the Second Division. There were the traditional optimistic calls to arms in the days leading up to the kick-off, with Tiler happy to lead the way at the annual meeting of the Dean Court Football

Supporters and Social Club. 'We are all trying to achieve the same thing,' the managing director told the members, who had just handed him a cheque for £24,000. 'There is an exciting time ahead, and this club has got a real chance. There is tremendous potential here, but it has got to be realised, not just talked about.'

Sadly these words proved to be far from prescient as Bournemouth lost each of their opening five Third Division fixtures and fell at the first hurdle of the League Cup during the same period. The opening-day defeat to Preston North End at Dean Court cast the die for the Cherries' worst start to the season in years. Megson, who had been quietly confident that he had a team ready to challenge at the top of the table, attempted to deflect the blame for the defeat on to the departed Tommy Heffernan. 'I had it all worked out,' he said, 'but Tom Heffernan's move has destroyed that. I hope it has not destroyed the understanding the players have built up.'

Unsurprisingly, Megson's judgement was soon called into question. Goalkeeper Ian Leigh chipped a bone in his thumb in a 2-1 defeat to Bristol Rovers in the Milk Cup, an injury which saw Megson take the surprise decision to replace him with the recently retired former Bradford custodian Neil Ramsbottom. Ramsbottom shipped 12 goals in four appearances for the Cherries that followed, leaving fans confused as to why he was hired in the first place.

The Bournemouth manager admitted he was under pressure, and following a fifth straight loss at home to Wigan, it did not abate. Just 3,161 fans could bring themselves to witness the 1-0 reverse and they did not shy away from venting their spleen in Megson's direction following yet another abject outing. 'I'm there to be shot at when things go wrong and this has to be accepted as part of the ups and downs of football,' he admitted. 'Every manager has been in this situation at one time or another and I am looking for the break that gets things going.'

What Redknapp made of this horrendous start to the season is unrecorded. It is, however, not difficult to imagine that despite his frustration at seeing the team he was coaching beaten match after match, part of him was feeling that the new board of directors should have stuck with him a little longer.

Victory was finally forthcoming at the eighth time of asking as Bournemouth won 2-0 at home to Gillingham. This result did not prove the springboard Megson hoped it would be. He showed his increasing desperation after a 1-0 defeat at home to Bristol Rovers in the following match when he chose to publicly bemoan the audacity of Pirates' keeper Phil Kite who pulled off a series of outstanding saves, including guessing the correct way to block a Trevor Morgan penalty. 'Why do keepers always come here and play blinders?' wondered Megson. A section of the Dean Court faithful blamed Kite's penalty save on there being a picture of Morgan taking a spot kick in the match programme. If this was the case, Harry Redknapp was impressed enough by Kite's commitment to research to make a note of the keeper's name for future reference.

Three weeks later, Tommy Heffernan returned to haunt Megson, scoring for his new employers Sheffield United in a 2-0 victory over the Cherries. The Bournemouth manager looked doomed and issued an appeal for the Dean Court faithful to join him in the doldrums. 'I ask the supporters to help the lads through this period because I feel a true supporter should share the bad times as well as the good,' he said. Any 'true' supporters hearing the manager's words would be forgiven for concluding that they had had more than their fair share of the former.

The midweek trip to Walsall that followed saw little in the way of improvement, with Bournemouth going down 3-1. It was their ninth defeat in the opening 11 games of the Third Division campaign and left Megson despondent. 'We lacked imagination and gave the ball away too much. There were too many players off form and we looked a poor side. Pre-season indications that we were going well are not there now. We need to make some decisions.'

Following a lengthy meeting with Brian Tiler the following Wednesday, a decision was indeed forthcoming. Megson was relieved of his duties and once again Harry Redknapp emerged from the backroom to take charge of the first team. Although it was initially described as a temporary appointment, it was a position Harry would hold for almost nine more years.

'After meeting with Don it was decided that he should step down as manager because we both feel that it is in the best interests of the club,' said Tiler. 'Don appreciates the fact that results have not gone well, and feels that this move will serve the club best. He will be staying at the club in another capacity and still has a role to play in the future development. It is a measure of the man that he would have the club's interests at heart.'

Megson was somewhat less expansive as he vacated the manager's seat, but was able to find some brief words of resignation. 'I am still keen to see the club do well,' he said. 'I can't argue with the disappointing results we have returned so far.'

Redknapp expressed surprise at Megson's departure at the time, and even today maintains that he was not clamouring for another spell in the manager's chair. 'Not really, I wasn't bothered,' he says. 'I was quite happy working with Don. He and Anton Johnson and Brian Tiler were quite pally, they were big friends. We got off to a bad start to the season and they all seemed to fall out. Suddenly Meggy was gone. It was a shame, I liked Don and I still speak to him.'

Despite this apparent reticence, Harry agreed to return to the Dean Court hot seat, and this time he was determined to hang on to the job. 'Meggy went and they asked me again to take over, which I did, but I didn't want to take over again as caretaker. I didn't want another month of doing it and then someone else comes in. But I took it on, and that was the start really.'

Once again he was thrown in at the deep end. In an ominous coincidence with his previous spell, Harry again faced the Third

Division leaders in his first match in charge. This time, it was Robert Maxwell's Oxford United at Dean Court. There would, however, be no repeat of the shambolic record defeat the Cherries suffered at Lincoln.

Twenty-two places in the Third Division separated Bournemouth and Oxford at the kick-off, but by the time referee Ken Salmon's final whistle blew, the Cherries had ripped the form book to shreds by recording a 2-1 victory that may have had the onlooking Megson wondering if he had gone too soon. 'Don't forget, this is Don's team,' said Redknapp as he took the post-match plaudits. 'The players are the ones who make things happen on the field and they are doing it for him as much as anyone else.'

Oxford had lost just once in the previous 14 games, and, despite rumours circulating that Tommy Docherty was about to assume the reins, Redknapp knew such an excellent result could do nothing but boost his claims to the job on a permanent basis. 'Now they have shown what they can do, it is important that the players keep this form going,' he said. 'This was a good all-round performance against tough opposition. The lads worked hard, created some good scoring chances and deserved their win.'

Meanwhile, Brian Tiler denied there was any truth in the Docherty rumour, but let it be known that there was plenty of interest in the job. 'We have had a number of people asking about the job. There has been no need to advertise and there are several managers currently available. But we are not making a decision just yet.'

Redknapp may have privately made it clear that he was not happy in a caretaker role, but he had little choice than to get on with managing the team, despite the uncertainty over what the future held. 'There is no problem,' he said. 'I will continue doing the job. The main thing is that we keep going now and pick up points. I am happy to hold the fort.'

The next fixture at fellow strugglers Brentford offered Bournemouth the opportunity to pick up their first away points of the season. Bobby Moore was in attendance at Griffin Park. The visit of the World Cup-winning captain afforded the press the opportunity to immediately link him with a renewal of the partnership with Harry last seen during their Portakabin days together at Oxford City. Moore, however, was still involved at Southend, a club where Anton Johnson had connections. Talk of him being in the running for a role at Dean Court soon evaporated when Redknapp appointed long-time friend and former Cherries team-mate Stuart Morgan as his assistant.

Morgan and Redknapp's first match in tandem was at Dean Court against another of Anton Johnson's clubs, Rotherham United. A swashbuckling 4-2 win had supporters and players alike clamouring for Redknapp to be appointed on a full-time basis. Harry, however, remained cautious, at least in public. 'I'm happy to carry on the same way for the time being,' he said. 'I can wait until I am sure I really want the manager's job, and the people who run this club are certain they want me. It will give us all time to think things over.'

On Wednesday 9 November it was confirmed that Redknapp had accepted the manager's position. It was just over 11 years since Harry had first arrived on the south coast and after the long period of uncertainty which followed the end of his playing days, he could at last look forward to some stability. Redknapp revealed he had turned down offers of coaching positions at Burnley and Brighton in the hope that he would continue to be employed at Dean Court and not have to uproot his family, who were happily settled in Old Barn Road in Christchurch. 'I know this job can bring pressure and I did not want them affected,' said the 36-year-old of his wife and boys. 'I have been happy with the way things have been going so I have decided to take the job.'

The tone of Redknapp's words suggests that he sought reassurances before accepting the position, and these appear to have included the transfer policy. 'I would like three or four new players in the club and I have been told there is a certain amount of money in the kitty,' he said on the day he was officially ushered in.

'We are obviously delighted that Harry has taken it on,' said Tiler, who was possibly the most thrilled person of all. 'Harry Redknapp has impressed everyone at this club. As a manager he is considered a popular choice by the directors and by the community as a whole.'

With results stabilising under their new manager and an FA Cup tie at home to Walsall to come, the squad jetted off to Jersey for the week. Training on the beach in the morning and a sports complex in the afternoon, it was not a relaxing trip for the players, but Redknapp was satisfied with the outcome. 'The lads really enjoyed the change in routine and it was a nice break,' he said, before taking charge of his first game in the competition that would make his name as a manager.

A thumping 4-0 victory to avenge the 3-1 reverse under Megson at Fellowes Park just a month previously meant that Redknapp's experience of the FA Cup could not have got off to a better start. 'I thought we would win this one,' said Harry after the game. 'I sensed my players were in the right mood for the challenge.'

Soon after, the board of directors published their annual report which contained details of the club's debts, the headline figure of which was almost £700,000. Such financial woe was not news to Redknapp, who, putting it to the back of his mind, promptly signed former Cherries defender Roger Brown from Fulham for £40,000. Finally breaking their away duck with a 2-1 win at Scunthorpe provided Bournemouth with a perfect platform going into their FA Cup second-round tie against Windsor & Eton. Befitting their title, the Isthmian League side counted Prince Philip among their patrons and played at Stag Meadow in the grounds of the Queen's garden at Windsor Castle.

Despite the lowly opposition, the FA Cup was still a huge draw for supporters and a special train was laid on to transport Cherries' fans to Berkshire for the tie. Unfortunately for them, referee Ken Salmon deemed the Stag Meadow pitch unplayable following heavy rain over the previous few days. Prince Philip's reaction to this development is unrecorded, although Harry was able to make his own frustration clear, commenting, 'It was cut up a bit and there was some clinging mud, but there was no surface water and we would have willingly played on it.'

The delay in getting the tie played meant that by the time the teams met the following Tuesday the draw for the third round had already been made. The winners would be awarded the money-spinning tie of Manchester United at home. Despite having mixed memories of when Bournemouth met United over two legs in the Milk Cup just over a year earlier, Redknapp could not disguise his glee at the draw, saying, 'This is the tie every club wants to be given. You couldn't hope for anything better because there is nothing better!'

Windsor & Eton were just as keen to face the Old Trafford giants. A crowd of 3,451, easily the highest attendance of the season at Stag Meadow, braved the muddy banks that made for terraces to watch a goalless draw on an equally sticky pitch in the rearranged tie. The Cherries dominated the match, but with the Royalists fighting for all their worth for the prize on offer, Redknapp's side could not make the breakthrough. Frustrated and a little forlorn at the final whistle, Harry was no longer so laid back about the soggy pitch. 'Conditions did not help us,' he said. 'We like to play football and that was not so easy here. The players had to dig the ball out in certain areas.'

A second-half defensive horror show saw Bournemouth go down 5-2 to Bradford at Valley Parade in the league match that preceded the replay. Fortunately for the Cherries, residing in the lower reaches of the Third Division still meant they had just about enough wherewithal to see off the Isthmian League side at home. Windsor & Eton had not lost in their past 15 matches but goals from John Beck and Ian Thompson in front of an attendance of 6,006 meant that Bournemouth could look forward to even more spectators coming through the Dean Court turnstiles for the visit of the FA Cup holders at the start of 1984.

The second-round victory was a game that would have been lost in the memory had it not preceded such an iconic FA Cup tie, as Redknapp admitted. 'Although we got the result, we did not play the football we are capable of,' he said. 'In this sort of situation, anxiety tends to creep in. I was more worried about the Windsor game than I will be about playing Manchester United. It was a relief, because against Windsor there was so much to lose, including our reputation.'

Reputation narrowly intact, the Cherries could now look ahead to a glamour tie and bumper payday. Before that, it was back to the Third Division Christmas programme, a period of fixtures Redknapp was looking towards to drag his side clear of any relegation worries.

It did not go well. With Roger Brown out with an ankle injury, the Cherries drew 1-1 with Newport on Boxing Day and then lost 2-0 at Orient 24 hours later. 'We have to start climbing the table,' said a disappointed Redknapp at Brisbane Road. 'The cup game will take care of itself, but our priority must be to get clear of the relegation zone in the Third Division.'

The only festive cheer for the Cherries was the 7,220 attendance at the Newport match. Traditionally a day when one of the season's highest attendances is recorded, Brian Tiler ensured an increase of over 3,000 on the previous league match at Dean Court by issuing each supporter who had torn themselves away from the mince pies with a voucher giving them the right to buy a Manchester United ticket.

Reports during Advent that the annual accounts would post a loss of £59,000 were greeted with satisfaction by the board of directors due to the figure being under half the previous year's debt.

Again, that was all the encouragement Redknapp required, and he returned to the transfer market to do a £12,000 deal for Stoke City's tough-tackling midfielder Bobby Savage. Savage was formerly in Bob Paisley's squad at Liverpool, although he never made a first-team appearance at Anfield. Within days of his arrival at Dean Court, millions of people would know more about him than they could possibly have imagined.

Savage's debut came on New Year's Eve when the Cherries entertained Exeter City. It proved to be an instant success when after just 40 seconds he scored with his very first touch for the club. This left-foot opener was the beginning of a rampant spell which saw Redknapp's side look anything but relegation fodder. After 25 minutes, Bournemouth were 3-0 up and, although the scoring ended there, they comfortably cruised to a 3-1 win. 'What a start for him!' said the Cherries' manager of his new signing's dramatic debut.

It was a happy end to a largely disappointing year for the Cherries, and once the New Year celebrations had died down, thoughts turned to an opportunity to start 1984 with a bang. At the start of the week several players were battling to be fit in time for the cup tie, with a bout of flu for John Beck rendering him the biggest doubt for selection.

United, who had beaten Brighton 4-0 in a replay the previous May to win the FA Cup, had injury problems of their own. Manager Ron Atkinson's regular centre-back pairing of Kevin Moran and Gordon McQueen were both ruled out, forcing the United manager to hand 19-year-old Graeme Hogg his debut in an era before wholesale line-up changes were common in cup competitions. The Old Trafford club were still able to field an all-star cast, and welcomed England captain Bryan Robson back into the side for the fixture.

'We can go and enjoy it,' said a characteristically optimistic Redknapp. 'The lads must go out there to run and work and, if we get the breaks, we can upset the opposition. United are there to be toppled.'

Rallying cries of this kind are commonplace in football, but there may have been more than bravado in the Bournemouth manager's words. Just 19 days earlier, United had been knocked out of the League Cup by the Cherries' Third Division colleagues Oxford after drawing the first leg at Old Trafford and then going down 2-1 at the Manor Ground.

'We were aware of a bigger build-up to the game than there had been for other matches that season,' says Ian Thompson. 'It captured the imagination of the town. I guess a lot of players may have been carrying little injuries but there was no way they were going to admit it because they wanted to get in the team.

'We stayed together the night before the game at the Roundhouse Hotel in Bournemouth. That was different, we didn't normally do that. I remember Harry saying, "This is a game where you don't need motivating because you are playing against some of the best players in the country." His whole attitude to it was, "If you don't believe you can go out and win then there is no point in going out and playing." Whilst I know that he has said since he didn't think we could win the game, he certainly didn't give that impression at the time. I think Harry's trick was that he made us believe we could win the game and take the opposition as motivation to win.'

Redknapp sought to relax his players, taking them to La Lupa Restaurant in the Charminster area of Bournemouth. It subsequently emerged that the Cherries' manager was a part-owner of the eatery, with the publicity doing business no harm.

On the Friday night before the game, Redknapp told his players they could win if they followed two simple instructions: match United for work rate; and concentrate on doing what they were good at. Harry's optimism may have appeared unrealistic to some of his squad, but it only grew when the game kicked off.

On 7 January, 14,825 packed into Dean Court to see the match that would make Redknapp's name as a football manager. With a back four of Phil Brignull, Everald La Ronde,

Chris Sulley and stand-in captain Roger Brown thwarting every United attempt to threaten the Cherries' goal, Ron Atkinson's side did not have a shot on target in the entire first half. 'With the big names they had we were almost expecting we would go a goal down at some point,' says Ian Thompson, 'but it didn't happen in the first half and I think our belief was then greater for the second half because we had comfortably held them to 0-0 and had a couple of half-chances ourselves. What Harry had told us before the game was clearly true at half-time and he only had to reinforce it. So our belief was stronger, United didn't really relish it and I think some of their players thought they could just turn up and turn us over.'

United finally recorded a goalbound effort in the 57th minute when Arthur Graham's fizzing strike was well saved by Ian Leigh. This suggested the tie was about to turn their way, but three minutes later Bournemouth were in front. Milton Graham, who had rattled Gary Bailey's crossbar in the first half, pounced on a mistake from the United keeper following a corner to volley home from inside the six-yard box. 'It was a very proud moment,' says Graham. 'I still get people asking me about it to this day. It was fantastic, one of those things you will never forget. I tell everyone the goal against Man United was from about 20 yards, but it really was only about a yard out. It was something we had worked on with Harry, a basic little walk back from the far post in case their keeper Gary Bailey spilt it or missed it and it just came to me perfectly.'

The delirium following this opening goal had barely subsided when, just two minutes after the Cherries had taken the lead, Ian Thompson seized the initiative when England's talismanic captain Bryan Robson dithered on the ball to fire home Bournemouth's second goal. 'For just a moment, Bryan Robson hesitated and I was on the move,' recalls Thompson. 'We both went for the ball at the same time, but I had a head of steam and got my foot in first. The ball then tangled in my feet a little bit but I managed to dig it out and I struck it really truly. Gary Bailey didn't get a hand on it and this was the moment when I remember thinking, "I don't believe this has just happened." I ran up to the crowd with some ridiculous celebration, but who cares?'

Bournemouth had not kept a clean sheet for two months, but United could find no way through, much to the frustration of their supporters. Lou Macari did manage to get the ball in the net, but the goal was ruled out for offside.

Around 100 United fans escaped the Brighton Beach End ten minutes before full time. They then evaded the clutches of the Dorset Constabulary to run the length of the main stand before entering the South End terrace through large gates that had been opened by stewards to allow any home fans who were too busy to stay until the conclusion of one of the most famous days in their club's history to leave early.

'Some Manchester United fans had got into the Bournemouth end and it all came to a sad conclusion,' remembers Thompson. 'I was standing next to United's Dutch midfielder Arnold Mühren and he said it was a shame that a minority could spoil such an occasion. It did hold the game up for several minutes towards the end and I guess that was the United supporters showing their frustration at the way their team had given up the FA Cup.'

A rusty crush barrier was broken as the United fans surged into the home terrace, and fighting spilled on to the pitch. Referee Brian Stevens had no choice but to suspend play as Redknapp and his team hoped the chaos would not force an abandonment and with it the chance of victory. Fortunately, the pitch was cleared after five minutes and the game was allowed to finish.

Amid the post-game celebrations, Ron Atkinson tore into his expensively assembled squad for a full 45 minutes after the match. As his players emerged with bowed heads after relinquishing their grip on the trophy they would win again the following season, Atkinson told the waiting press, 'I'll give you two seconds and that's it,' before making his self-imposed time limit count by labelling his team of internationals a disgrace who could only make up for the embarrassing defeat by going on to claim the First Division title, a challenge they subsequently failed to meet.

Across the corridor, the Bournemouth dressing room teemed with national press keen to get a piece of the shock of the season. The decision of news broadcasts to go live to the scene demonstrated the magnitude of their victory, although this decision may have been regretted by production staff after viewers were left choking on their tea leaves when confronted with the sight of Bobby Savage rising from the team bath in all his glory shouting, 'Who's Bryan Robson?!'

'The media flooded our dressing room and I just wasn't expecting it,' recalls Thompson. 'That was when we all realised that it was a significant result. You couldn't move for the media. We had the "Let's all get in the communal bath" photo which you don't have these days for all sorts of reasons. And then, of course, there was Harry's brilliant interview afterwards, in which he had no thoughts of sadness for United whatsoever. He almost said "No, why should I?" The Bournemouth fans were standing behind him cheering and I think it was that and events afterwards that made me think how significant the result was.'

Out on the pitch, Redknapp was thrust into the national spotlight for the very first time and took it all in his stride. Surrounded by a gaggle of Bournemouth fans wrapped in homemade scarves and holding tinfoil-covered cardboard reproductions of the FA Cup, the victorious manager told television cameras, 'It's got to be the greatest day of my life, and I'm sure it's the greatest day of all the players' lives. It's a great afternoon for everybody in Bournemouth. I've had a strong feeling we could beat Man United today. The supporters were tremendous. The players are the ones who did it, not me. The game is about players, not managers, it's about the men that get on the park and play. We keep seeing managers on TV and they're becoming more famous than the players. The lads have done it today with great support from all the people.'

Whilst it's easy to laugh about the reaction of Mrs Redknapp to this very public statement, it is in some ways a shame that Harry has subsequently retracted his words, quite reasonably making light-hearted reference to the 'stupid things' people say in times of excitement. Nevertheless, in the light of what followed in subsequent decades, it could be argued that it was the greatest day of his working life as a whole, even greater than winning the FA Cup itself whilst at Portsmouth. After just 13 games in his two very short spells in management, Redknapp had achieved what most managers could only dream about. Furthermore, his already firm popularity with Cherries' fans was fortified, as he brought them a day of genuine joy after a miserable 18 months following promotion out of the Fourth Division.

After spending the rest of the evening celebrating with friends and family, Harry and Ian Thompson found themselves appearing on *Good Morning Britain* as the nascent breakfast show did its best to inform anyone who had missed the news that a genuine giant-killing had occurred less than 24 hours earlier. It was the beginning of Redknapp's celebrity, a development that he looks back on without regret. 'You get known, don't you?' he says with a shrug. 'Suddenly you are on TV after winning a game like that. It was a massive win because they were cup holders, full of international players and we were struggling in the league. It came completely out of the blue. No one could see that coming, including myself. I couldn't have said, "I think we will beat Man United" that day. It was amazing really.'

A reception in the mayor's chambers was planned for later in the week, but Monday morning brought a reality check for the suddenly famous Bournemouth players. Redknapp has delighted in telling the tale of the post-United training session which saw him and his squad scaling a perimeter fence after being locked into King's Park by a curmudgeonly park-keeper who many have suggested was from the red side of Manchester. Contemporary reports suggest that regardless of the ex-Bournemouth manager's reputation for occasionally distorting the facts, this anecdote is entirely true. Brian Tiler, who had been unequivocal in his condemnation of the United fans' behaviour towards the end of the cup tie, showed no restraint whatsoever when giving his opinion of the park-keeper. 'He just came along and locked the gates,' said Tiler. 'The players had to climb over the fence to get out. One of them could have slipped and injured himself. We are trying to find out who the man was. If the fans get hold of him he could be tarred and feathered.'

Once they had regained their freedom, Redknapp and his players joined chairman Rodney Barton and the still-hungry press pack to listen to the draw for the third round. In a wonderful piece of theatre, someone at the club had dug out the same steam radio that Freddie Cox's Bournemouth players had used to listen to FA Cup draws after defeating Wolves and Tottenham Hotspur on their way to a quarter-final meeting with Manchester United in 1957. Unfortunately, the old wireless had used up all of its luck 27 years earlier. Instead of another glamour tie or winnable draw at home, the Cherries' reward for the shock of the third round was a trip to Second Division Middlesbrough's Ayresome Park.

Boro's defeat of Arsenal in the third round had been overshadowed by the Cherries' heroics, but that did not make a visit to the north-east any more palatable to Redknapp. 'It could hardly have been worse,' said the Bournemouth manager. 'I'm disappointed. It will not be easy at Middlesbrough. I've played in the cup up there before and it is not an enviable prospect. Still, we'll take it as it comes.'

'I think we were all disappointed,' says Ian Thompson, 'but Brian Tiler, bless him, said, "We've had United, so what do you expect?" He said his only challenge was to find a cigar as big as Malcolm Allison's!'

With that, life at Dean Court began to return to normal. Bournemouth were 17th in the Third Division with exactly half the season's fixtures completed. The prospect of relegation was far from remote and Redknapp was keen to use the United result as a springboard to better form. 'The players showed what they could achieve,' he said. 'After a performance like that they should not be short of confidence as they come back to the league programme.'

It was, therefore, almost inevitable that Bournemouth would lose their next match, which they duly did away at Preston. There was no ebullient Redknapp this time. 'The performance today showed we are a long way short of being a good Third Division side. The conditions were bad but they were bad for both teams. And the test of character should have come today in the league. For some, it only came in the cup.'

The fourth round tie at Middlesbrough was due to be played the following Saturday but melting snow littered the Ayresome Park pitch with icy puddles and referee George Tyson postponed the game on the morning of the match. The delay did not help the Cherries who, with around 500 hardy fans making the 700-mile round trip on a Tuesday evening, went out of the competition they had lit up after losing 2-0 on the back of a performance far more in keeping with their poor league form than their heroics against Manchester United.

When a midweek game away to Rotherham fell victim to thick fog at Millmoor in February, Redknapp kept himself busy by using some of the proceeds from the cup run to sign striker Billy Rafferty from Portsmouth and bring in future Bournemouth manager Sean O'Driscoll on loan from Fulham. The 26-year-old midfielder had been ever-present as Malcolm Macdonald's Cottagers narrowly missed out on promotion to the First Division the previous season, and his arrival on the south coast began an association that would last for the next 22 years. 'Sean is a player who has got quality,' commented Redknapp upon sealing the loan. 'He's deceptively quick and I'm glad we have got him.'

With the Cherries far from out of the relegation dogfight in the league, their first game in the new Associate Members' Cup provided a welcome distraction. The cup was the latest attempt to establish a meaningful knockout competition for lower league clubs following the demise of the Anglo-Scottish Cup and the Group Cup.

Bournemouth began their participation with a match against nearby Aldershot. The Shots were flying high in the Fourth Division and had already scored 50 league goals by mid-February, but the Cherries rekindled their cup form and blew the Hampshire side away in a 4-0 victory.

Redknapp's team then found themselves fourth from bottom of the Third Division table after losing to Jim Smith's Oxford United. The Bournemouth manager took the novel step of handing over one of the midweek training sessions to an aerobics instructor, and his side duly saw off Walsall 3-0 at Dean Court. This thumping victory did not prove to be the catalyst for dramatically improved form, and the patchy results continued to leave supporters looking nervously at the foot of the Third Division table.

Bobby Moore and Anton Johnson, whose shadowy connections with both clubs continued in almost parodic cloak and dagger fashion, were at Dean Court for Bournemouth's meeting with Southend in mid-March. Moore, who remained close to Redknapp and spoke to the Bournemouth manager on the phone several times a week, had been in caretaker charge at Roots Hall since Peter Morris's departure on Valentine's Day. 'It's a funny thing,' said Redknapp before the match, 'but I haven't spoken to Bobby for some days now.' After a Bobby Savage penalty had given his side a valuable 1-0 win, Harry was keen to pal up once again with the World Cup-winning captain. 'Sorry Bobby,' he said at the final whistle, 'but we needed those three points.'

The win also boosted confidence going into the second round of the Associate Members' Cup, which pitted the Cherries against Millwall at The Den. On a night of mounting tension in south-east London, Bournemouth managed to win away from home for just the second time all season. It took a penalty shoot-out in which goalkeeper John Smeulders, who was deputising for the injured Ian Leigh, emerged as an unlikely hero.

Redknapp used the tie at The Den to trial a sweeper system he was considering using in games away from home in the Third Division as he attempted to improve the Cherries' abysmal record on their travels. The system came good as the Cherries won 3-1 at Wigan two games later. It was just their second away victory in the Third Division all season. 'We can keep out of trouble with the players we have got on the books now,' said Redknapp after the very welcome three points had put daylight between Bournemouth and the drop zone.

Subsequent defeats to high-flying Sheffield United and Wimbledon did not prevent Harry from putting pen to paper on a new contract that promised to keep him from having to worry about applying for a taxi driver's licence until at least the end of the 1985/86 season.

The offer of an improved contract to Redknapp came after Rodney Barton regained the majority shareholding of the club. This purchase was spun as an act of altruism by Barton, who painted himself as carrying the burden of guarding the ownership of the club until a suitable buyer could be found. 'For the past 12 months the affairs of AFC Bournemouth have been dictated by people outside the town, whose main aims have not been clear to either the directors or the management,' said the Bournemouth chairman of the recent ownership saga. 'We've got to make this club a viable proposition, and attempt to get more people in the town interested. Otherwise there could be a real danger of the club going out of business.'

Redknapp, who was still only 36, represented a beacon of hope for directors and supporters alike. He was a young, talented and charismatic coach, and although the details of his new contract were not revealed, it is safe to assume that a comparatively small salary was required to secure the signature on his first permanent deal than would have been the case if a more experienced candidate were brought in to replace him. 'He has a stabilising effect on the club. The players were lacking in confidence and he changed all that,' said Brian Tiler, Harry's staunchest ally. 'His relationship with the community is second to none. Harry is so vital to our future.'

Following another run of poor form in mid-April, the immediate future brought a meeting with Orient at Dean Court on the Tuesday after Easter. Redknapp was under no illusions as to the importance of the outcome. 'We have got to battle, we must all pull together – everyone connected to the club. A result tonight will mean more to us than the win over Manchester United. We must collect this three points.'

Collect them they did in a 3-2 win, but only after enduring a nervous final five minutes as the O's pressed for a late equaliser. 'That's better,' grinned Redknapp, before pragmatism took hold of him. 'It's not over yet. We still need more points.'

In the days after the victory, it emerged that Redknapp himself had been the main fitness doubt before kick-off. Whether or not his feeling under the weather was induced by the stress of the job was not revealed, although the evidence of his subsequent career in management suggests this was not the case. 'Really, Harry should not have been at the midweek match as he was feeling pretty groggy,' reported his assistant Stuart Morgan.

The triumph over Orient may have been just the tonic the Bournemouth manager required, as he then guided his side to three wins and a draw in their final four games of the season to finish above the relegation zone in 17th place.

Just after safety was achieved, Bournemouth faced Bristol Rovers in the area semi-final of the Associate Members' Cup. Buoyed by a recent win over the Pirates in the league, Redknapp could already smell glory. 'It's been a good run and now that we are within reach of the final itself we want to go on and win the trophy,' he said.

In a tight game against Rovers, Bournemouth came out on top thanks to a Bobby Savage penalty which was awarded after John Beck was brought down on the edge of the 18-yard box. The Cherries' reward was £1,000 and a home draw against Millwall in the Southern Area Final.

In what Redknapp described as a 'fine contest', Bournemouth emerged 2-1 victors to take their place in the final against Hull City. After Ian Thompson's 17th goal of the season was levelled by a Dave Cusack header on 62 minutes, Sean O'Driscoll scored what proved to be the winning goal four minutes from time.

Trouble flared late in the game when defender Cusack blasted the ball past Ian Leigh only for the linesman to raise his flag for offside. 'The linesman was standing right in front of the Millwall fans and it was not a popular decision to say the least,' recalls Thompson. Hundreds of the London club's fans invaded the pitch, first to celebrate the goal and then to berate the officials.

The playing area was eventually cleared, but at the final whistle the away supporters again swarmed across the pitch which led to referee John Martin sustaining a punch to the face. Unfortunately, this violence came as no surprise to Mr Martin, who told the *Evening Echo* after the match that he had made his way over to the touchline nearest the tunnel before he blew the whistle, saying, 'It was time and I could see there was going to be trouble.'

Despite being delighted with advancing to the final, Redknapp admitted he was unable to focus towards the end, saying, 'To be honest, I lost interest in the game in the closing stages. I was worried what was going to happen to our fans.'

The venue for the final was uncertain until 48 hours before kick-off. As Redknapp explains, 'Wembley was unavailable as the Horse of the Year Show stopped the final being played there. The horses had cut up the pitch. It was a shame for the players that we couldn't play the final there.' Villa Park was strongly mooted, but never confirmed, and Redknapp expressed his desire to play Hull over two legs. In the end, the Tigers won a coin toss and unsurprisingly elected to play the game at Boothferry Park.

Hull had missed out on promotion to the Second Division by the slimmest of margins less than two weeks earlier. Needing to win by at least three goals at Burnley, they could only manage a 2-0 victory and their league campaign ended in depressing fashion. A further blow came soon after when manager Colin Appleton, who had guided the Yorkshire club to promotion from the Fourth Division just 12 months previously, unexpectedly resigned.

Caretaker Chris Chilton led the Tigers into the final on Thursday 24 May, but whatever the outcome, it could at best only be a small consolation for the players and fans. Bournemouth, on the other hand, were unusually buoyant, having successfully staved off relegation and won six of their last seven games.

Hull took a 12th minute lead through Bobby McNeil's curling drive and having only lost twice at home all season, put themselves in pole position to take the trophy. On 28 minutes, Milton Graham, who had only been selected following a late injury to Billy Rafferty, received the ball from Chris Sulley on the left-hand side of the pitch. Pushing it past Tigers' defender Dale Roberts, the young Londoner then audaciously chipped the ball over goalkeeper Tony Norman into the net via the far post. 'It was exactly the same as the famous goal Glenn Hoddle scored for Spurs about a month before against Watford when he chipped the ball over their keeper,' says Graham. 'I remember it vividly, that was exactly how it happened. It was a tough game because Hull were a big, tough side. Their striker Billy Whitehurst was a beast, really strong.'

Whitehurst had a goal ruled out for offside before Paul Morrell, the Cherries' only home-grown player on the night, took centre stage. After missing a gilt-edged opportunity ten minutes after half-time, Morrell made amends in the 73rd minute when he headed home after John Beck's corner was touched on by Roger Brown.

Morrell's goal gave the Cherries only their second-ever trophy, the first coming when they claimed the League Three (South) Cup just after the Second World War. It was their 55th match of a season that threatened more than once to end in tears. 'This is a marvellous night for the club and I am very thrilled for Harry Redknapp and the boys,' said chairman Rodney Barton. 'We've been building a side and with the new players settling in it is making a difference.'

For his part, Harry looked back on a challenging job completed in very satisfying fashion. 'It finished up as a good season after all,' he said following the game. 'It was nice to bring a trophy back for the sake of the supporters. I'm delighted for everyone concerned with the club, and the players take credit for their hard work in the past few weeks – and the cup run has made some money.'

Celebrations among management and players were somewhat limited on a journey back to the south coast that was not completed until the small hours of the following morning. 'It was a long coach trip from Hull,' says Redknapp. 'Different world in those days, as we got back here about four o'clock in the morning. We stopped on the motorway coming home for a bacon sandwich and a cup of tea. All very tired, long, long journey but it was great to have won a trophy, even though it was only the Associate Members' Cup. Just to win it was nice, it was pleasing.'

'We didn't get an open-topped bus,' remembers Milton Graham. 'People used to call it the Mickey Mouse Cup. But we were proud we'd won it.'

It is unlikely that Redknapp was too put out by the less than glamorous rewards for the team's triumph, as he could look back on his first few months as a full-time manager with a great deal of satisfaction. For winning the Associate Members' Cup, Bournemouth received £5,000 and made a total of £20,000 from their participation in the competition. It was money that Redknapp would not let go to waste.

Chapter Nine

Making Do

1984/85

PRE-SEASON matches in Hamburg and the west of Ireland over the summer were funded by the Cherries' German hosts and the Bank of Ireland, but when the latest set of the football club's accounts were published in August, they predictably had the Dean Court faithful shaking their heads in bewilderment.

Chairman Rodney Barton reported annual losses of £90,000 and a total debt of half a million pounds. In what was described as 'one last attempt to keep football at Dean Court', the club had received planning permission to build 27 houses on the land behind the Brighton Beach End which was currently occupied by the rusting relic of the abandoned Walker Stand.

Little of this was of any pressing concern to Harry Redknapp, who went about the business of taking his first pre-season as a football manager with apparent ease. As well as securing the permanent signature of Sean O'Driscoll, Redknapp also brought in Liverpudlian Colin Russell from Huddersfield Town for £15,000 in the hope that the striker, who at one point had been Kenny Dalglish's understudy at Anfield, would spearhead a push for promotion.

After fighting off enquiries for Ian Thompson, his star striker from the previous season, and almost losing Billy Rafferty to Dutch outfit Den Haag on the eve of the campaign, Redknapp declared himself happy with the players he had at his disposal. 'It is the best squad we have had at this football club for many a year. I feel we are going to do something very good. We will be pushing for promotion this season.'

Thompson, who saw Redknapp from his earliest days in management, remembers his young manager demonstrating a natural aptitude for the role from the very beginning. 'Harry was cutting his teeth as a professional manager,' he says. 'He just instilled this belief in players most of the time that you could go out and win games. He took things a little personally sometimes and we all had our little ups and downs with him, but he was a great tactician and a great motivator. He very much knew his stuff on the training ground and was learning as a manager. I've got nothing but praise for the guy and I think he did a superb job. It was really interesting working with him as a new manager making his way in the lower leagues.'

On the back of the previous year's successes, optimism abounded come the start of the season. Following a 1-0 triumph over promotion favourites Derby County, it threatened to go through the roof, before a hard dose of reality brought supporters back down to earth. A 5-0 aggregate defeat to Fourth Division Aldershot in the Milk Cup bookended a less than glorious return to Hull in the first league away game, a 3-0 defeat.

Little appeared to be going in the Cherries' favour. On their way to face Plymouth Argyle in mid-September, the team coach broke down and only the goodwill of Clifton Rugby Club, who were taking the same route in their own bus, ensured Bournemouth did not have to default on the fixture.

The goalless draw at Home Park was followed by another draw when the Cherries played Newport a few days later. Redknapp's captain Roger Brown sustained an ankle injury to further add to the manager's woes. 'We're not having a lot of luck in that department,' he said. Harry's mood did not brighten when goalkeeper Ian Leigh injured a hand in training before the match with Bristol Rovers. 'It's unbelievable,' said an exasperated Redknapp. 'When your luck's out it really is out.'

On this occasion, Redknapp's words proved accurate as not only did Bournemouth lose 1-0 at Eastville, but Paul Morrell was stretchered off with concussion. To make matters worse, Bristol Rovers' matchday doctor was absent from the fixture, leading to a hospital visit for Morrell, and when the defeated Cherries trudged off the pitch at full time, they discovered that no water was available in the dressing room to shower.

By October, Bournemouth found themselves in the Third Division relegation zone. Redknapp, however, remained optimistic. 'It's been a difficult spell,' he said. 'Once we get a fully fit squad and I can field the team I want, the league record will be improved. There is no cause for panic. We have played some good football at times, without getting the results we deserved.'

Prior to a goalless draw at Lincoln, more light was shed on the machinations behind the scenes at Dean Court in recent months. Self-styled 'King of Clubs' Anton Johnson was the subject of an investigation by ITV's flagship current affairs programme *World in Action*. When the programme was aired on Tuesday 16 October, Cherries' fans watched on as Harold Walker was presented with a document confirming that Johnson was the figure behind Channel Islands-based Wigbourne Holdings, which owned the majority of the shares in AFC Bournemouth for the ten months between March 1983 and January 1984.

Walker, Brian Tiler and Rodney Barton had all been economical with the truth regarding Johnson's involvement, but had no choice but to come clean in the light of the very public evidence. 'I knew when we exchanged contracts,' admitted

Walker. 'Anton took complete control from then on. But it was a complicated business.'

Brian Tiler had arrived at Dean Court as a direct result of the Wigbourne takeover, but was keen to distance himself from Johnson. 'I quickly became disillusioned,' said the Cherries' managing director of his appointment by the Essex businessman. 'I was supposed to be running the club, but I had no powers. It was intolerable. There is no question about my loyalty to AFC Bournemouth. I have moved my family down here and I believe in its potential.'

'It was hard,' says Redknapp of the penurious circumstances in which he was managing. 'We had no training ground and just trained wherever we could in those days. Anywhere we could get basically. That went on for years. We sometimes used to train on a cinder pitch in the forecourt of the ground. It was awful.'

Fortunately, Harry has never let financial issues hinder the performances of his teams. As players began to recover from their injuries to strengthen the squad, Ian Leigh's replacement John Smeulders did not concede a goal in any of the next seven Third Division games, a club record.

A 4-0 thrashing of York City at Dean Court provided some evidence that Redknapp's confidence in his team as they plummeted down the table was justified. 'I would have been worried if we had not been playing well,' said the Bournemouth manager, 'but I knew the only thing we were lacking in most games was effective finishing.'

With Ian Thompson and Billy Rafferty suddenly finding their goalscoring form, Redknapp watched on as his confidence in his team proved well founded.

Both strikers claimed braces as Preston and Reading were seen off in the next two matches and Rafferty's sixth goal of the season was enough to extend the winning run to four games at home to Wigan. As the Cherries moved into the comfort of mid-table, chants of 'going up' were heard around Dean Court. 'We want to keep this nice little run going,' said Redknapp. 'We have been playing well and getting some good results lately. If we maintain those same standards, we will be all right.'

A goalless draw at Walsall saw the Cherries remain in tenth place in the Third Division going into an FA Cup first-round tie against Kettering Town of the Gola League. Despite their excellent recent form, Redknapp's side were held to a goalless draw at Rockingham Road. Before the replay, Harry promised to 'finish the job' but the match proved far from straightforward.

After keeping a clean sheet for some 671 minutes, John Smeulders suddenly found himself picking the ball out of his net twice in short order as Kettering took a commanding early lead in the replay. The Cherries clawed their way back into the tie courtesy of goals from Bobby Savage and Colin Russell but had to rely on an own goal by Poppies' full-back Nigel Thrower to see them through.

Normal service was resumed when the next league game at home to Brentford ended 1-0 to Bournemouth. That was the end of the clean sheets and the winning run as Redknapp's team went down 1-0 to table-topping Bradford at Valley Parade at the start of December. Redknapp had promised John Smeulders a box of 50 cigars if he had kept his eighth clean sheet in a row in the Third Division, but the gift was never to materialise.

Before setting off for Yorkshire, Redknapp played his part in fooling long-serving groundsman John Harriss into thinking his precious playing surface was being overrun by moles. It was, in fact, an elaborate practical joke staged by Noel Edmonds' *Late Late Breakfast Show*, a popular Saturday evening television programme which regularly pulled in in excess of ten million viewers at a time when there were only four television channels to choose from.

'I wasn't very happy, I can tell you,' says Harriss. 'Harry was in on it, but it was Brian Tiler that was the main player in stitching me up. They sent me to pick Brian up from a hotel but he wasn't registered there. They must have been setting it up whilst I was gone. When I got back to the ground the chairman took me out to the pitch and said, "What's going on out there?" There were little explosions going off everywhere. Of course, it turned out to be Noel Edmonds. I nearly hit him.'

Unsurprisingly, the television cameras did not follow the Cherries to their next match, an FA Cup tie against Gola League club Dartford Town. As in the previous round against Kettering, Bournemouth made hard work of the tie, drawing the first game 1-1 at Watling Street.

The draw for the third round took place before the replay. Incredibly, Bournemouth were given the opportunity to reacquaint themselves with Manchester United for the third straight season in cup competition, with the tie due to take place at Old Trafford this time around.

Redknapp's team made no mistake when Dartford came to Dean Court, thumping the non-league side 4-1. However, victory was only sealed with two goals in the last five minutes, up until which the Cherries had put in a nervy performance. 'We didn't want to miss out,' said Redknapp after the game. 'It will be quite different in the next round. We will be the side with nothing to lose and the pressure will be on United. It will be Ron Atkinson going through something like I have tonight. Of course it's a tough one. We will need a slightly bigger miracle than last time if we are to get the right result.'

Despite the Bournemouth manager's pragmatism, the club had boldly issued supporters with a voucher giving them the right to buy a ticket for a possible replay at the league match against Gillingham on New Year's Day.

Stung by their shock defeat 12 months earlier, United manager Ron Atkinson was determined to finish the job at Old Trafford. 'It's time to get our act together and have a good cup run,' he said. 'We are all very much aware that it was Bournemouth who put paid to our FA Cup hopes at this stage last season, another good reason why we must get our act together. We want revenge.'

Redknapp had a full squad to choose from, with the little niggles some of his players had been complaining about miraculously clearing up in the days before the team travelled north. Unfortunately, Atkinson also had no selection worries, and was able to bring back top scorer Frank Stapleton in place of Alan Brazil.

Icy conditions across the country meant the match was briefly in jeopardy as the newly installed undersoil heating at Old Trafford was required for the first time and did not function properly in all areas of the pitch. A late inspection resulted in the game going ahead, much to the relief of the thousands of Cherries fans who had made the trip. Whilst club staff and their families, including Redknapp's sons Mark and Jamie, had flown to Manchester from Hurn Airport, supporters catching one of the two chartered trains had a less comfortable journey as the heating failed and they arrived late for kick-off.

Sadly, those fans may have missed the best of Bournemouth's performance on the day as a Gordon Strachan-inspired United looked every inch the footballing aristocrats that had failed to turn up at Dean Court the previous January. United keeper Gary Bailey had to pick the ball out of his net in the opening stages of the match after Ian Thompson had headed home, but the goal was disallowed following an infringement by Colin Russell.

Strachan then opened the scoring on 22 minutes and his compatriot Gordon McQueen doubled United's lead with a header six minutes before half-time. There was little Redknapp's team could do to bridge the gulf in class, and when Frank Stapleton scored a third just before the hour mark, the game was up.

Redknapp had no complaints at the final whistle. 'United deserved their win. They are a pretty good team with one or two useful players,' he joked, appearing significantly less disappointed about the outcome than after other defeats. Upon returning to his home in Christchurch, Harry reviewed his side's performance via video cassette, wryly commenting, 'It didn't do any good. The result was still the same.'

Decades later, Redknapp still remembers the encounter fondly. 'It was a great experience, obviously,' he says. 'For players who have only played in the lower divisions, they dream of playing at Old Trafford and most of them never get the chance to do it. It was great for me to take a team there. It was a good little cup run we had; they were a good group of lads.'

Aside from the chance to visit one of English football's most iconic venues, consolation for the Cherries came in the shape of around £25,000 in gate proceeds from the 32,080 crowd.

This very welcome opportunity to put a dent in the club's arrears was not taken in the spirit of prudence by chairman Rodney Barton, but as a sign of things to come. 'This is another page in the history of AFC Bournemouth,' he said post-match. 'Today we played Manchester United in the FA Cup, but we hope to be returning on a more regular basis as a First Division club in the not too distant future.'

It's easy to scoff at Barton's optimism in the knowledge that it would take three decades and much heartache before the Cherries would reach the summit of English football. However, at the time the club appeared to be on an upward trajectory under Redknapp and the manager would provide further evidence that he might deliver the seemingly impossible in the coming years.

For now, Harry was faced once again with the task of refocusing his players on the Third Division campaign. A draw on an icy Dean Court pitch with high-flying Hull was followed by a 1-0 defeat at fifth-placed Rotherham United. With just five goals in their 12 away games to date, Redknapp threw on teenager Steve Claridge in the hope that the former Fareham Town striker would provide the scoring touch. 'The lad has done well in a short

After a promising start to his playing days at Bournemouth in 1972, a fit and healthy Redknapp became an increasingly rare sight at Dean Court. (Getty Images)

Redknapp's team-mates Mel Machin (left) and John Benson led the exodus to Norwich in 1973/74, but both returned to manage the Cherries, with Benson's struggles leading to Harry's first taste of coaching. (Getty Images)

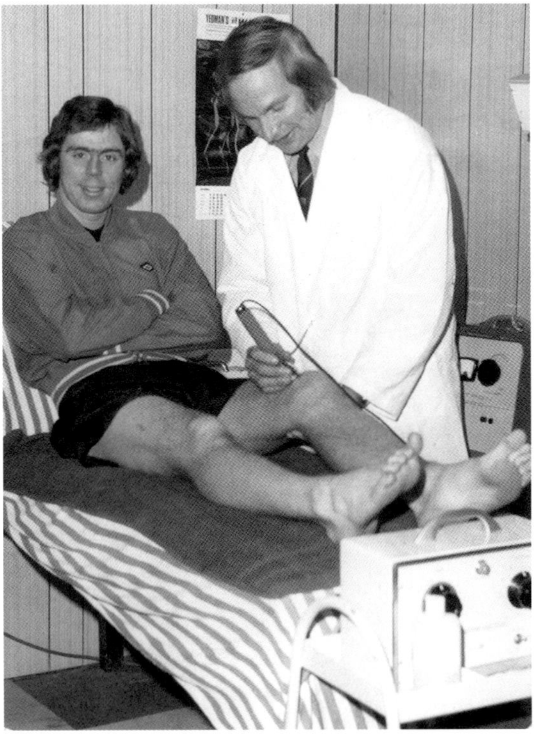

Harry in 1975, benefitting from the ultrasound machine that physio Arthur Cunliffe did not know how to operate until Redknapp explained. (Bournemouth Daily Echo)

By 1981, Redknapp was first team coach at Dean Court. Taking a break from his duties, he and former Bournemouth manager Don Megson race a bath chair on the seafront against a rickshaw pulled by a Zulu warrior. (Bournemouth Daily Echo)

Described as 'a right boy' by Harry, comedian Jim Davidson became a director at Dean Court in 1981 through his friendship with Dave Webb. He stepped down when Webb resigned in December 1982, resulting in Redknapp's first opportunity in management. (Getty Images)

George Best made five appearances for Bournemouth in the spring of 1983. Despite his failure to attend training sessions and away fixtures, Redknapp praised his attitude, describing the Irishman's stint at the club as 'fantastic'. (Getty Images)

Redknapp picks up the Bell's Whisky Third Division Manager of the Season award for 1986/87. (Getty Images)

Harry leads the celebrations at Dean Court before an end of season friendly between Bournemouth and old foes Norwich City to celebrate the 1986/87 Third Division title triumph for the Cherries.

Mark Newson and Ralph Milne tussle for the ball in the FA Cup fifth round in 1989. Bournemouth drew Manchester United four times in knockout competitions during Redknapp's tenure as coach and manager. (Getty Images)

By the late 1980s, Redknapp's unprecedented success at Dean Court saw him linked with a succession of high profile jobs in football management. (Getty Images)

The final game of the 1989/90 season that saw Bournemouth relegated and the Leeds supporters riot throughout the weekend. Redknapp described the fixture as 'the most intimidating game I have ever been part of'. (Getty Images)

Redknapp returns to take training for the first time since almost losing his life in a car crash at the 1990 World Cup in Italy 14 weeks previously. (Bournemouth Daily Echo)

A forlorn Redknapp at Victoria Park in May 1992 after an injury-time winner for Hartlepool saw the Cherries miss out on the play-offs in Harry's final game as Bournemouth manager. (Bournemouth Daily Echo)

With his career in management winding down, Redknapp regularly attends matches at Dean Court, both as a television pundit and season ticket holder. (Getty Images)

Despite the controversy surrounding his departure as manager in 1992, Redknapp retains his place on the wall of fame at Dean Court. (Getty Images)

time,' said Redknapp of a man who would go on to play for 20 different clubs.

Claridge made his first start for the Cherries as they began their defence of what was now known as the Freight Rover Trophy at Plymouth. Bournemouth tasted defeat again, but Billy Rafferty's close-range effort in injury time gave Redknapp's side a lifeline going into the second leg.

After a four-game winning streak saw Bournemouth rise to fourth place in the Third Division, supporters gave their wholehearted approval as Redknapp was rewarded for his endeavours with another improved two-year rolling contract. 'The players have been magnificent during this spell,' beamed Redknapp, before putting pen to paper just in the nick of time.

Bournemouth lost four of their next five Third Division games, scoring just twice. The only bright spot in this barren run was a 2-1 win over Dave Webb's Torquay United in the second round of the Freight Rover Trophy. The chance of promotion appeared to be receding rapidly, but Harry remained confident in his team's quality and blamed only poor finishing for the downturn in fortunes. 'It's all about putting the ball in the back of the net,' he said. 'For some reason we have not been cashing in on the chances we have been creating.'

Seven goals in the opposition net in the next two home games against Lincoln and Bolton soothed Redknapp's frustration and delighted the Dean Court faithful. Bournemouth then won at Burnley and drew at Wigan to put themselves within stretching distance of the top three once again. The Bournemouth manager knew it was asking an awful lot of his depleted playing squad to maintain their form until the end of the season. 'It's not impossible. We need to keep pegging away,' he advised. 'It will be difficult but the chance is not gone. It is up to us. All we need is another eight or nine wins!'

In the event, Bournemouth only won three more times in the nine remaining games of the campaign. Over the Easter weekend at the start of April, a goalless draw at home to Cambridge United and defeat at Gillingham meant the glimmer of hope that the league season would end in unlikely glory was all but extinguished. However, thumping 4-1 wins in consecutive home games over Walsall and Bradford had supporters sighing ruefully over what might have been had the Cherries shown a little more consistency and not been hampered so severely by injuries. Whilst Walsall had had a similar season to the Cherries and would finish just one place below Redknapp's team, Bradford were already promoted by the time the teams met having run away with the Third Division, suggesting their surprise collapse at Dean Court may have been caused by lengthy celebrations in Yorkshire.

A chance of glory remained in the shape of Bournemouth's defence of the Freight Rover Trophy. No sooner had the Walsall players begun to recover from their mauling at Dean Court than they were forced to return to the south coast in the Southern Area quarter-final of the competition just five days later. The Saddlers gave a better account of themselves second time around but fell to a 2-1 defeat courtesy of goals from Manchester United's conquerors Milton Graham and Ian Thompson.

Redknapp knew progress in the competition could salvage the season and lead to a further cash injection to fund new recruits to the playing squad. 'We won it last year,' said the Bournemouth manager. 'Now we want to collect that trophy with the added thrill of playing at Wembley.'

Bournemouth faced Brentford in the Southern Area semi-final of the trophy. On a bright evening at Dean Court, 4,617 supporters watched an enthralling tie which was decided when future television pundit Chris Kamara scored the Bees' winning goal in a 3-2 victory. Bournemouth did not relinquish their grasp on the trophy easily, with Milton Graham ending up in hospital with a neck injury sustained when attempting to equalise two minutes from time. 'We're all disappointed, of course,' said a crestfallen

Redknapp. 'It would have been great for everyone, and especially the supporters, if we had made it all the way to Wembley.'

Although the season was effectively over, the Cherries still had four more Third Division fixtures to fulfil. Defeat at Ashton Gate kept Bristol City's promotion hopes alive before Redknapp's team faced another high-flying club in the shape of George Graham's Millwall. With the Lions being in the grip of an ugly hooligan element in the 1980s, the game was staged on the Wednesday after the Bank Holiday, with the unusual kick-off time of 6pm. Although somewhat ham-fisted, this approach largely worked as little trouble was reported at the game or in the area surrounding Dean Court. However, an attendance of 2,983, one of the lowest of the season, was the outcome. Millwall ran out 2-1 winners, a result which may not have been cheered by the Cherries' faithful, but was welcomed if it meant the Lions would not be on the fixture list the following season.

Bournemouth's final away game of the campaign saw them travel to east London to face Orient at Brisbane Road. The O's were deep in the relegation mire, but their disappointment at gaining just a point in a turgid 0-0 draw with the Cherries soon became muted as the perilous state of English football in the 1980s became tragically palpable.

As the players at Brisbane Road were trudging off the pitch at half-time, news began to filter through of a fire at Bradford City's match against Lincoln City. The match began in a mood of great celebration, the Bantams having claimed the Third Division title the week before with a 2-0 victory over Bolton. Captain Peter Jackson, born and bred in the Yorkshire city, was presented with the silver champions' trophy before kick-off and the majority of the first half, although goalless, was a scene of joy for a club that had not played in the Second Division since 1937.

Five minutes before half-time a fire broke out in Bradford's wooden main stand. The blaze spread rapidly, engulfing the stand where around 3,000 supporters were sitting. Fifty-six people lost their lives, making it the worst disaster in the history of English football.

As the families of the victims buried their loved ones, the world around them moved on surprisingly quickly. Just two days later Bournemouth completed their Third Division fixtures with a 3-0 victory over a Newport County side who had secured their safety in the division despite only gaining one point in their previous eight games.

Redknapp gave Steve Claridge another chance to impress and the skin-headed striker gratefully accepted, heading the first goal past County keeper Mark Kendall after Billy Rafferty's chip had rebounded to him off the crossbar.

With a tenth-placed finish achieved in his first full season in management, Redknapp looked ahead to mounting a serious assault on the Second Division next time around. 'I feel we are two players short of being a very useful side capable of launching a real promotion challenge,' he said, before confirming he intended to oversee something of a clear-out of the playing squad in order to balance the books. 'It will mean getting rid of a few players so that I can keep within the overall wage structure.'

With the campaign under his belt, Redknapp would be busy over the summer, his hard work scouting in the lower leagues and aptitude for playing the transfer market coming to the fore.

Elsewhere, just 18 days after the tragic events at Bradford, 39 fans were killed at the Heysel Stadium before the European Cup Final between Liverpool and Juventus when a wall collapsed under the weight of Italian fans trying to escape onrushing Liverpool supporters. In the weeks leading up to the final, both clubs had lobbied UEFA to find a more suitable venue than the crumbling Belgian national stadium to host the game, but their pleas fell on deaf ears. It would take further loss of life before football would finally wake up to its responsibilities.

Chapter Ten

Striking Out

1985/86

PROMOTION was very much on Redknapp's mind in the summer of 1985. With genuine improvement shown in both the results and the quality of the football at Dean Court since he took control of team affairs, he had every reason to feel that a crack at the second tier was within his team's grasp.

Moving into the transfer market to bolster his attack following the departure of leading scorer Billy Rafferty to Portugal, Redknapp unearthed Colin Clarke at Tranmere Rovers. The Northern Irish forward had scored 22 goals in 45 Fourth Division games the previous season for Tranmere and Harry was convinced he could repeat the feat at a higher level. Initially offering £10,000 for the striker, the Cherries were forced to attend a tribunal to set the fee when Rovers demanded eight times that amount. At the hearing, Tranmere's representatives produced a letter from Chelsea confirming they had bid £70,000 for the player, but this only had a modest impact, with Bournemouth eventually being required to pay a £22,500 fee. Even that price was too steep as far as the Bournemouth directors were concerned. 'I tried to sign Colin and the chairman Rodney Barton said to me, "Harry, we haven't got £20,000 to sign a striker,"' recalls Redknapp. 'I said to him, "I think he would be a great investment." I had followed Colin for a long time, watched him all over when he was at Tranmere and even been over to Ireland to watch him. Mr Barton said, "Well, we can't afford him," so I got three of the vice-presidents who were friends of mine to put up £5,000 each and we could buy the player and split any profit if we sold him. I think the chairman thought, "Hang on, Harry is so confident about this there must be something to it," so in the end the club put up the £20,000.'

Tranmere's citing of Chelsea's bid for Clarke hinted at how close Bournemouth came to losing out to the west London club for his signature. 'When we agreed the deal with Colin, we shook hands on it but for some reason it took an awful long time to get the contract drawn up,' says Redknapp. 'Whilst we were waiting, the phone went and it was Colin's wife ringing from the hotel to tell him that Chelsea had just been on the phone. He took their call and spoke to Chelsea. They said they would get him a car and get him straight to London and whatever we had offered they would double. They were a First Division club and we were only a Third Division club, so we were not offering him very big wages. And he was a Chelsea fan, so basically it was a dream move for him. He put the phone down and I said, "It's OK, I understand Colin. I'm choked obviously but you've got to do what you've got to do." He said, "No, no. I shook hands with you. If I shake hands and give someone my word that's it. I can't go back on that." It was unbelievable.'

Of all the transfer deals Redknapp has been involved in, his favourite appears to have been the acquisition of defender Mark Newson from Maidstone United, who were managed at the time by Barry Fry. Newson had been in the youth ranks at Charlton and had represented England at non-league level. From within his ever-expanding army of contacts at all levels of the game, Redknapp was aggrieved to learn that Newson was soon to play in a trial match at Tottenham, who were preparing a six-figure bid. But his sources also disclosed that Newson was not actually under contract at Maidstone and was a free agent.

That was all the encouragement Redknapp required, and he did the deal with Newson behind Fry's back. Redknapp's punchline to this story understandably focuses upon Fry's furious reaction when he phoned him to break the news. 'Barry said, "I'll tell you what Redknapp, there'll be two blokes coming down the motorway to shoot your f***ing kneecaps off."'

Among the warm-up matches for the coming campaign was the final of the Hampshire Cup against Portsmouth. It was a competition the Cherries still took reasonably seriously despite its low-key parochial status and the town becoming part of Dorset when local government was reorganised during Redknapp's playing days in red and black 11 years previously. The Bournemouth manager's disappointment at a 1-0 defeat was significantly overshadowed by his rage at Portsmouth's Mick Tait who had broken the leg of Cherries' key midfielder Bobby Savage in the 27th minute of the fixture after launching a reckless challenge. Tait's immediate dismissal was little consolation to the baying Dean Court crowd who had heard the sickening sound of Savage's fibula snapping from the stands. Savage was out for the season, taking his dynamic energy and important goals with him. 'A terrible setback' in the push for promotion in Redknapp's view. 'We are going to miss the little fellow.' Fortunately, although not for Bobby Savage, Harry had re-signed Tommy Heffernan from Sheffield United at the end of the previous season, and the popular Irishman was able to fill in for Savage in midfield.

Redknapp remained optimistic about his team's prospects for the campaign that lay ahead, 'We have a lot of ability and a lot of character among these players. They are capable of doing well for this club.' A 3-0 defeat at Derby in the opening league fixture of the season was not the hammer blow to Redknapp's confidence it first appeared. Bournemouth went on to beat Reading 3-1 at Elm Park in the Milk Cup and Bristol City 5-0 in the first Third Division game of the season at Dean Court. The Royals, who would go on to set a record of 13 league games unbeaten from the start of the season, were duly dispatched after a 2-0 victory for Bournemouth in the second leg.

Harry's prediction regarding Colin Clarke's potential proved prophetic as the Irishman bagged five goals in the first four fixtures, including a hat-trick against Bristol City. With just a handful of Bournemouth appearances under his belt, Clarke was delighted to discover that he had been called up into the senior Northern Ireland squad by manager Billy Bingham. It was the first occasion in 37 years that a serving Cherries player had been called up to an international squad since goalkeeper Tommy Godwin represented the Republic of Ireland in 1948.

These rare developments were described as 'smashing' by Redknapp, but left the Cherries' manager fending off speculation about his latest acquisition after just three appearances in a Bournemouth shirt. 'I've seen the same people at our games,' he said in relation to the scouts that were already circling from bigger clubs. 'Colin is here to do a job for this club. He is on a three-year contract and will get even better. He's popular with the supporters and I'm not interested in selling him.'

Whilst fending off Clarke's suitors, Harry's desire to find new blood to improve his squad did not abate and he continued to travel widely and frequently to scout potential signings and run the rule over future opponents. Following the Cherries' defeat at Brentford in a midday kick-off on the August Bank Holiday, Redknapp dragged Brian Tiler across London to watch games at Fulham and Wimbledon on the same day. 'I've never done that before,' said a weary Tiler, who may or may not have known that the previous day his manager had taken in four youth team games in the Bournemouth leagues and would go on to watch Southampton the following evening at The Dell. 'I love watching football at all levels,' said the indefatigable Redknapp. 'It's always interesting to see individual players and, of course, at league level, you need to keep in touch in this way.'

Despite this impressive dedication to his work, Redknapp was unable to build upon the positive start to the season as his team went on to win just twice in the next seven league games. The nadir of this patchy run of form came at home to Blackpool in mid-September when Bournemouth crashed to a 4-1 defeat. Redknapp's anger at the final whistle over the way his side allowed the Tangerines to dominate the second half was barely concealed, and he did not find any consolation in the fixture list which paired the Cherries with early pacesetters Wigan Athletic. 'I could not think of a tougher fixture at the moment,' bemoaned the Bournemouth manager, who travelled to Springfield Park with a squad shorn of eight injured players.

It came as no shock to anyone when the home side cruised to a 3-0 victory, dumping Bournemouth into the relegation zone with just seven points from five matches in the process. 'It's been a bad week,' said Redknapp. 'From a good position we have sustained three bad results.'

Relief came in the form of yet another plum draw, this time in the Milk Cup. Bournemouth's reward for seeing off Third Division leaders Reading in round one was a two-legged tie with Football League champions Everton. The Toffees were in the middle of the most glorious period in their history, with Redknapp's old England Youth team-mate Howard Kendall breaking the hegemony of city rivals Liverpool on English football. The Goodison Park side had already proved their mettle in Europe as well, winning the Cup Winners' Cup at the end of the previous season, but they were prevented from usurping the Anfield side in the European Cup when English clubs were indefinitely banned from UEFA competitions following the tragedy at the Heysel Stadium.

'It's a fantastic draw,' said Redknapp, who rated Kendall's side as the best in Europe. 'We have been lucky again and the club could not wish for anything better. Whatever happens it is going to be a tremendous experience for the players and supporters.'

Harry's excitement at the prospect of another cup upset was somewhat diluted in the days leading up to the game when his assistant manager and most trusted lieutenant Stuart Morgan left Dean Court to take the manager's job at Torquay United. Whilst the Cherries were enduring the defeat at Wigan, Morgan was on scouting duty at Anfield for the Merseyside derby in what turned out to be his last engagement under Redknapp for some time. 'Stuart's move came as a bit of a surprise,' said the Bournemouth manager, 'but we wish him well.'

This disappointment was temporarily forgotten when Bournemouth took a remarkable two-goal lead in the first 11 minutes at Goodison Park. Footballer of the Year Neville Southall's first task in the match was to pick the ball out of the Everton net after Colin Clarke hammered Ian Thompson's cross past him within ten seconds of the kick-off. Liverpudlian Colin Russell then nutmegged Everton and Wales captain Kevin Ratcliffe before firing past Southall to render the home crowd silent and threaten another famous cup scalp for the Cherries. However, unlike the victory over Manchester United the previous year, Everton had the time to regain their composure and were level by half-time. Gary Lineker added to his growing tally of goals with an impressive header from a Gary Stevens cross and Ian Marshall scored his first goal for the Toffees from a Graeme Sharp flick-on. Bournemouth's players were generously applauded by the Everton faithful as they returned to the pitch after the break, but the applause turned to cheers when Tommy Heffernan headed into his own net from a Kevin Sheedy corner in the 55th minute.

'Everton must be worried,' said a grinning Redknapp of the prospect of an overall Bournemouth victory in the tie. 'Against that class of opposition it must be one of the best-ever results for this club and it gives us a real chance going into the second leg.'

Worries regarding the Cherries' league form were somewhat allayed as, boosted by their performance on Merseyside, Bournemouth took six points from the three games that preceded the second leg. A 4-2 win at home to Darlington saw Mark Newson score his first goals in professional football, and although Redknapp's side went down 3-2 to Lincoln at Sincil Bank after Chris Sulley was sent off before half-time, a 1-0 win at Cardiff meant confidence was high when Everton arrived on the south coast.

Bournemouth began the return leg well, matching Everton throughout the first half and having the majority of the chances. Unfortunately, none of these were taken and Gary Lineker delivered the sucker punch two minutes before the break when he headed in from close range. The second half was played out in driving rain, and, despite more saves from Neville Southall, it was Howard Kendall's side that grabbed the next goal through Kevin Richardson and the tie was all but over.

Redknapp admits that he is not a good loser, but on this occasion he was uncharacteristically sanguine. 'We proved it tonight – we can compete with the best of them. We have the makings of a successful side,' he said after the final whistle.

The real disappointment on the night was the lower than expected attendance of 8,084. When the draw was made, Brian Tiler justifiably predicted a 12,300 sell-out for the second leg. Ultimately, he was reduced to applying to Dorset Police to extend the sales period for tickets into the afternoon of the day of the match as it became clear that a combination of a public unfamiliar with all-ticket matches and a poor weather forecast would reduce the size of the payday the club had anticipated. Although it would prove to be Bournemouth's highest attendance of the season, the £25,000 that the Cherries made from the tie was only half of what Tiler and the board of directors were hoping for.

Following this latest brush with glamour, Redknapp's team continued to blow hot and cold in the league. Victory over Bury was followed by defeats at home to Gillingham and at York City. Both matches were lost in the latter stages, with Tony Cascarino grabbing a late winner for Gillingham and City scoring just two minutes from time.

Supporters' frustration with the Cherries' inability to put a sustained run of results together was given some succour in the next game at Dean Court where the home side put six goals past Bristol Rovers. It was Bournemouth's best win since they put seven past Doncaster Rovers in February 1979. 'I knew we would get this sort of result one day,' said Redknapp, who had seen his side take a four-goal lead in the first half. 'We've been playing well without too much luck, but this time we got the breaks and made the most of them.'

Relying on fortune's favour did not prove to be a successful strategy going forward. Bournemouth lost the following game to Bolton 1-0, a defeat which a raging Redknapp put down to the inadequacy of the officials despite Wanderers' manager Charlie Wright not knowing which players he would have available until the morning of the match as a flu epidemic swept through the Burnden Park dressing room. Referee John Key sent John Beck off five minutes before half-time and awarded a free kick for a Mark Newson disputed handball four minutes from time from which Steve Thompson scored the Trotters' winning goal. The Cherries' manager did not mince his words at the final whistle. 'It seems when you go up north you have to expect these kinds of things,' he said. 'The refereeing is disgraceful, the standard has gone. They are not up to it any more.'

Whilst the FA disciplinary panel were considering Harry's comments, the Bournemouth manager was watching his side go down to another defeat at Plymouth. Again, Redknapp described himself satisfied with his team's performance, but the significance of playing well and losing was not lost on supporters. 'We have played well and lost,' said Redknapp. 'It is not the first time we have outplayed a team and got beaten. It is happening too often. People will be getting fed up with me saying how good we were but did not get the breaks, but that was just how it was.'

Victory over Wolves, in the first meeting between the clubs since the Cherries famously knocked the Molineux side out of the FA Cup in 1957, briefly brought hope that the winter months would see a turnaround in results and see Redknapp's confidence in his charges vindicated. However, just one win in the final five games of 1985 meant the remainder of the season would focus on avoiding the drop into the Fourth Division.

'It's very disappointing,' said the Bournemouth manager. 'We look good going forward, but defensively we are not doing what we should be doing and are conceding too many goals. There are no excuses.'

The final fixture of 1985 saw a goalless draw at Brentford played out in freezing conditions that would have seen the fixture called off under current guidelines. Redknapp was not impressed with the conditions under which his squad was required to perform. 'I didn't think the pitch was playable,' he began. 'Conditions out there were worse than they appeared from the stand. The players from both sides did the best they could but it was difficult to create anything. They could only play the ball in the direction they were facing and turning was treacherous.'

The start of 1986 did not go that well either as the Cherries conceded a last-minute goal to draw with Swansea in a game they dominated on New Year's Day and they did not record a league victory until the final day of January when they won 3-2 at Chesterfield. In between times, the chance of another dose of cup fever to brighten an already disappointing campaign was lost when Redknapp's side were unceremoniously dumped out of the FA Cup by Third Division high-flyers Wigan Athletic. A 3-0 hammering in blizzard-like conditions at Springfield Park, in which future Bournemouth midfielder Warren Aspinall scored after coming on as a substitute in the second half, left Redknapp considering his options. 'One or two players have disappointed me. They have not been consistent enough in producing the form of which they are capable. I called them in on Sunday and last week they were training in the afternoons,' he said after the 2-1 reverse against Newport at Somerton Park. 'When you're in this sort of situation the only answer is to work harder at putting it right, and that's what we are doing.'

There was little evidence of a desire from his players to bring the extra training sessions to an end in the 3-1 defeat that followed at Leyton Orient in the opening match of the Freight Rover Trophy campaign. By the following weekend, the penny had begun to drop and the Cherries had the better of a 1-1 draw at Dean Court with Derby County. Prior to the match, Redknapp outlined both the gulf in spending power of the two clubs and the poverty at Dean Court when he told the *Bournemouth Evening Echo*, 'I have added it up; Derby are a million-pound outfit.'

Following a run of just one win in the previous ten games in league and cup, the Cherries' players emphatically demonstrated to Redknapp they would very much like their free afternoons back by thumping runaway Third Division leaders Reading 5-0 in the second match of the Freight Rover Trophy. Having dumped the Royals out of the League Cup at the beginning of the campaign, Bournemouth continued their dominance over the Berkshire side in knockout competitions with Colin Clarke scoring four goals on the night. Reading's ace marksman Trevor Senior did not appear in the fixture having been injured in training, allowing Clarke to race ahead in the season's goalscoring charts, his total of 21 bypassing Senior's 19.

With a ten-day break in prospect due to going out of the FA Cup, Harry took himself off for a few days' relaxation in Jersey and gave his much-relieved players the same leave of absence. By the time he returned, the scouts were once again showing up in numbers wherever Colin Clarke played. The Ulsterman scored in the 3-2 victory over Chesterfield and found himself under the watchful gaze of representatives from north London rivals Spurs and Arsenal in the 2-0 defeat to Gillingham at Priestfield. Redknapp knew he couldn't lose whether his star striker stayed at Dean Court or moved on, although he was not naive enough to admit as much in public. 'I want him to stay here and keep scoring his goals,' said the Bournemouth manager. 'The big clubs have got to check on a player of Colin's ability, but nobody has come in with a bid so far.'

Yellow paint was used to mark the snow-covered pitch at Priestfield and with Bournemouth's next match at Blackpool falling victim to the bleak winter weather, Redknapp endeared himself further to supporters by travelling to The Dell to see Southampton play Millwall in the FA Cup before declaring after a less than thrilling tie, 'Most of our games at Dean Court have been far more entertaining.'

When the pitches thawed, Redknapp may have been forgiven for praying for another cold snap as the Cherries failed to win in five games to the middle of March. It was a spell during which the Cherries struggled to find the net and could only draw at home with fellow relegation battlers Lincoln and Cardiff in the space of four days. Colin Clarke remained the only source of enjoyment for the Dean Court faithful, scoring twice during this barren run and picking up his first cap for Northern Ireland against France in Paris, a game which inevitably ended goalless.

After struggling to score for three months, Bournemouth then briefly went on the rampage in front of goal, with Clarke leading the way. He followed up his brace against Bolton with another against Bristol Rovers and scored in each of the Cherries' four wins in their next five games as relegation worries eased. Redknapp was now taking calls about his star player on a daily basis from First

Division clubs, but made his determination to hike up the price clear when he announced, 'We would like to keep Colin at least until the end of the season. He's happy with the club and is in no rush to get away. Neither are we in any hurry to sell him. He will be going to the World Cup in Mexico this summer as a Bournemouth player.'

It was during this purple patch that the Cherries again faced Third Division champions-elect Reading. The teams had met four times during the season already, with Bournemouth winning on three occasions. Yet again Redknapp's team confounded followers of the Biscuitmen and their own supporters by recording a 2-1 victory at Elm Park, their best result of the entire season. The Bournemouth manager had recalled youth team coach Keith Williams to bolster the midfield and swooped for left-winger Mark O'Connor from Bristol Rovers on transfer deadline day, and both men were key in the Cherries reaching the all-important 50-point mark after the victory.

With safety assured, Redknapp did not demonstrate a total commitment to victory as the season petered out, electing to 'give a couple of the kids a chance' to appear in the first team. Teenagers Billy Clark, Tommy Keane, Adrian Randall, David Coleman and Tony White all featured before the end of the campaign, and the Bournemouth manager was keen to see how they would cut it at league level with the prospect of cuts to his playing staff looming in the close season. 'There is no other way,' he said of the requirement to trim his roster. 'The squad for next season will probably have 14 senior players with the support of the youngsters. It seems that I will have to release one or two players I would have liked to retain. Their contracts are up and we have not got the cash to offer them.'

Prior to the penultimate fixture of the season at Blackpool, it was confirmed that Colin Clarke had been selected in Billy Bingham's Northern Ireland squad for the World Cup finals in Mexico. It was the first time a serving Bournemouth player would feature at a World Cup, a fact not lost on Redknapp. 'This is great news for everyone concerned,' said Harry, a statement in which he clearly included himself as he knew it would further ramp up Clarke's transfer value and thus the potential to dodge the financial black hole currently enveloping Dean Court. 'Of course they are all interested in Colin because of his tremendous scoring form,' he went on, 'but it will take a big fee to get him. A lot of clubs would like the player, but not too many could afford him, because we are not going to give him away.'

'It was a massive season for me and my most prolific in terms of goalscoring,' recalls Clarke of the year he spent at Dean Court. 'I got on well with Harry Redknapp and they were a great bunch of lads at the club. It was a really positive season for me and showed I could get goals on a consistent basis.'

Despite only finishing a disappointing 15th, Clarke considered the team potential candidates for the step up to the Second Division that would not be realised until a year after he moved on.

'I think we had the players capable of doing a lot better. One of the regrets I have, looking back on my career, is the times I've been with teams capable of getting promoted when we had the ability to do so. Bournemouth was definitely one of those examples.'

With the Football League season at an end, Cherries' fans could turn their attention to the tournament in Mexico and enjoy the unique prospect of seeing one of their own feature on the pitch. The striker did not disappoint. After coming on for goalscorer Norman Whiteside in the 81st minute of the opening draw with Algeria, Clarke was selected by Bingham to start in the second match against Spain ahead of Oxford United striker Billy Hamilton.

Northern Ireland had shocked the world by beating the Spanish hosts in the previous World Cup in Madrid's Bernabeu Stadium, but in Guadalajara four years on they struggled to repeat the trick and found themselves trailing 2-0 after just 18 minutes. At the start of the second half, Clarke beat Andoni Zubizarreta and defender

Ricardo Gallego to a high, bouncing ball to head over the flailing Spanish goalkeeper and score before a global audience of hundreds of millions. 'It wasn't my greatest goal,' reflected the Bournemouth striker years later, 'but it was one of my most memorable.'

Clarke limped off late in the game with a knee injury, forcing him out of training for two days. It was, however, no surprise when he declared himself fit for the final group match against Brazil. Although Northern Ireland exited the tournament following a 3-0 defeat, Clarke returned home a wanted man. The striker gave the shirt he wore against Algeria to Redknapp as a gesture of thanks when he got back to the south coast, saying, 'Harry has done a lot for me since I came to the club.'

Clarke's return from Mexico was greeted by what appeared to be a clamour involving several big-name clubs to secure his signature. Foremost amongst these, at least as far as the media were concerned, were Italian aristocrats Torino, with reports that a 'substantial bid' had been submitted from the Alps to secure the services of the Northern Irishman. Consequently, it came as both an anticlimax and a bitter frustration for the Dean Court faithful when, on the last day of June, Clarke decided the south coast was good enough for him and signed for Southampton. The deal was sewn up at Gatwick Airport before the striker flew out to Majorca for a holiday with his wife and young son.

A payment of £400,000 doubled the previous record transfer fee Bournemouth had received when Ted MacDougall left to join Manchester United in November 1972. Yet the move stuck in the craw of supporters who had cheered their man on with immense pride at the World Cup, only to see him sign for their nearest rivals.

Redknapp, by contrast, had no such qualms. 'When we signed Colin and he turned down Chelsea,' recalls Harry, 'he said, "If someone comes in for me in a year or two if I do well you won't stand in my way?" I said, "No, if a First Division club come in, I'll let you go." Sure enough, we had one season and Southampton came and offered £400,000 for him. It was a lot of money in those days. Great profit.'

Under the terms of Clarke's £22,500 transfer from Tranmere the previous summer, a third of the money would go to Prenton Park. That still left Bournemouth with a profit somewhere in the region of £250,000 and Harry Redknapp planned to make every penny count.

Chapter Eleven

Glory

1986/87

BOURNEMOUTH fans may have felt let down by the departure of their best player to local rivals for a price which was significantly less than some of those being bandied about in the press following the World Cup, but, for Redknapp, the deal was exactly what was required. As well as the fee, Southampton threw in striker David Puckett and defender Mark Whitlock. Harry knew the players plus cash was best for his purposes as a straight money deal would have seen more of the fee siphoned off to service the football club's debts.

Redknapp's tireless scouting had reaped rich rewards in Colin Clarke's case, but Bournemouth supporters were hoping their manager's eye for a player remained as keen when more new recruits joined Whitlock and Puckett at Dean Court during the summer months.

Harry himself was confident he could find the right mix without breaking the Dean Court bank. 'I didn't think we needed to spend big money,' he remembers. 'I felt there were players around who could do a job.'

Carl Richards, who had scored 35 goals in the Gola League the previous season and gained amateur international recognition, arrived for a fee of £10,000. 'I took Carl from Enfield,' recalls Harry. 'I went to watch on a Bank Holiday weekend. My wife said to me, "Where are you going on such a lovely day?" "I'm going to Nuneaton to watch a player," I said. I drove down there on my own to watch the England non-league team play the Welsh non-league team because Stuart Morgan, who was my chief scout, had told me about Carl. He said, "He's quick, he's strong. You want to go and have a look at him." I liked what I saw so after the game I hid behind a shed waiting for Carl so I could tap him up. That was how it worked in those days. So he came past and I said, "Carl, can I speak to you?" He walked over and said, "Who are you?" So I told him. Carl said, "Bournemouth? What league are you in? You're not in the Isthmian are you?" "No, we're in the Football League," I said. That was good enough for him, so I did a deal with Enfield's manager Eddie McCluskey. Carl came in during pre-season and he has the worst pre-season I have ever seen. I thought I'd done my money with him. We had a meeting and I slaughtered him and he just said, "Wait until the real games start." And he was as good as his word. Carl turned out to be a fantastic player. I loved him.'

Richards' immense confidence in his own ability meant that when he underperformed, his self-belief was barely bruised. However, the striker's opinion of his own prowess saw Redknapp miss out on the chance to sign a player who would go on to make a much greater impact on English football. 'Before the first game of the season, Carl comes to me and says, "Can my mate have a trial?" I said, "Is he as good as you Carl?" He said, "No, he's not as good as me." So I said, "Well tell him not to bother!" Anyway, the following week we had a friendly against Crystal Palace and this mate who Carl reckoned wasn't as good as him was on trial there and played in the match. It was Ian Wright.'

On the same day as he signed Richards, Redknapp signed 27-year-old Tony Pulis after the midfield enforcer had been released by Newport County. Harry had driven to Wales through a torrential storm to run the rule over Pulis at Somerton Park during the previous campaign, only to discover upon his arrival that the man who would eventually succeed him as Cherries' manager had been left out of the starting line-up. Undeterred, Redknapp snapped up Pulis once the Welshman was out of contract at the end of the season.

Next, the Bournemouth manager turned his attentions to the goalkeeping position. He had let both Ian Leigh and John Smeulders go after neither had convinced him that they were capable of consistently making the crucial saves that could be the difference between success and failure in the Third Division. After pulling out of a £5,000 deal for Shrewsbury Town's Paul Malcolm saying 'I've changed my mind', Redknapp then rejected West Bromwich Albion's Paul Bradshaw before landing 29-year-old Fulham custodian Gerry Peyton. Peyton had made several appearances for the Republic of Ireland and Redknapp considered his new purchase an important part of the squad he was attempting to assemble from cheap deals and other clubs' cast-offs. 'Gerry is a big, strong and experienced keeper and will do a great job, I am certain,' Redknapp confidently predicted.

Despite the disappointment over Ian Wright, the hastily arranged friendly against Steve Coppell's Crystal Palace saw Redknapp tying up a £15,000 deal to bring the Eagles' 28-year-old target man Trevor Aylott to Dean Court. 'We needed someone we could hit with the ball,' said Harry, in a revealing comment on the reality of life in the third tier.

Pre-season did little to dispel the doubts that supporters had about the Cherries' ability to improve upon their 17th place finish in May. Playing ten warm-up matches in 16 days, Redknapp's team won just three.

When the season proper kicked off, evidence that the relevance of the results in the friendlies could be disregarded was in short supply. Captain Mark Newson headed the equaliser in a 1-1 draw at Brentford on the opening day of the league season. This was followed by an early exit from the Littlewoods Cup at the hands of Bristol Rovers as the individuals in Redknapp's team struggled to become a cohesive unit. 'The way it was going I thought I wouldn't last a month into the season,' says Redknapp. 'I thought I was going to get the sack.'

Brian Tiler, who had recently expanded his portfolio to become the chairman of the Dean Court Supporters' Association as well as managing director of the football club, was keen to persuade those in the region's extensive catchment area that the hooligan blight that had reached its apotheosis in the mid-1980s should not put them off coming to watch the Cherries play. 'We have a great relationship with the police and we rarely have any problems. Parents can feel happy in bringing their families to Dean Court,' said Tiler, before going on to extol the appeal of the club's manager. 'Parents and children feel they can identify with Harry Redknapp. He has been part of the community for quite a long time now and he has got such a good personality that parents feel confident in approaching him. Harry's policy is to be involved as much as he can in schools and youth clubs. He knows every player in this area so much that he could probably tell you what they have for breakfast.'

Although Redknapp found reasons to be optimistic after his side battled to a 2-1 win against Newport in the first league game of the season at Dean Court, it is unlikely that even he would have predicted the sudden turnaround in form the Cherries demonstrated in the ensuing two months as they proceeded to win seven and lose just one of their next ten Third Division matches.

It was a run that would see Bournemouth hit the top of the table by mid-September and send the red and black faithful into paroxysms of stunned excitement. The sequence of positive results also coincided with further confirmation of Redknapp's status and popularity in and around Dean Court in the shape of the debut appearance of his 'Harry's View' post-match column in the *Evening Echo*. Redknapp used his first column to take credit for a Gerry Peyton penalty save in a 1-1 draw at Notts County, claiming, 'I had a word with Gerry Peyton before the game – and it worked!'

Harry was certainly solely responsible for team selection and tactics and prior to Bournemouth's 2-1 victory over Bolton Wanderers he took the somewhat surprising step of announcing that he was dispensing with the five-man defensive unit he had been attempting to implement. 'I like the sweeper system,' he said, 'but it is foreign to the players in this country. It is hard to get them to change the way they have played since they first kicked a ball. It wasn't as successful as I thought it would be.'

Knowledge of this revelation was not enough for Wanderers' manager Phil Neal to plan a victorious assault on Dean Court. The Trotters had two players sent off as the home side ran out 2-1 winners in what was Bournemouth's 2,500th league game since entering the old Third Division South in 1923.

After reaching the summit of the Third Division, Bournemouth saw off Bristol City with a 2-0 league victory thanks to two penalties from the newly revived Bobby Savage. The credit due to Redknapp and his players for their performance was, however, somewhat diluted by an outbreak of crowd trouble towards the conclusion of the match. The catalyst for the hooliganism which erupted between rival fans sitting near each other in the main stand was the sending off of City defender David Moyes for dissent after the Cherries were awarded their second penalty. Moyes, the future Everton and Manchester United manager, was adjudged by referee David Hodges to have fouled Carl Richards in injury time and the contentious decision proved a flashpoint for the seething resentment that had built up throughout the fractious encounter.

Moyes was soon joined in the hall of shame by his manager Terry Cooper, who took it upon himself to run on to the pitch and remonstrate with Hodges, who in turn sent the Robins' boss to the stand. Cooper's ill-advised actions precipitated a pitch invasion by scores of Bournemouth fans from the South End terrace. Remarkably, this idiocy was rapidly quelled by the intervention of the Cherries' players, whose diplomacy was as surprising as it was effective, inspiring the *Evening Echo* to report their actions in a purple prose rarely deployed to describe any aspect of football:

'The fans erupted in a sweeping rush,' reported the *Echo*, 'yet they advanced scarcely a yard beyond the penalty area, scene of glory and despair. Towards them, at the run in agonised formation, palms outstretched, came the Bournemouth players. The fans' team, their gladiators. "No! No! Go back! Go back!" they shouted. And the wild ones did. It was as if some tribe from the dark ages had seen the light.'

It can be safely assumed that, despite the recent appearance of 'Harry's View' in the local paper, Redknapp himself had not penned the above. When when questioned about the actions of the City fans he elected to comment, 'They just could not take losing.'

Despite the infraction of the 'wild ones' on to the playing surface from the home end of the stadium, the Bournemouth manager sought to place the blame for the incident squarely at the feet of the opposition. 'It's a great shame it ended like that. Our fans behaved ever so well but it's not the first time that Bristol City followers have caused trouble. Unfortunately, there is that very small element of troublemakers at several clubs. We are very fortunate here because we don't have them.'

Bournemouth's first league defeat of the campaign at fellow high-flyers York City proved nothing more than a blip as the Cherries then won four games out of four in October.

Days before that successful run began, Redknapp's burgeoning sideline in journalism was once again to the fore as he launched his own midweek column in the *Daily Echo*. In 'Harry's Game' he promised to answer correspondents' questions about AFC Bournemouth and other football matters, writing that it would also be 'a good chance for me to air a few of my views'.

Bournemouth remained in the north after the defeat at Bootham Crescent to prepare for the next match against Darlington. With the always thin budget stretched to cover the costs of accommodation, no specific training facilities were hired and the squad instead made use of a nearby park. It is unlikely Redknapp's players would have complained, as this was little different to their regular routine in King's Park, and the Bournemouth manager saw it as a team bonding opportunity. 'It was a bit of a change for us. It has given the players a chance to get to know each other better. We have a lot of new lads and they have only seen each other in training until now.'

Whatever training Harry put the players through was sufficient preparation for them to record their first away win of the season going into a two-week break due to the scheduled home fixture against Gillingham clashing with the arrival of Prime Minister Margaret Thatcher in Bournemouth for the Conservative Party Conference.

Successive victories over Bury, Doncaster and Wigan saw the Cherries regain top spot in the Third Division table, replacing Middlesbrough going into the meeting of the two sides at Ayresome Park on 1 November. With such fine form, Bournemouth were confident of passing the first serious test of their promotion credentials.

Prior to the fixture, 39-year-old Redknapp was the recipient of his first-ever Manager of the Month award as a result of his side's fine run of form in October. Unfortunately, this personal highlight proved to be another opportunity for those who believed in the curse that accompanies the award to add to their folder of evidence as Bournemouth were clinically defeated 4-0 by Bruce

Rioch's Middlesbrough side. But with only 13 games played and his team still riding significantly higher than even he would have predicted, Harry was able to take a philosophical stance, saying, 'That's the way it goes sometimes,' after the final whistle.

The Bournemouth manager may not have been quite so sanguine had he known that the defeat was to be the first of four the Cherries would suffer in their next six league games. After losing to relegation candidates Walsall in the subsequent fixture, Harry outlined the challenge facing his side. 'This is going to be a long, hard struggle if we are to get promotion this year,' he said, but went on to praise the spirit in the squad. 'Our efforts to keep in the promotion race are unlikely to be undermined by dressing room disruptions. Harmony behind the scenes is a major factor at any football club, and we have that.'

A welcome break from league action followed as the Cherries next prepared to face non-league side Fareham Town in the first round of the FA Cup at Dean Court. The appeal of the apparently low-key tie to the home fans was boosted by the presence of 24-year-old midfielder Simon Jackson in the Fareham line-up. Jackson was a PE teacher at Twynham School in Christchurch, where amongst his pupils he counted 13-year-old Jamie Redknapp.

This coincidence provided ample material for a week of 'magic of the FA Cup' themed copy in the local and national press, giving Jamie his first taste of the spotlight. 'Whatever happens, it's going to be a special day for us,' said Jackson, who had at one time been a member of Bournemouth's youth team. 'We will be there to enjoy the day, and anything we get on top of that will be a bonus.'

Jamie was sprung from his lessons to participate in a staged photo shoot where he and Jackson engaged in friendly battle for a football borrowed from Twynham's PE shed. Mr Jackson was full of smiles, and this continued throughout the gentle ribbing he got from his Bournemouth-supporting pupils in the week leading up to the game.

These same pupils and a number of their interested mates took their places on the South End terrace come the kick-off in order to make the most of a unique opportunity to replace the acceptable banter of the school changing room for full-scale foul-mouthed sledging with no fear of retribution from Sir. Jackson did well to ignore this tirade of taunts and briefly thought he may have had the last laugh as Fareham took a surprise lead in the 14th minute through Malcolm Wilkes before the Cherries found their feet. A second-half hat-trick from David Puckett eased the home side to a 7-2 victory, their best in the FA Cup for 15 years. Jackson's reward, upon returning to his day job, was to find that a pupil had scrawled the result of the match on the blackboard in two-foot-high numbers, although a short investigation failed to establish if Redknapp junior was the culprit.

Victory over Chesterfield in the next match extended the unbeaten home record to nine games since the beginning of the season and talk of this at long last being the Cherries' year again reached fever pitch. Redknapp, however, was less than impressed with the long-circulating rumour that promotion was not wanted by either club or town. It was a long-held theory among sections of the fan base who speculated that the expense of Second Division wages, requisite stadium improvements and the increased frequency in which hordes of supporters of bigger clubs would descend upon the still somewhat sleepy region meant it was not a desirable outcome.

After the 2-0 win over the Spireites, Redknapp counted five supporters who approached him to ask if the club really wanted to go up, and with each, his patience thinned. 'The next one who says that to me will get a right mouthful,' he began. 'I am absolutely sick and tired of people coming up to me and asking, "Is it right Bournemouth don't want promotion?" What a load of cobblers.'

Even today, Harry's frustration at this suggestion is palpable. 'People used to say to me, "You won't go up, the council won't allow it,"' he says. '"They don't want Second Division football at Dean

Court. They have always stopped it over the years." So many people said that to me. I asked them, "What do you mean the council won't allow it? You think I'm going to walk in the dressing room on the day of a match and tell the team we have to lose because the council don't want us to get promoted?" And those people genuinely believed it.'

Whether they desired promotion or not, Bournemouth then faced their worst period of the season upon returning to action. Defeat at home to fellow title contenders Gillingham was swiftly followed by an exit from the FA Cup at the hands of Orient and, just a few days later, a 4-2 reverse at Rotherham. 'There are one or two in the side who are not doing enough to retain their places,' he said as his team looked to slip off the promotion pace. 'I'm looking for improved performances all round. It's time for changes.'

One change Redknapp was not keen on was the departure of Bobby Savage to Bradford City. Savage, one of Redknapp's first signings as a manager, was an important and versatile member of the Cherries' side who the Bournemouth manager was keen to see rediscover the form he had shown prior to the badly broken leg which had kept the tenacious midfielder out of the entirety of the previous campaign. But the Liverpudlian had failed to settle in the south and he and his wife were keen for a return closer to home.

Redknapp may not have been so disappointed with Savage's departure had he known that most of the £35,000 he had received for him would be spent on the player the Bournemouth manager would in later years describe as his 'best-ever signing'.

John Williams was a 6ft 1in defender who had first come to Redknapp's attention when the Bournemouth manager had attended Colin Clarke's transfer tribunal. Like the Irishman, Williams was also on his way out of Prenton Park, having played 173 games for the Merseyside club. His next stop was Port Vale, a move which required the services of the same tribunal panel that Clarke's did.

Williams had to wait a few weeks to make his debut upon arrival at Dean Court. Issues with his registration and an ankle injury picked up in one of his first training sessions on the south coast ruled him out of contention for the defeat at Rotherham and a 4-3 reverse at Wolves in the preliminary round of the Freight Rover Trophy.

Although he was unable to contribute on the pitch, Williams was soon making his voice heard in the Bournemouth dressing room. Immediately after the reverse at Millmoor, Redknapp invited the defender to deliver a critique of his new team-mates. 'We were in the changing room after the game and Willo was there in his long trench coat,' remembers captain Mark Newson. 'Harry being Harry, he slated a few players and then he looked at Willo and said, "Go on John, tell them what you think of them." He put Willo right on the spot because he didn't really know any of us. But he let us have it, he laid into us.'

Williams made his first appearance for the Cherries on Boxing Day as Bournemouth travelled to Bristol Rovers' temporary home at Twerton Park in Bath. Rovers had played at Eastville Stadium in Bristol for 89 years, but a fire in 1980 destroyed their South Stand and contributed to ongoing financial problems which saw the Pirates ultimately move 12 miles east to the home of Bath City FC. Redknapp, for one, was less than impressed with Rovers' new address. 'It's not a nice ground,' he said just before Christmas. 'The pitch is an awful surface to play on. We like to play attractively, but I think we will have to adapt our game, getting the ball forward earlier and missing out our midfield.'

This rare reversion to the much-derided long ball did no harm on the day as Bournemouth plundered a valuable 3-0 win with John Williams scoring the third when he pounced on the rebound after his initial shot from Gary Howlett's cross had come off the post.

The triumph came at a high price, however, as David Puckett was stretchered off in the 13th minute when Darren Carr clattered the diminutive forward from behind. Days later, it would emerge that Puckett's leg was broken and his knee ligaments were torn to shreds. He would not be seen in a Bournemouth shirt again that season, depriving Redknapp of a striker who, with 16 goals to his name, was on course to beat Colin Clarke's total from the previous campaign.

With Carl Richards limping off ten minutes from time at Twerton Park, Redknapp was forced to pair his captain and right-back Mark Newson up front with midfielder Sean O'Driscoll in the meeting with Fulham at Dean Court the following day. Trailing 2-1 at half-time, Newson justified Redknapp's tactics by equalising immediately after the restart and then Williams secured a place in the hearts of the Bournemouth faithful that remains to this day by heading in from Tommy Heffernan's free kick in the 83rd minute to give the makeshift Bournemouth side the maximum return over the festive period.

Despite the injury crisis, 1987 started brightly for the Cherries, with successive 1-1 draws against Chesterfield and Brentford seeing Redknapp's side stretch their unbeaten run to five Third Division games despite the injury crisis. During a two-week break from action precipitated by a waterlogged pitch at Newport, Redknapp moved to sign 20-year-old Spurs winger Richard Cooke. When Cooke pulled out of a deal to sign for Dutch Eredivisie club Groningen, Redknapp tabled a £25,000 bid for the pacy Londoner.

Haggling over an extra £5,000 demanded by Spurs briefly threatened the deal, but a compromise figure of £27,500 was reached and the Bournemouth manager looked forward to the impact Cooke might have on his attack. 'He's an out-and-out winger who has a lot of pace. He can beat people and get behind defences, and that will be a great asset for the team. Richard is a natural right-winger, and that means a lot to me, reminding me of my own playing days.'

Following the conclusion of the Cooke deal, Harry gave a summary of his approach to transfer activity, which, despite the caricature which he would help create of the wheeler-dealer manager in future decades, spoke of painstaking research. 'Before I take on any player I like to know everything about him,' explained the Bournemouth manager. 'Not only his form on the field. I want to know if he is going to be the right type to fit in at the club. And I like to see any possible transfer target in action three or four times in home and away games before I make any move.'

Today, he recalls the dedication that was required in the lower leagues to build a successful side on a limited budget. 'It was different then managing,' he says. 'The manager was almost a one-man band. You went out and looked at players and you put the team together. You didn't have a lot of help like now with video systems and all the rest of it. Managers were out every night watching games because all of the players came from the UK.'

Both Cooke and Williams scored in extra time to give Bournemouth a 2-0 advantage in the first round Freight Rover Trophy tie at Swindon's County Ground. Two contentious goals for the Robins, including a penalty in the 118th minute, took the tie into a shoot-out, in which the home side held their nerve to win 4-2. 'I consider that result an extension of our unbeaten run,' said Redknapp, in reference to a string of positive results which now stretched back some eight games, and went on to make his most optimistic pronouncement yet regarding his team's potential. 'There is no team in the division playing as well as us at the moment, so we must fancy our chances. We are looking strong.'

It was the arrival of the two new signings during this period that Redknapp points to as the catalyst for the tremendous run of results that ultimately led to glory. 'I didn't start the season thinking about promotion to be honest,' he says. 'And then suddenly, we started OK and we were up there but then Willo and Cookie came in around Christmas time and made a massive difference. Suddenly we went from being amongst the four or five teams with half a chance to having a real chance.'

When Mansfield were thrashed 4-1 on Valentine's Day and Redknapp's team returned to the top of the Third Division table after going undefeated in ten league games, 'half a chance' appeared an understatement. The string of positive results came to an end in the next match against fifth-placed Bristol City. With Redknapp's future backroom coach Joe Jordan and former striker Trevor Morgan spearheading the Robins' attack, the Cherries suffered a bruising 2-0 defeat. But Harry knew his players had put the club in with a shot of a historic promotion, and used the defeat as an opportunity to highlight the progress his team had made. 'I am still optimistic. In fact, I am more optimistic than I was before today. The Second Division is not on my mind yet. We will let other people talk about it because we know there is an awful long way to go and how difficult it is going to be.'

With David Puckett out for the season, Harry scoured the country for a replacement, eventually landing the loan signing of Tony Sealy from Leicester City. Upon the conclusion of the deal, the Bournemouth boss gave a ringing endorsement of the Dean Court board. 'I believe I am working for the best chairman in the league,' said Redknapp of Rodney Barton. 'He is a great man to back your judgement and let you get on with your job. I believe he and the board would back my judgement now. They realise we have a good chance of getting promoted. They're desperate to go up to the Second Division.'

With an unlikely harmony reigning at Dean Court, Redknapp's side quickly bounced back from the disappointment at Ashton Gate by winning their next five games to consolidate their position at the summit of the Third Division. The undoubted highlight of this run of victories came in the game on Tuesday 3 March against second-placed Middlesbrough. The two sides had been neck and neck in the title race since Boro humiliated the Cherries at the start of November. The heavyweight clash pitted the side with the best home record against the team with the best away record and, despite there being almost a third of the season's fixtures still to play, it felt like a winner-takes-all encounter.

Redknapp was in no mood to play down the fixture, his raw emotion seeing him encourage the Dean Court crowd to spur their heroes on to greater heights. 'I want the place to erupt when we run out on to the field,' he said. 'We want noise for all the 90 minutes; we want to raise the roof.'

He was not to be disappointed. In the days when few matches were all ticket, Brian Tiler predicted a crowd of around 10,000. Come the kick-off, upwards of 14,000 fans arrived to set a new record for an evening fixture at Dean Court. With car parks full, King's Park became an impromptu car park, fans abandoning their cars on grass playing fields in what proved to be the correct assumption that everyday regulations would be waived as a matter of crowd control.

The official attendance was given at 13,835, but hundreds of fans were let in after kick-off in an attempt to prevent crushing outside the ground. In the pre-Hillsborough tragedy days, repeated appeals were made on the decrepit public address system for fans in the Brighton Beach End to shuffle along the terracing and make room for more spectators.

This largely worked, although many season ticket holders found that they could not get to their seats with Brian Tiler himself being forced to watch the match from behind the goal after the directors' box also fell victim to interlopers.

With his rallying cry emphatically answered by the faithful, Redknapp guided his team to a thrilling victory to match the sense of occasion. Towards the end of a frantic first half, future England and Manchester United centre-half Gary Pallister sustained a nasty gash on his leg in a challenge with Trevor Aylott. Pallister was replaced by winger Stuart Ripley, meaning the key defensive partnership of Pallister and Tony Mowbray was broken, giving the Cherries an opportunity to strike for all three points.

Seven minutes after the break, Mark Newson headed the opener following a well-worked set piece. Benignly chaotic celebrations on the terraces had barely died down when Boro equalised from the kick-off. Hesitation between Newson and Gerry Peyton allowed the prolific Bernie Slaven to latch on to a through ball and slot home from two yards. The away side's tails were up, but Redknapp's team rode the storm for almost 20 minutes before taking a lead they would not relinquish. A sweeping move from defence saw Trevor Aylott delicately lay the ball into the path of the onrushing Sean O'Driscoll who fired home off the underside of the crossbar from 15 yards. Bournemouth made it three just five minutes later when Aylott converted the penalty he had won after referee Keith Cooper adjudged Boro captain Mowbray to have pushed the powerful target man.

Once the ecstatic scenes at the final whistle had abated, the league table made very happy reading indeed for Harry. His team were now six points clear going into the business end of the season, and the Bournemouth manager heaped praise upon the supporters' impact on the result. 'The ground is still buzzing,' he enthused. 'Things like that happen when you get a crowd like that, and it made a huge difference to the players. We are looking for the top spot. Now we have got as far as we have, I wouldn't settle for just a place in the play-offs. Until John Williams came I didn't think we were quite good enough. He suddenly made such a difference and from his first game you could see an improvement. The players believe they can do it. They believe they are as good as anyone in the division.'

Even today, Harry looks back on the victory proudly. 'Look at that Middlesbrough team that year,' he says. 'What a strong team that was. They had Gary Pallister, Tony Mowbray, Bernie Slaven. We did fantastic to beat them.'

It wasn't just points the players stood to gain from beating Middlesbrough. Paul Morrell, who spent the evening keeping the likes of Ripley and Slaven at bay, recalls Redknapp motivating his squad with the prospect of modest material gains. 'The guy who owned Simone's, a leather shop in Bournemouth, was at a sportsman's dinner a few days before the Middlesbrough game,' says Morrell. 'He went up to Harry and he said, "Your boys aren't going to go up this year." Harry said, "You want a bet?" The guy was so confident he bet a leather bomber jacket for each player if we went up. At the end of the season, he had to fork out for 16 of them.'

The opportunity to benefit from the momentum gained after the victory over their nearest rivals was threatened when the Cherries' next match at Wigan was abandoned after 61 minutes in a snowstorm in Lancashire. With the score at 1-1, Redknapp was keen to see the match to its conclusion and save his team another trip north. Referee George Courtney was in no mood to listen, calling the players off the field of play when he could no longer see the markings on the pitch. The Bournemouth manager was not impressed. 'I thought it was a disgrace for the game to be called off like that,' he said as the players attempted to warm themselves in the Springfield Park dressing room. 'The conditions were bad when we started, and I don't believe they got any worse. It was a bad decision to abandon the match.'

The Cherries were not to be stopped, however, and beat both Bury and Doncaster in the space of three days upon their return to action. Harry's delight with his side's continuing good form was tempered somewhat by concerns closer to home. Son Jamie had reached the final selection for the FA School of Excellence in Lilleshall. Sixteen boys were to be offered a place from a pool of the 33 most promising youngsters in the country, but Redknapp's fatherly pride at his son's precocious talent was dulled by concern that the school was not the best place for Jamie to continue his footballing education. 'I have mixed feelings about it,' he said. 'I'm not sure if two years away from home would be a good thing for Jamie or not.'

Young Bournemouth starlet Paul Mitchell was already at Lilleshall, and Redknapp had high praise for the work of former England manager Dave Sexton and his staff at the centre, saying, 'The kids get the best possible treatment and there is no doubt the standard is extremely high.' However, as a father, and doubtless taking the views of wife Sandra into consideration, Harry was not keen to see his youngest son fly the nest at such a tender age. 'I am not convinced I would like one of my sons to go away for two years. I have always felt they should grow up at home, but for some lads it is ideal.'

Harry's inner turmoil was not soothed when his team's record of five straight wins came to an end against bête noire Gillingham at Priestfield. The Bournemouth manager's frustration at a disallowed header from Trevor Aylott in a 2-1 defeat may have been eased had he known that it would be the last time his side would be on the wrong end of a result until the end of the season.

The 11-game run-in began in fortunate fashion when a below-par performance at home to Darlington ended in victory following an own goal from Mark Hine as he attempted to clear the ball but only succeeded in beating his goalkeeper Mike Ashley who had kept the Cherries' attack at bay from the kick-off. With ten matches now to go, Redknapp set out his aspirations in detail. 'I am looking for another seven wins this season. I don't care where they come from, but I believe that is what we need to go up.'

Two set-piece goals from captain Mark Newson and late heroics by Gerry Peyton saw the Cherries take a 2-1 win in the rearranged fixture at Port Vale, a victory that put the visitors eight points clear of Middlesbrough at the top of the table.

It couldn't have been going any better for Redknapp, and he was the envy of every other manager in the division. Behind the scenes, however, it was by no means plain sailing, as Harry struggled to keep the exuberant characters in his side under control. 'Every day there was something,' he says. 'It was a real test, especially after Willo and Cookie arrived. I remember we stayed up in Blackpool before we played Port Vale and Carlisle. We were top of the league. I said the night before the match, "Everyone, ten o'clock, bed. No one is going out." So I sat in the bar at the hotel having a coffee with Blackpool's manager Sam Ellis. All the lads were going off to bed about 9.30pm and Sam said, "They're good lads them." I said, "Well they can be a bit of a handful." Anyway, I saw Sam off in the car park at about quarter past ten and went to the lift. So I'm waiting there, and when it arrives the door opens and I thought it was John Travolta. It was Willo, dressed up like you had never seen. He had all the gear on and all the other lads were there behind him. I told them to get back up to their rooms or they would all be going home. Years later, I discovered they did manage to sneak out after all. The next day we only won 2-1 and got a point at Carlisle a few days later.'

Meanwhile, a period of deliberation in the Redknapp household resulted in the announcement that young Jamie would not be accepting England manager Bobby Robson's offer of a place at the FA School of Excellence after all. In his first public statement, the 13-year-old schoolboy told the *Bournemouth Evening Echo*, 'It was a very difficult decision to make, but I did not look forward to being away from my family. I hope we have made the right decision. I want to play as a professional and I hope I get the chance.'

Whilst Jamie returned to his studies at Twynham School, there was a sure sign that history beckoned for his father's team when the Dean Court ticket office announced a voucher scheme was being put in place to ensure there would not be a repeat of the overcrowding which threatened supporter safety at the Middlesbrough fixture. The final three home games of the season would be all-ticket affairs, with extra staff drafted in to deal with the unprecedented demand. In a move that was spun as a significant step towards modernisation but seems laughably quaint today, postal ticket applications were accepted for the very first time by the club. 'The voucher scheme has been introduced at the request of the police, with the safety and comfort of the crowd being the important factor,' explained Brian Tiler. 'We hope that this system will ensure the fans who watch the club week in week out will be there for the last crucial matches.'

The first of these vouchers was issued as fans passed through the turnstiles for the fixture against Walsall. A crowd of 8,626 were in attendance to endure 88 minutes of tension after Richard Cooke bagged his fifth goal of the season just after kick-off. In the closing stages of the game, Walsall were awarded a goal by referee Darryl Reeves after Saddlers forward David Kelly swept home from a Nicky Cross pass. Cross had clearly fouled Mark Whitlock as they battled for the ball in the lead-up to the goal, and Dean Court erupted in a hail of protest. Reeves took Tony Pulis's name for dissent before consulting with his linesman. Two minutes of heated discussion later, Reeves took the rarely seen step of reversing his decision and awarding Redknapp's team a free kick, much to the relief of all but the visiting fans and players.

Three days later the Cherries returned to Springfield Park to replay the match which was abandoned in a snowstorm in early March. Redknapp's rage that day was replaced with delight as his team won a record 25th game of the season thanks to a brace from Mark O'Connor. 'It was a marvellous display by the whole side,' gushed the Bournemouth manager. 'I could not single out any individual player because they all played an important part in giving us complete control of the game.'

The win put the Cherries 11 points clear of Swindon at the top of the Third Division table with the two teams set to meet in the next match on Easter Saturday. Four thousand Bournemouth fans made the relatively short trip to Wiltshire, blocking approach roads to the County Ground in the hours prior to kick-off. They were not to be disappointed for their efforts, as John Williams continued his knack of scoring against the Robins when he headed home in the 16th minute from a Mark Whitlock cross. The home team equalised seven minutes into the second half, but Redknapp boarded the coach for the return journey to Bournemouth a happy man in the knowledge that Swindon had made no dent in the Cherries' lead at the top of the table. The trip, however, proved hazardous for many of the travelling fans, some of whom were greeted with a hail of missiles as they alighted from supporters' coaches and then came under fire from bricks, concrete and masonry hurled from outside the stadium into the away terrace.

On Easter Monday the Cherries soothed the injuries sustained by the Dean Court faithful with a 2-0 win over Bristol Rovers, leaving their manager eyeing the biggest prize on offer. 'Now it's got to be the championship,' he insisted. 'It would be disappointing to me if the players did not collect medals at the end of the season. They deserve the title.'

Success in football is often fleeting, and a manager can go from flavour of the month to *persona non grata* in the space of three or four results. By the end of April 1987, Redknapp was enjoying his ascent to the status of Next Big Thing, saying modestly, 'I'm sure other clubs must look and think about making a move. I did a great deal with Colin Clarke, buying him for £20,000 and selling him for £400,000. Obviously people will look, but I am very happy here. I said it when I took over that it would be my ambition to take Bournemouth into the Second Division and that is still true. It would be a dream come true.'

When it came to blowing his own trumpet, Harry wasn't finished there. As a historic promotion to the second tier looked increasingly likely, fans and pundits drew comparison between the class of 1986/87 and the side which previously stood undisputed as the greatest ever Cherries team – John Bond's vintage from the early 1970s. Although he missed out on their best seasons, Redknapp played for Bond alongside all of his star players, yet the current Bournemouth manager was in no doubt who was number one now. 'Few can now argue that this team is not better than that of the early 1970s,' he claimed. 'It is on the threshold of achieving something Bondy's boys never did. John's side may have been better individually, but the team of 1986/87, in terms of working for each other and dressing room spirit, is way out in front.'

Redknapp went on to compare the two sides man for man, rediscovering his modesty to state, 'I'd put Richard Cooke ahead of the right-winger they had then,' when measuring his younger self against the player he had recently signed from Tottenham. Humility was in shorter supply when it came to comparing the managers, with Redknapp saying, 'As to the managers? Ah well, I don't think I am the person to compare Harry Redknapp to John Bond. If there has been a major difference, it might be that John changed the side too much.'

A 3-1 win at Blackpool took the Cherries to 90 points, causing an excited Redknapp to comment, 'We are almost there now.' Just four points were required from the final three league fixtures to secure promotion, and with two games in three days over the May Day weekend, the town began to prepare for a celebration.

However, Redknapp's team froze as nerves took hold in the first of those games against Port Vale at Dean Court. A goalless draw was the best the Cherries could produce in front of an expectant crowd of 9,556, and suddenly a kernel of doubt crept into the minds of the long-suffering supporters.

Two days later on Bank Holiday Monday, over 4,000 of them made the journey to London to see if their side could finally get across the line with a win over Fulham at Craven Cottage. Another jittery first-half performance almost ended in disaster for Redknapp's team when a fierce shot struck the hand of Mark Whitlock in his own 18-yard box and Fulham were awarded a penalty. Midfielder Peter Scott, who would become one of Redknapp's final signings as Bournemouth manager five years later, stepped up to take the spot kick. Gerry Peyton, who had played with Scott for five years at Craven Cottage, guessed correctly and enhanced his status as the recently voted player of the season by saving with his legs.

This let-off was short-lived, however, as things got worse for the Cherries 12 minutes after the break. From a free kick, Fulham defender Jeff Hopkins headed goalwards and, in trying to clear the danger, John Williams saw the ball bounce off him and into the goal.

Just as hearts on the packed away terrace began to sink, fortunes suddenly turned. A minute after going behind, Bournemouth were awarded a penalty of their own when future Manchester United and England defender Paul Parker brought down Carl Richards in the area. Richards' strike partner Trevor Aylott placed the ball on the spot and, making light of the pressure of expectation, fired the Cherries level. In the 81st minute the headbanded Aylott put Redknapp's team ahead, his miscue of Richard Cooke's cross confounding Fulham keeper Laurence Batty to bobble inside the post.

Delirium on the bench and in the away end turned to ecstasy five minutes later when Tony Sealy, whose wife Michelle had given birth to a baby boy earlier in the day, celebrated in unforgettable fashion by rifling into the top corner of Batty's goal from 25 yards. Understandably overcome with emotion, Sealy proceeded to attempt a Samba-style jig before being mobbed by his team-mates. 'Right now, I couldn't be any happier,' said Sealy after completing a joyful lap of honour with his team-mates.

'Magic,' was all Harry Redknapp had to say, and his uncharacteristic economy with words could not have been more well chosen. It was the apotheosis of the 15 years he spent at Dean Court as player, coach and manager. Harry himself would rank the achievement as possibly the greatest of a career in management that included among its highlights winning the Championship of the second tier and the FA Cup whilst in charge at Portsmouth years later.

Celebrations among Redknapp and his squad were not muted despite all involved making it clear that the season could not be considered a total success unless Rotherham were defeated at Dean Court the following weekend to secure the Third Division title. After they had left the pitch, players immediately availed themselves of whatever beers, wines and spirits were available and joined fans on a balcony at Craven Cottage overlooking the Thames. The party continued on the coach home where Redknapp and his squad toasted their success and, for those that were still standing, the good times continued at Bournemouth's Royal Bath Hotel well into the small hours.

After a day of supposed rest and recuperation, Redknapp and his squad reconvened for training in the middle of the week. With further glory on offer, there was no question of Harry allowing the players to ease up now that promotion had been secured. 'We want to win the league,' said the Bournemouth manager. 'It would be a superb finish for the fans, a great thing for the town and it would earn the players the medals they deserve after their efforts.'

Redknapp's team shook off any lingering hangovers and the visiting Millers, who were safely ensconced in mid-table, put up little resistance to the Cherries' final push. Following the dangerous overcrowding that mercifully ended without serious injury in the epic defeat of Middlesbrough in March, the club's all-ticket policy kept the attendance down to a manageable 11,310. Trevor Aylott had a goalbound effort cleared off the line after 20 minutes but recorded his fourth strike in five games eight minutes later after fine work by Paul Morrell. Five minutes later the Third Division trophy was all but in Mark Newson's hands when Carl Richards raced clear of the Rotherham defence to latch on to a Richard Cooke through ball. After lobbing the advancing O'Hanlon in the visitors' goal, Richards then followed his own effort towards the goalmouth and headed the bouncing ball over the line.

As the second half drew to a close, fans on all sides of the pitch left the stands to crowd around the perimeter of the playing surface. A premature pitch invasion inevitably ensued when referee Lester Shapter blew for a minor infringement. Gerry Peyton was relieved of his shirt before the pitch could be cleared and played the remaining 90 seconds in 'skins'.

'Let's enjoy it,' said chairman Rodney Barton at the final whistle, and wasted little time in announcing that he had secured the man who was now undisputed as Bournemouth's greatest ever manager on a longer three-year 'roll over' contract. 'A new era began for this club when we appointed Harry Redknapp as manager,' said Barton. 'This contract is giving him ever more security. We want him to stay for ever.'

Barton may have overlooked the circumstances that led to Redknapp's appointment, but nobody was particularly bothered, least of all the man himself. 'This is fantastic,' said Harry as the champagne corks popped. 'You have to enjoy the good times in football because you get some bad ones as well. It has been a tremendous effort by the players, who have displayed great character, as well as ability all through the season. I would not like to pick my player of the year. They have all been great, even those who have been out of the side. Now we are ready for the Second Division, and we can do well at that level too.'

Brian Tiler, who had developed a close bond with Redknapp since the two had been thrown together four years previously, continued the verbal love-in. 'He is the most popular manager in this club's history and we have a duty to the supporters to ensure that he stays with the club for a long time,' said Tiler. 'We have been building for the future and stability at management level has to be an important factor. Harry loves the area and has an affinity with the fans that is second to none.'

Redknapp's love affair with the region has yet to abate, and despite the success he went on to have later in his career, the title win is one he remembers with great fondness. 'It's right up there with the FA Cup win and winning the Championship,' he says. 'That game at Fulham will always be special. We had a couple of Irish directors, Peter McDonagh and Jimmy Craven, and they enjoyed a drink and our vice presidents were good lads and they all got into the boardroom at Craven Cottage. I think they drank the bar dry. Jimmy Hill wanted them to go home. He couldn't get rid of them. We came back to Bournemouth and a few of us went to the Steakhouse on Holdenhurst Road with our wives and that was where we celebrated.'

Bournemouth finished the season with 97 points, a record haul for the third tier which stood for 13 years. Redknapp was duly installed as Bell's Whisky Third Division Manager of the Year at the Savoy Hotel in his native London before returning to the south coast to lead his team into a celebration friendly against his old mate Ken Brown's Norwich City two days after the title triumph.

Prior to kick-off in this well-attended but meaningless fixture, Mark Newson was presented with the glass pentagon that passed for the Today League Third Division Trophy by Chelsea chairman Ken Bates. The moment was oddly anticlimactic, the thrilling rush of glory that enveloped the Rotherham fixture having subsided in the somewhat more mundane circumstances.

Norwich, for so long the bogeymen in the Cherries' seemingly endless struggle against mediocrity, did the decent thing and rolled over to give the 6,113 supporters a 4-2 victory to accompany the occasional 'Champions' chants. The less than febrile atmosphere did have the silver lining of allowing the squad to complete a lap of honour at the final whistle, a tradition rendered impossible at the conclusion of the Rotherham fixture.

Two days later, the celebrations wound up with an open-top bus parade which snaked its way from Dean Court to a reception at Bournemouth Town Hall in bright sunshine as thousands of fans lined the streets to acknowledge Redknapp and his unlikely heroes. Again, the details of the parade appear laughable in the age of stage-managed celebrations. Lolling about on the top of a yellow bus, the squad faced their adoring public with a handwritten 'Champions' sign taped to the front.

The star attraction, of course, was Harry Redknapp himself. He did not disappoint, arriving in a shiny beige suit, looking tanned and youthful. His charisma was there for all to see, and for a few weeks at least, everything was rosy in the Redknapps' garden.

Chapter Twelve

Learning Curve

1987/88

IT was not long before the thrill of winning the Third Division came to an abrupt end. Upon returning to Dean Court after the promotion celebrations had finally wound up, Harry Redknapp found himself unwittingly caught in the crossfire of another bout of the type of boardroom machinations the club would continue to suffer throughout his tenure and beyond.

Over the summer, Rodney Barton's Macbar Construction, which effectively owned the club, went into liquidation and he was forced to sell his 75% shareholding. Midlands-based Coventry fan Eric Groves, who owned Canberra Properties, stepped in to snap up the shares for a knock-down price rumoured to be around £70,000. Groves soon realised he had bought a club almost permanently on life support, and within months was looking for a way out.

Before long, a local consortium led by board member Jim Nolan took control. 'I made an approach to Canberra, and after a bit of hustle, things came together,' explained Nolan. 'They had done nothing wrong but they are property developers and we have seen all too often what they can do to football clubs.'

Once in control, Nolan inspected his new acquisition closely, and was unimpressed with what he found. 'I walked around the ground, around every nook and cranny, and I was ashamed. The terracing was crumbling; the place looked awful. I was so ashamed.'

The new owner could at least take solace in on-field matters, even though the boardroom drama had disrupted preparations for the season ahead. 'I'm Harry's number one fan,' he said after the takeover. 'We work extremely well together and I know Harry is happy here. He is on a very good contract and it is one he deserves. His knowledge of the game and particularly of players is amazing.'

Redknapp had grown used to instability in his years as Bournemouth manager, but with the contract Nolan referred to in place, he chose to soldier on despite interest from elsewhere. 'I went away on holiday and then suddenly when I got back the club had been sold,' he recalls. 'I didn't even know the owners. It wasn't a great situation. It was always difficult, changing chairman every year. But we got through it in the end.'

As a result of government recommendations, the Cherries installed closed circuit TV and cage-like fencing behind both the goals and in front of the away seating adjacent to the Brighton Beach End. This fencing, of which a similar version would prove tragically insurmountable at Hillsborough less than two years later, wasn't exactly the improvement in spectating conditions most fans would have hoped for. Unsurprisingly, it wasn't long before attendances began to dip, a situation certainly not helped by an ill-thought-out membership scheme which required that fans attempting to enter the ground had to show a club-produced identity card as well as their hard-earned money when approaching the turnstile.

'There were lots of different changes at that time,' says Redknapp of this tumultuous period in English football. 'Suddenly the government and everybody seemed to be getting involved in everything in the game.'

Somehow, funds were found to allow Redknapp to strengthen his squad and the elevation into a higher level of football made his sales pitch to potential signings a little more convincing. Former England international midfielder David Armstrong made the well-worn trip from Southampton, whilst Shaun Brooks arrived from Leyton Orient in a £20,000 deal.

Sheffield United's Bramall Lane was the venue for the Cherries' first-ever Second Division match on 15 August. With the team still full of confidence after the previous season's triumph, Redknapp was bold in announcing his ambitions for the campaign on the eve of the match. 'We are aiming to win another title,' he declared. 'That's my ambition for 1988. It's going to be hard but you have to say at the start that is what you want to do. I know the lads are as excited as I am. We can't wait for everything to start.'

Seasoned supporters and football followers nationwide may have laughed at Redknapp's bullishness, but they were given cause to think again in the early weeks of the historic campaign. Following a heroic display from Blades' goalkeeper Andy Leaning, Bournemouth took a deserved maiden win in the second tier after new signings Armstrong and Brooks combined for the latter to unleash a 30-yard screamer that even Leaning was powerless to prevent hitting the back of his net six minutes from time. 'It was a dream start in the Second Division for us,' said a satisfied Redknapp.

Bournemouth faced Bradford in the opening Second Division fixture at Dean Court. Gerry Peyton missed the match after picking up a groin strain against Exeter, and was replaced by the ever-faithful John Smeulders. Smeulders was plying his trade with Poole Town in the Beazer Homes League but, as Redknapp had not secured a permanent back-up for Peyton, 'The Bear' was on non-contracted standby.

During the days leading up to the match, the local press made hay with the prospect that Redknapp himself was preparing to fill in between the sticks. The Bournemouth manager had been photographed fielding penalties from ladies in St Trinian's-style fancy dress at a charity event. 'I wouldn't mind some of these ladies in my team,' quipped the ever-quotable Redknapp. 'They've certainly got better legs than John Williams. But then again, who hasn't?'

It was a push on Williams by Bantams' defender Dave Evans that gave David Armstrong the opportunity to put the Cherries ahead from the penalty spot in the 70th minute. Bobby Savage had moved from Dean Court to Valley Parade the previous season and his return to his old stomping ground was not a happy one. Richard Cooke ran the injury-cursed midfielder ragged throughout the encounter and following a vicious tackle in the 86th minute, Savage took an early bath. The Cherries took full advantage of the brief period they found themselves with an extra man, as Trevor Aylott robbed City's Gavin Oliver of possession and found strike partner Carl Richards who had all kinds of time to pick his spot from 20 yards. The 2-0 win was enough to see Redknapp's team reach the giddy altitude of first place in the division on goal difference.

'That was a smashing result and we couldn't have made a better start to the season,' said a beaming Redknapp, before issuing a note of caution, 'but you cannot get carried away after two games. It is such a long season, but it is so much nicer to be sitting here with six points than it is to have nothing.'

After seeing off Exeter City over two legs in the Littlewoods Cup, the draw for the second round paired the Cherries with Southampton. Brian Tiler was so overcome with the prospect that he speculated that the intervention of a higher power around King's Park may have been responsible. 'It is absolutely marvellous news,' he said. 'It is as if the Good Lord is smiling on us. We couldn't have had a better start to the season.'

With excitement mounting as the tie approached, the Cherries faltered after their winning start. Just one win in the six league matches that preceded the meeting with Southampton meant that

Redknapp's side were less than buoyant when they welcomed their neighbours to Dean Court.

Although the First Division side had won 3-0 at Dean Court in a pre-season friendly, it was the first meeting of the two clubs in a competitive fixture for over 27 years. This absence of matches meant the flames of a rivalry were never really fanned, with the vitriol of Southampton supporters only ever directed at nearby Portsmouth. Desperate for a derby of any kind, Cherries fans haphazardly worked themselves up into a dislike of Southampton nonetheless. Fuelling this one-way rivalry was the weekly exodus of Bournemouth residents to watch Southampton instead of the Cherries. The representation of the two clubs in the local media was also a sore point for the Dean Court faithful, who to this day feel they are given less airtime and less respect by presenters and journalists across the region.

Always confident in the cups, Harry again saw no reason to play down his side's chances before the first leg. 'We are the underdogs and no one really fancies us. It's a good night for an upset,' he said the afternoon before the match. 'We've done it before, and there's no reason why we shouldn't do a bit of giant-killing tonight. I think we are capable of it.'

With a red-hot atmosphere expected, Mark Newson was installed as a makeshift centre-forward, a role he had undertaken six times during the title-winning campaign. Tommy Heffernan filled in for Newson in defence as the Cherries shrugged off their poor recent league form to dominate their neighbours from the kick-off. Gerry Peyton was rarely troubled and a Richard Cooke header two minutes after the break gave Bournemouth a narrow but deserved lead to take into the second leg at The Dell a fortnight later.

Redknapp's team received a standing ovation from the ecstatic Dean Court faithful, and Harry shared their delight. 'That's a great result for us,' he said. 'You can never tell if one goal will be enough but it gives us a great advantage.'

Coming after a dip in fortunes in the Second Division, the result led to a minor improvement in league form, although it was by no means significant. A missed penalty from Trevor Aylott saw Bournemouth lose out on a point in a 3-2 defeat to Leicester City before Aylott scored to help his team gain a point at home to Plymouth Argyle. A 1-0 defeat at Stoke City was next, and it was in the days leading up to this reverse that Harry was linked for the first time in the media with a move to West Ham to succeed long-serving Irons boss John Lyall.

Lyall had been at the helm at Upton Park for 13 years but poor results and dressing room unrest led to speculation that the Hammers' board were preparing to move him upstairs. Redknapp's lengthy association with the East End club and recent impressive success at Dean Court inevitably saw his name feature alongside the likes of Terry Venables and Billy Bonds in the bookies' list of favourites. Ultimately, Lyall would be replaced by Lou Macari at the conclusion of the season, but a return to the Boleyn Ground at some point from Harry appeared inevitable in the eyes of both Bournemouth and West Ham fans.

Three days after the defeat to Stoke, Bournemouth travelled to The Dell for the second leg. Southampton launched a fierce offensive on Gerry Peyton's goal in the first half, but the Cherries' keeper was equal to the test. With the home crowd growing impatient for the breakthrough, Bournemouth took the lead on the night when Mark Newson headed past Tim Flowers from a Shaun Brooks free kick.

Redknapp's team now held a commanding 2-0 lead in the tie, but were pegged back almost from the kick-off. Poor defending of an Andy Townsend corner saw the ball drop to Matthew Le Tissier on the edge of the penalty area and the man who would become the home side's greatest-ever player had no trouble beating Peyton with his majestic right foot.

Nine minutes later, Southampton levelled the tie when Derek Statham unleashed an unstoppable shot from the edge of the 18-

yard box which flew past the stranded Peyton. The Dell crowd were now in full voice, but Redknapp's team refused to fold. Flowers pulled off the kind of save from a John Williams header that would see him go on to win 11 England caps in the 1990s, but was forced to come off his line when a Mark Newson pass put Sean O'Driscoll clean through on the Southampton goal. The dynamic midfielder had played superbly in both legs and crowned his performance by dummying Flowers before putting the ball into the empty net.

The draw for the third round paired the Cherries with the holders of the trophy, Arsenal. In his early youth, before a number of London clubs beat a path to the Redknapp family home in Plaistow, Harry was a committed Arsenal supporter due to his father Fred's lifelong support of the Highbury club. 'He'd better support us, I'm getting his ticket,' Harry joked of Redknapp senior before the meeting with the Gunners. 'Seriously though, blood's thicker than water and I am sure he will be behind us all the way.'

Prior to meeting the Cherries, Arsenal had won each of their previous nine games with a team built around the home-grown talents of Paul Davis, Tony Adams and David Rocastle. In such a rich vein of form going into the tie, the Gunners had little trouble sweeping Bournemouth aside in a comprehensive 3-0 victory in front of 26,050 fans. The result came as no surprise to Redknapp. 'To be honest I expected the game to go that way. They were much better than us and I have no arguments about the result.'

A few days later, Bournemouth made a swift exit from their first season in the Simod Cup at Sheffield Wednesday. The competition had been introduced by the Football League in an attempt to redress the revenue gap created by the indefinite ban on English clubs' participation in European competition following the Heysel Stadium tragedy.

The fixture at Hillsborough was notable for Redknapp giving a debut to American striker Brent Goulet. In an era when footballers from the United States had yet to gain any sort of profile in Europe, the protracted acquisition of the 21-year-old international was something of a novelty on the south coast.

Goulet had trained with both QPR and Celtic during pre-season but neither club were able to obtain a work permit for the striker. After months of delay, Redknapp and Brian Tiler finally secured clearance to sign the former Seattle Storm forward. With little riding on the tie at Hillsborough, the Bournemouth manager was happy to include the Oregon native in his starting eleven. 'We've succeeded where half a dozen other clubs have failed,' said Redknapp. 'We persevered and convinced people he has sufficient talent to be granted a permit and it has paid off. The lad has real potential. He's very quick, very strong and he can get goals. He will be a great asset.'

In fact, Goulet proved to be a strong contender for Redknapp's worst signing during his tenure as Bournemouth manager. Just a fortnight after securing the American's long-coveted signature, Harry was backtracking on his previous optimism. 'Brent's nowhere near the finished article,' he said, before adding with only a hint of the faintest praise, 'He's not bad, but he's still got an awful lot to learn.'

Twenty-three clubs populated the Second Division in the Cherries' debut season, a figure which resulted in a bye week twice in the season for each team. Using the profits from the Littlewoods Cup run, Redknapp took his team on a short break in Tenerife. 'A little break like this will be nice,' said Harry before jetting off to the Canary Islands. 'We made a little bit of money from the Arsenal game and the board thought it would put some of it towards a holiday for the squad.'

Whether this small luxury was deserved or not was debatable in the eyes of the Dean Court faithful. The Cherries were slipping towards the relegation zone and a crucial fixture with bottom-of-the-table Huddersfield Town awaited them on their return to the south coast. Arriving back at Bournemouth airport, Harry spoke positively of the benefits of the trip. 'We were there for a bit of sun, sure, but mainly to get together and help team spirit,' said the newly bronzed Bournemouth manager. 'It was a smashing week and hopefully it will brighten us up a bit.'

Although Harry was positive about the trip in public, Paul Morrell's recollection of events paints a picture of a squad less than fully focused on football. 'During the break, the first one Bournemouth had ever had, Harry took us off to Tenerife,' says Morrell. 'Harry had just signed David Shearer from Gillingham and when we got to the airport we saw Shearer sitting on the luggage carousel going around and around. Harry comes up to me and says, "I think I've done my money here Moz." Mark Newson had broken his arm, but he made it on to the trip because Harry liked him. When we got there, we did a bit of training, then Harry gave us all some time off. We abused it as usual and went to a few bars.'

This carousing may provide an explanation for Bournemouth's performance against Huddersfield. The Terriers were the whipping boys of the Second Division and had been beaten 10-1 by a Mel Machin-managed Manchester City a few weeks earlier. However, the Yorkshire side took all three points after a 2-0 victory at Dean Court. Redknapp's sunny disposition from the Canary Islands rapidly evaporated. 'I am sick with what happened against Huddersfield. They were the worst side I've seen this year. They were absolutely awful and we still couldn't beat them.'

Defeat at Swindon and at home to table-topping Manchester City followed, with both Morrell and Tommy Heffernan being sent off at the County Ground after letting their frustration get the better of them and launching wild late challenges on the Robins' players. Bournemouth found themselves deep in the relegation mire, and Redknapp was running short on patience. 'I'm not a miracle man. I can't keep working wonders. I did that last year and I've run out,' he said, in a plea for a bigger transfer budget. 'There is no doubt about it, we are not good enough in certain positions.

The present board are doing a fantastic job, but mistakes were made before they took over and we are having to live with them. I just want a fair chance like everyone else to put a team together.'

These comments proved to be the catalyst for a brief spat between Harry and the *Bournemouth Evening Echo*. Despite the deal for 'Harry's View' to feature weekly in the newspaper, Redknapp withdrew access to both himself and his squad to *Echo* journalists after the newspaper published letters from supporters on its sports pages criticising individual players and Redknapp's management.

By no means unique in the history of relations between football clubs and their local newspapers, it was the first time such a circumstance had occurred between the Cherries and the local press. Fortunately, cordiality was soon restored without the need for a public stand-off. Redknapp remained a popular figure in the local press throughout his tenure and was not averse to using his relationship with journalists to campaign for a larger transfer kitty. After a creditable 2-2 draw at home to Oldham Athletic followed the City defeat, Harry was back in the press extolling his management skills. 'I rate myself, but I'd be so much better with money to carry through deals,' he said. 'John Docherty at Millwall must have spent £800,000 on building a promotion team. If that sort of money were available to me, I'd be very, very disappointed if we were not in the top six pushing for the First Division.'

Redknapp was not quite so keen to allow the players in his squad to fulfil their ambitions. Paul Morrell had starred in the title-winning team and had made the step up to the Second Division with apparent ease. In the days before England's top teams looked abroad to strengthen their squads, he soon began to attract attention. 'We were playing away up north, and Tommy Heffernan showed me a copy of the *Liverpool Echo*,' remembers Morrell. 'It said Liverpool were about to bid a quarter of a million pounds for me. So we played the game and afterwards I saw Harry talking to

Kenny Dalglish. On the coach coming back I said, "Can I have a word H?" So I sat down next to him and said, "Look, what's this about Liverpool?" Harry said, "I don't know anything about it," so I threw the *Liverpool Echo* at him and he said, "Oh. Come and see me tomorrow, we'll have a chat."

'Next day I turned up at the club and phoned my agent because I thought I needed him in there with me. My agent arrived and we knocked on Harry's door. Harry is in there with Brian Tiler and the first thing he said is, "I'm not seeing you with him." I said, "But he's my agent." Harry said, "F**k that. I ain't seeing you with him." I told him we weren't moving, so eventually Harry gave in and we thrashed out this contract. We didn't think it was enough, so I asked Harry, "What if I don't sign it?" and he replied, "I'll stick you in the reserves for the rest of the season." It was a bit cruel really. I wanted to go, as it was a great move for me to go to Liverpool, but in the end I did sign a two-year extension.'

After defeat at Bradford in the next game, the Cherries began a run of positive results over the crucial Christmas period which corroborated Redknapp's rarely diminished confidence in his squad and his own ability as a manager. Victories over the Midlands trio of Leicester, West Brom and Birmingham saw Bournemouth pull clear of the relegation mire by the new year.

Unfortunately, there was to be no FA Cup run to illuminate the second half of the season. A third-round visit to Brighton's Goldstone Ground ended in a 2-0 defeat. Around 2,500 of the Dean Court faithful made the journey along the south coast to Sussex, only to be rewarded with a performance that was described as 'timid and toothless' in the *Evening Echo* match report.

Redknapp's persistent haranguing of his board of directors over the transfer budget paid a small but ultimately important dividend before the upcoming fixture with fellow relegation battlers Sheffield United. Jim Nolan was able to loosen the purse strings sufficiently to allow his manager to sign 21-year-old

Tottenham striker Shaun Close on a month-long loan, a piece of business partly funded by a similar move for struggling Brent Goulet to Crewe Alexandra.

Close would go straight into the starting eleven for the match against the Blades, and although the Cherries lost 2-1, the player himself made a strong impression on what he considered to be a four-week trial at Dean Court with a view to a permanent move. According to the forward, Redknapp had had little trouble persuading him to consider leaving White Hart Lane. 'I told Spurs' manager Terry Venables I wanted a loan, and being a player once himself, he knows what I meant. I want first-team football and, let's face it, I probably won't get that at Spurs. As Harry Redknapp said to me, they will go for a big-name player when they want a new striker. What chance have I got?'

A blizzard in Barnsley and the early exit from the FA Cup meant it would be three weeks before Bournemouth resumed their campaign to remain in the Second Division. With the enforced lay-off providing the unexpected luxury of what amounted to a winter break, Redknapp had time to outline his approach to squad discipline at Dean Court. QPR defender Mark Dennis had recently received an eight-game ban from the Football Association as a consequence of picking up the 11th red card of his career. 'I've met him at a few games and off the field he seems quite a nice bloke,' said Redknapp. 'But when he gets his gear on, he seems to lose all self-control. I think the most important thing at a football club is if you have got someone who is causing problems you get rid of them. With most players, if you treat them right, you shouldn't have a problem in the first place. Basically, if a player doesn't know how to behave, you are wasting your time.'

With his players left in no doubt as to what was required in terms of conduct, they finally returned to action against Hull City in the first week of February. The Tigers were chasing a play-off place at the very least, but in a result that ranked among the best of the season for the Cherries, Redknapp's team won 6-2, with Shaun Close opening his account with two of the goals. It was a game that saw Harry return to his favoured sweeper system due to Mark Newson once again being available for selection after an ankle injury had ruled out the man his manager described as 'the best player at the club' since October.

The result against Hull also heralded the end of the Cherries' revival. Following a defeat at Manchester City in the next game, Redknapp set his players a target of at least five more wins in the remaining 14 fixtures, commenting forlornly, 'I can't say where we are going to get them. We have a horrible programme coming up. It is going to be very tight and we have to show some character.'

Desperate for more punch up front, Redknapp convinced the Bournemouth board to meet the £70,000 Terry Venables was demanding to secure the signature of Shaun Close from Tottenham. However, no sooner had the ink dried than Close turned his ankle in the defeat to Aston Villa in the next match, ruling him out for the second half of a 2-1 defeat at Dean Court.

Prior to the fixture against Ipswich at Portman Road, an anonymous Town player made the mistake of telling the press that a team of Ipswich's size and history should not have to demean themselves by sharing a pitch with minnows like Bournemouth. This classic error was a gift to Redknapp in his pre-match preparations and he was as optimistic as ever prior to kick-off. 'We've got a job to do and we are looking forward to it,' he said. 'The spirit among the lads is great. There is no feeling down or anything like that.'

Football managers often make such claims during poor runs of form, but regardless of the veracity of Redknapp's words, spirits soared come the final whistle at Portman Road. First-half goals from Trevor Aylott and the fit-again Shaun Close gave the Cherries a very welcome 2-1 victory and pushed them out of the drop zone with a game in hand on most of the five teams below them. 'We played very well,' said a grinning Redknapp, who may or may not have thanked the Ipswich player responsible for the derogatory comments that presumably added extra motivation to his team's performance.

One reason cited for the positive outcome in Suffolk was the team reverting to a flat back four. Redknapp's desire to play the sweeper system was strong and he was often convinced he could make it work, as he had with such success against Hull City. But the perilous nature of his team's position meant that it would be abandoned yet again. 'I think I'll stick with four at the back from now on,' he said. 'The system worked well against Ipswich and I can't see myself changing back.'

Meanwhile, Harry had the pleasant distraction of seeing son Jamie make his international debut for England Schools Under-15s at Carrow Road against Northern Ireland. Jamie was called into the squad at the last minute and seized the opportunity to showcase his precocious talent in a convincing 4-0 win.

Following a defeat at Crystal Palace which saw Ian Wright sent off after just 20 minutes for lashing out at Mark Newson, Bournemouth faced a crucial encounter with fellow relegation strugglers Shrewsbury Town. So keen was the Cherries' manager to achieve a positive result at Gay Meadow that he convinced Jim Nolan and his fellow directors to fund the unusual luxury of an overnight stay at Shropshire's Prince Rupert Hotel for the six-pointer. 'The importance of this match is worth the extra few quid,' said Redknapp. 'We have to give ourselves every chance. It's an absolutely vital game. We cannot afford to lose this one and let them get a three-point advantage at our expense.'

Harry's careful preparations lay in ruins minutes before kick-off when his key defender John Williams tweaked his Achilles tendon in the pre-match warm-up and then failed a rapidly arranged fitness test. To make matters worse, heavy rain left the Gay Meadow pitch resembling a muddy marsh. This led to the Cherries' downfall when Williams' replacement David Langan chose to pass the ball back to Gerry Peyton five minutes before half-time. Inevitably, the ball became stuck in the quagmire, allowing Scotsman Jim Melrose to reach the ball ahead of the Bournemouth goalkeeper and put the Shrews a goal to the good.

At the final whistle, the home side had taken all the points with a 2-1 win and Redknapp was understandably apoplectic. 'I have told the players time and again I don't want back-passes to the goalkeeper. I repeated it three times before kick-off; I tell them until I am sick and tired of it. It was the last thing we wanted. It was a scandalous goal to give away.' One can only imagine the choice words he would have delivered to David Langan behind closed doors.

As if the manner and implications of the defeat were not enough, Billy Whitehurst scored for struggling Reading in the second minute of injury time to secure victory for the Royals over Barnsley and bring them within three points of Bournemouth. The two teams met five days later in what proved to be a ferocious encounter at Elm Park.

With survival on the line, no quarter was given and both teams emerged from a goalless draw nursing a variety of cuts and bruises. Redknapp was less than impressed with what he considered the Biscuitmen's physical approach. 'They were brutal, there was no other word for it. I don't know what that performance has got to do with football,' he seethed. 'Every time the ball was in the air there was an elbow in the neck or a kick in the ankle. They came out to batter and beat us up. Billy Whitehurst is more frightening than Mike Tyson. In the circumstances, I think our lads did superbly to keep their cool.'

It was a hard-won but vital point that kept the Cherries' fate in their own hands. With one of their remaining two fixtures at Dean Court against top-of-the-table Millwall, Bournemouth still had it all to do to avoid automatic relegation or a bizarrely established play-off in which the third-from-bottom team would face the teams finishing fourth, fifth and sixth in the Third Division.

John Docherty, who had briefly managed Redknapp during his short spell at Brentford, had guided Millwall to the top of the Second Division on the back of a nine-match unbeaten run, sending shudders through the corridors of power at the Football League's Lytham St Annes headquarters as they struggled to contain the blight of hooliganism in the English game.

On the night, it was Millwall who successfully dealt with the pressure. Richard Cooke was seen leaving Dean Court in tears after spurning the opportunity to give his side a share of the points when missing a penalty in the 89th minute, with the Lions' 20-year-old goalkeeper Brian Horne preserving his side's 2-1 lead. Captain Mark Newson summed up the mood around Dean Court after the match. 'Right now,' he said, 'I feel as low as I can remember for a very long time indeed.'

Bournemouth now occupied the dreaded relegation play-off position. Relief of a kind came in the shape of the second bye weekend of the season before yet another crucial clash at Plymouth. Argyle were mid-table and with their season threatening to peter out, star striker Tommy Tynan elected to spice things up by taking to the press to declare, 'If we win, Bournemouth might as well say to themselves, "That's us down," and I've got some bad news for Harry Redknapp's boys – I'm desperate for a goal.'

Tynan had not scored for six games, but his loose tongue provided all the motivation the Cherries required to extend the drought to seven with a come-from-behind 2-1 win that proved the catalyst for a perfectly timed mini-revival. 'That was a fantastic result for us,' said the once again buoyant Bournemouth manager. 'We knew we wanted to win and showed fantastic character to come back into it after going a goal down.'

A 2-0 win at the division's whipping boys Huddersfield Town four days later put the Cherries just a point shy of securing at least another season in the second tier with two matches left in the campaign. Bournemouth sought to finish the job when they entertained perennial rivals Swindon on May Day Bank Holiday. The Robins were safely in mid-table and Redknapp's team took control of the contest from the kick-off. On 34 minutes, a Colin Calderwood push on Trevor Aylott saw referee Keith Miller award the home side a penalty. Spot kick duties had been passed to Shaun Close following Richard Cooke's late miss against Millwall, but with Close preparing to place the ball, Redknapp issued instructions from the dugout that his captain Mark Newson should be handed the responsibility.

Redknapp's confidence in his skipper may have briefly stuttered when Swindon keeper Fraser Digby got a hand to Newson's strike and pushed the ball on to the post. To the relief of almost everyone inside Dean Court, the ball then rebounded into the net. Whilst celebrations were still dying down, the Cherries scored again when Close got to a long Paul Morrell throw-in ahead of Digby and finished first time into the far corner of the Wiltshire club's net. It was enough to secure survival in the Second Division with a game to spare.

The post-match revelry continued well into the night, but the following day Redknapp was able to face his public with another feather in his cap. 'We played some smashing football yesterday and we fully deserved the three points,' he said with a smile. 'It was a nice way to wrap up the season at home, and to get our third win in a week. We couldn't have timed a run like that at a better stage of the season. We've come good when we've needed to and we've proved we don't deserve to go down.

'It's been nerve wracking, there's no doubt about it, and I could have done without all of the pressure we've been under in the last few weeks. But when you sit down and look back on it, this has been the best season there's ever been at Bournemouth. In terms of football quality and excitement, there hasn't been a better one in the 64 years we have been in the Football League.

'There has been a great atmosphere at Dean Court every week, and I think we have responded to it. We played some lovely stuff this year. We played better this year than we did when we won the championship. As a football season, it has been a wonderful experience. If we are honest about it, every year we keep Second Division football at Dean Court we will have done very well.'

In the days after safety was secured against Swindon, chairman Jim Nolan spoke in detail about the transfer budget for the following season. 'Harry will have money available to spend on the team during the summer,' he promised. 'I cannot say how much it will be at the moment, as we are in the middle of doing our finances for the next campaign, but he will be able to deal in the market when he wants. It will be a substantial sum, and it will be at his fingertips to be drawn on when the need arises. It will mean Harry will not need to go cap in hand to the board asking for money for a player. If the board cannot be brought together during the summer due to holidays or whatever, the manager will still be able to wheel and deal for the player or two that he wants.

'Obviously, Harry does talk to us and would tell us as soon as possible out of courtesy if he was signing a player. That's the way he is and that's the kind of excellent communications we have here. But he is the manager and we always trust his decisions. We all believe we have one of the best young managers in the game at this club and everybody gives him the support he needs to do the job. In the transfer marketplace his record is second to none. He has done a marvellous job here and we all know he will continue to do so.'

Jim Nolan's words revealed much about life at the sharp end of running a provincial football club, but they did not tally with his manager's thoughts when it came to assembling his squad for the following season. Redknapp was looking to bring in as many as four new players, and felt he would have to move some of his current squad on to fund the improvements to his playing staff. 'I am looking to make a few changes and that means bringing in three or four players,' he said at the season's conclusion. 'If the right offer comes in for one of our players I'll take it. I need some fresh blood, and selling someone is the only way I can see of raising the money I will need.'

If proof were needed, Redknapp provided it the very next day when he let stalwart defender Tommy Heffernan go after 212 appearances and years of success together. 'He's been superb for Bournemouth and kept everyone on their toes,' said the manager with a heavy heart. 'It is possibly the hardest decision I have had to take.'

There would be equally challenging decisions to come.

Chapter Thirteen

Record-Breaker

1988/89

THE close shave with relegation convinced Harry that he needed to strengthen his squad, and his eye for a player was now finely tuned. Southampton defender Kevin Bond rejoined the club where he had once been on the books as a youth team player. Bond's association with Redknapp went back to his childhood when his father John and the Bournemouth manager were team-mates at West Ham United. 'If it hadn't been for Harry Redknapp, I believe Kevin would have stayed at Southampton,' said Bond senior when the transfer was completed. 'I know he has got a lot of respect for Harry Redknapp, and I believe this was the only club outside the First Division that he would have left The Dell for.'

David Armstrong had been forced to retire from football after an injury-hit first season at Dean Court. With little money to fund a replacement, Redknapp plucked Ian Bishop from Carlisle United. The Liverpudlian midfielder would prove to be such a hit on the south coast that when the new houses were finished on the land once intended for the Walker Stand, it was named Bishop's Close in his honour.

Redknapp was pleased with this pre-season transfer business, but the extra revenue and kudos from staying in the Second Division did not stretch far. 'We signed some experienced players like Kevin Bond,' he recalls. 'They were good professionals and good lads. We still had the same problems, like nowhere to train. No training ground as such, but they all got on with it.'

As pre-season wore on, Redknapp used this slightly less demanding period of the calendar to expound his views on how football should be played and what he saw as worrying developments in the game in the late 1980s. 'I've always believed in producing skilful players and exciting football. And while I am manager here, this club will always be known for those qualities,' he confirmed.

Harry went on to passionately condemn what he saw as the darker side of the beautiful game. 'I won't resort to thuggery,' he said. 'I won't let Bournemouth become another Wimbledon. It was a black day for football when they won the FA Cup last year. I wouldn't sign Vinnie Jones for anything. Not on a free transfer, not ever. He is a thug in football boots and he sets a terrible example. He'll breed dozens of skinheads in shorts coming into the game and ruining it. He sickens me more than anything else in the game at the moment.'

Harry was also at pains prior to the 1988/89 season to extol the virtues of his football club and question that of the domestic game after England had lost each of their three group games at the European Championships over the summer. 'Bournemouth will always be an example to youngsters over how the game should be played,' he said. 'That's where the future lies, where our responsibility lies and where the success of our national team lies. No wonder we muck up at the European Championships if we can't produce players with any skill.'

As for the season ahead, there was no shortage of optimism from the Bournemouth manager, and it turned out to be prescient. 'All I can realistically hope to achieve is to finish higher than we did last year,' he said. 'If we do that, it will be three years in a row this club has finished in its highest ever position in the league – an incredible achievement. Bournemouth will entertain at Dean Court this year, just as we always do. The standard of football here this season will be the best this club has ever seen. I'm confident and I just want to get started. I can't wait. This is going to be the best year in the history of AFC Bournemouth, mark my words.'

Those words appeared to be no idle boast when the Cherries began the season undefeated in their first six. An opening-day draw at Roker Park against hotly tipped Sunderland began the run, although Redknapp's post-match comments seemed slightly at odds with his football purist mantra of a few weeks earlier. 'You've got to get stuck in,' he said, after his side had secured a point. 'There's no point coming to these places to play open football with two wingers as we did last year. You've got to make sure you get a result. We are a big, strong side and we have fierce competitors. It's not realistic to expect to have the ball that much at a place like this.'

Chelsea were the first visitors to Dean Court in the league. Although the west London club were some way off being the moneyed aristocrats they would become under the ownership of Roman Abramovich years later, Bobby Campbell's side had the status of a star attraction in the second tier, and Redknapp was gunning for another notable scalp in the days leading up to kick-off. 'This is the sort of place the Chelseas of this world hate coming to,' said the Bournemouth manager of Dean Court. 'It's not a big ground. The stands are closed in, so we can really build the atmosphere.'

Harry was unwittingly given a helping hand by Bobby Campbell, who upon being relegated from the First Division told the press that 'playing the likes of Bournemouth will be like playing clubs from the Fourth Division'. It was a comment guaranteed to leave players and fans sensitive regarding any perceived slight at the best of times, broiling with indignation.

So it was that in the eyes of the Dean Court faithful, justice was done when Richard Cooke belied his 5ft 6in stature to head past Kevin Hitchcock in the second half. It was the only goal of a keenly fought contest and another triumph for the Bournemouth manager's favourite formation. 'Today showed the value of playing with a sweeper. We weathered the storm at the start and came back into it. We haven't conceded any goals, but if we hadn't had a sweeper today we would have had real problems. In the end we deserved the result.'

Despite this famous victory, the sight of Graham Roberts in the away side's defence stuck in Redknapp's craw. Redknapp had been in charge of the Cherries' youth team in his final year as a player at Dean Court and saw Dorchester-based Roberts progress through the ranks as a youngster. Whilst Harry was in America in the late seventies, John Benson had dispensed with the youth set-up due to financial pressures, leaving the 17-year-old future Spurs and England player a free agent. 'That was the most stupid thing this club has done for years and years,' commented Redknapp. 'There was no doubt in my mind that Graham Roberts was going to be a tremendous player. He was a fantastic lad.'

Confidence around King's Park rose even further when Bournemouth had by far the better of a goalless draw with Leeds at Dean Court in mid-September. The Yorkshire side's £190,000 summer signing Vince Hilaire had cost more than Redknapp's entire squad, but it was the Cherries who dominated the game. So impressed was Leeds manager Billy Bremner with the home side's performance that he sought out Redknapp after the final whistle to praise the 'miracle' that he was overseeing at Dean Court.

Miracles do not happen frequently, however, and Harry had little opportunity to enjoy this high praise before Bournemouth hit a run of patchy form. Defeat at Swindon was followed by victory over Oxford United, but the Cherries would not win any of the following eight games in league and cup.

During this barren spell, Bournemouth faced First Division Coventry City in the second round of the Littlewoods Cup. Since gaining promotion to the First Division in 1967 under Jimmy Hill, the Sky Blues had been perennial relegation scrappers until a dramatic FA Cup Final triumph over Tottenham Hotspur in 1987 under joint managers John Sillett and George Curtis precipitated a brief period of top-half finishes. Sillett, who had grown up in the village of Nomansland in the New Forest, was in fighting form as the tie approached, keen as he was to avenge his side's narrow pre-season defeat at Dean Court. He need not have worried as a flu virus in the home side's dressing room proved to be the Cherries' downfall in a 4-0 hammering.

Despite being one of those who had fallen ill, or perhaps because of it, Redknapp was angrier than ever at the final whistle. 'That is the worst performance I have seen since I have been at this club,' he fumed. 'Before tonight I wouldn't have believed we could play that badly. We were lethargic at the start and got worse as the game went on. That was rubbish.'

It emerged the following morning that eight of the Bournemouth players had been laid low and that along with Redknapp, Jimmy Gabriel and physio Brian Gant had also been struck down. With a visit to Stoke City just days away, Dean Court was shut and training cancelled in a bid to stop the spread of the virus and to provide Harry with 11 fit players for the match at the Victoria Ground. In the light of these developments, Harry significantly softened his attitude towards the Coventry humiliation. 'I didn't know how bad the thing was,' he relented. 'I thought it was just a cold, something brought about by a change in the weather or something. But having gone down with it myself I know how bad it was. Just before the game started, I began to feel lousy and I must admit I was a bit fearful. And certainly, the way I was feeling afterwards, there was no way I could have gone out and played football. To be fair to the lads, I'm not sure some of them should have played.'

One bright spot in this difficult run of results was the fifth anniversary of Redknapp becoming Bournemouth manager. Prior to a match against Shrewsbury, former West Ham and England manager Ron Greenwood presented Harry with a silver salver to commemorate the milestone before making a surprising observation about his former winger. 'He is a quiet personality,' said Greenwood. 'He's not got there by being aggressive, but by earning the respect of his players through his knowledge of the game. And Bournemouth play football the right way. Harry was brought up in that atmosphere and some of it has rubbed off. That he has been successful at Bournemouth is evidence, I hope, that he came from a good background. West Ham have done well with the number of managers who have emerged from the club and Harry merits alongside them. He has made history.'

Reflecting on his time at the helm, Harry revealed the prospect of managing the club on a permanent basis was not one he relished. 'I must admit, I didn't want the job when it was offered to me,' he said. 'There were so many things happening off the field at the time and I was really enjoying my coaching. I enjoyed being popular with the players. I know that when you become a manager, that popularity goes almost instantly. Everybody likes to be liked and I was no different. I've learned since then and it doesn't bother me now. I don't want to be just popular. I want to take decisions and do the job.

'The thing that decided me, the biggest reason for taking the job, was that I felt I could do it as well as the other people being mentioned. There were names being talked about and I knew I was as good as all of them. So I said, "What the hell! I'll do it." The last five years have been great and we all aim to keep it going. I'm glad I became manager, that's for sure.'

Redknapp was less than keen to make a further entry into the history books by being the first man to manage Bournemouth to relegation to the third tier. But with his entire first-choice defence carrying injuries and little to clutch on to in terms of performances, Harry was at something of a loss as to how to turn things around. 'Things are going very wrong and I don't know why,' he confessed. 'The players have become fearful of making mistakes and it shows in what they are doing. When that happens, it becomes hard to get your game together and everything becomes a lot more difficult. The crowd becomes apprehensive and that is communicated to the players. You have to be a very strong character to come through a spell like this.'

Another defeat on Oldham's plastic pitch followed, confining the Cherries to fifth from bottom of the table. With the sweeper system again faltering, Redknapp reverted to the flat back four for the next fixture against promotion-chasing Ipswich. Twenty minutes from time, Town's Canadian goalkeeper Craig Forrest inexplicably spilled a mishit Ian Bishop free kick into the net, gifting the Cherries' 23-year-old summer signing his first goal for the club. With some semblance of health breaking out amongst the players, fortunes took a rapid upturn as Bournemouth claimed successive 1-0 victories over Bradford and Crystal Palace, a run only interrupted by a 1-0 reverse at Derby County's Baseball Ground in the Simod Cup.

Mel Machin's high-flying Manchester City then brought the Cherries' mini-revival to an end as a goal just before half-time from future Bournemouth striker Paul Moulden settled the match. Machin had played alongside Redknapp at Dean Court, and his return to his old stomping ground brought back memories of when the Bournemouth manager was still donning his boots. 'Harry was a comedian, a character,' recalled the former defender. 'For example, just after he arrived, we were all sent on a man management course in Jersey. Harry, just arrived from West Ham, couldn't believe it. He just wanted to play football. So he took the chairman Harold Walker to one side and had a word with him. "I've come from West Ham," he said, "and I didn't like school when I was a lad. I've come from a big family and when I was younger I used to take as much time off school as I could. I can hardly read and write." Mr Walker, who was a lovely man, said not to worry, he would write everything down for him when Harry gave him the nod, and he did. The lads all knew he was having him on. We spent four days in stitches. I think they were the funniest four days of my life.'

Redknapp would soon be laughing himself, as watching on from the stands at the City match was former England and AC Milan striker Luther Blissett. Harry had been in the market for a proven goalscorer and had been linked recently with Preston's Gary Brazil and West Brom's Don Goodman, but kept his interest in Blissett under wraps for fear of other clubs swooping for the Watford striker should they learn of his availability.

At just £60,000, the price for the 30-year-old represented a potentially huge bargain for the Cherries, with Blissett commanding a £1 million fee just five years earlier when he went to play in Serie A.

'Watford played at home to Millwall on the Saturday and I heard that Bournemouth were watching me,' says Blissett. 'That didn't make a lot of difference to me because I always went out and tried to do the very best I could anyway. I scored twice that day and then I heard on the Monday that Bournemouth wanted me to come and see them. I watched them play and liked their style of football and thought I could score goals in that team.'

It was a confidence that, in Blissett's opinion, was shared by Harry Redknapp. 'I think having seen and heard what I had done in my career, he felt that I was the right player to come in and do that,' says the former England striker. 'I just came in and got to it with the players.'

Blissett's home debut came against Hull City, and his prowess in front of goal would secure all three points for the Cherries and immediately endear him to the home supporters. After missing a good chance in the first half, Blissett ran riot after half-time, scoring four times in a 5-1 win. 'It was fantastic to watch,' beamed Redknapp. 'We were superb in the second half. Luther looked fantastic. What a great start. The crowd have taken to him and I'm delighted. I just hope people don't expect him to do it every week.'

It was an audacious signing that demonstrated the strength of Harry's pulling power. 'Luther was great,' says Redknapp. 'He changed the habits of the players in lots of ways. The drinking culture was everywhere in English football. Luther came in here and he got the players to eat better, stop drinking too much and look after themselves better. He'd been to Italy and come back with the habits he picked up there and tried to get the lads here to live the same type of life. I'm not saying he succeeded with Willo and a few of them, but he certainly tried!'

'Many of the players were of a lower division mentality in terms of diet and fitness,' Blissett remembers of his arrival at Dean Court. 'I always conducted myself professionally and picked up a lot of good habits in Italy. I think that rubbed off on some of the players, as they realised they couldn't go out partying and drinking if they wanted to perform at a higher level.'

As well as attempting to curb some of the excesses of his new team-mates, Blissett made some revealing observations regarding Redknapp's style of management. 'I found out when I got there that Harry wasn't really a coach,' says Blissett. 'He was a manager in the true sense of managing because he had a very clear picture in his mind of how he wanted the team to play and he would pick the players that he thought would gel accordingly. Then, in his conversations with his coaches, he would say, "This is what I want. Make it work." Harry's thing was to pick players that he could trust to go out and do a job.'

Blissett went on to score in four of the next five games as Bournemouth picked up 13 points out of a possible 15 from the start of December to Boxing Day. He was not left to carry the burden of goalscoring alone, however, as Redknapp delighted his public again when just days after Blissett's stunning first outing at Dean Court, he secured the return of Colin Clarke on loan from Southampton.

Clarke had been struggling to get game time at The Dell and had yet to score all season. He soon put that right in his second debut for the Cherries, driving past Blackburn keeper Terry Gennoe from the edge of the penalty area just three minutes after replacing a wounded Trevor Aylott in the second half. Rovers were level soon after, but the Northern Irish international completed his dream return when he set up his new strike partner Blissett for the winner in the 89th minute.

In the week after the Blackburn match, Redknapp shared his thoughts on the trickle of foreign talent that was beginning to enter the English game. 'There are not many that have been successful,' said Redknapp of the overseas talent that would flood into the Football and Premier Leagues in the decades that followed. 'You would be taking a bit of a gamble. You have to be sure when you spend a lot of money for these people and there are a lot of problems like language and work permits.'

A second Boxing Day win at Leicester in a row saw Colin Clarke sign off from his brief loan spell with the only goal. Defeat at Watford on New Year's Eve did little to dissuade the Bournemouth public from turning out in their numbers. A season-high league attendance of 10,629 watched Redknapp's side see off Brighton 2-1 to start 1989 in the top six of the Second Division. The pressure to add to the points tally was then relieved for a week, as Bournemouth joined the rest of the First and Second Division clubs in launching their FA Cup campaign. Drawn away at Blackpool, Luther Blissett scored his tenth goal in nine games to take the Cherries through to the fourth round.

Following the cup tie, Redknapp busied himself in the transfer market. Protracted negotiations with Weymouth manager and good friend Stuart Morgan led to the signing of 24-year-old Shaun Teale for a fee of £50,000. The transfer saw Morgan and Redknapp briefly fall out. It was a dispute that did not last long. No sooner had Teale headed up the coast than Morgan followed him to Dean Court after having resigned in disgust over the sale of the defender and accepted an offer to be his old friend's chief scout.

No doubt the Dean Court board would not have been pleased to see their manager depart in similar circumstances and the regard in which Harry was held at the club was further confirmed when he signed an improved three-year rolling contract. The package brought Redknapp's salary in line with other top managers in the Second Division and chairman Jim Nolan was satisfied it was a good deal for the club as well. 'We value our manager very highly and we believe he is the man to take us into the First Division,' said Nolan. 'We don't want other clubs coming along and poaching him and getting the success we feel he can bring to Bournemouth. We have had no approaches recently for him and this is not linked to rumours that Harry may be going elsewhere.'

Nolan's denials may have done little to quash any of the rumours, but with the deal signed, his manager was happy to confirm his commitment to the Cherries. 'At no time have I thought of leaving Bournemouth,' said Redknapp. 'Although I am as ambitious as everybody else, my ambitions are for this club. I genuinely love Bournemouth. I have a great board behind me and I know other managers have far more problems at work than I do. We have built something here and it would be hard now to leave it. I want to keep developing Bournemouth and providing the sort of quality football that has come to be associated with us. They wanted to tie things up for me here and make sure I am happy. I'm glad to do that because I don't want to leave.'

With the ink still drying on the contract, the Cherries promptly lost their next two games to Hull and Sunderland. Fortunately, the fourth round of the FA Cup arrived in the nick of time to stem the blip in results. Bournemouth were drawn away to Hartlepool and although the north-east club were residing in their traditional position near the bottom of the Football League, the Cherries only managed to escape with a 1-1 draw. It was a poor performance from Redknapp's side, although Luther Blissett emerged from Victoria Park with a degree of satisfaction after converting a 45th-minute penalty for his side after enduring a half of horrific racial abuse from a section of the home support.

The replay on the south coast came three days later, and by then the draw for the fifth round had handed the winners a home tie against Manchester United. With a potential six-figure windfall for the club that went through, motivation was not in short supply come the kick-off at Dean Court. Redknapp's side did not disappoint the 10,142 supporters who braved the January evening and romped home with a 5-2 victory.

Despite the excitement and glamour on offer, Cherries' defender Kevin Bond conceded that the Old Trafford club represented 'the worst team we could have possibly been given' in terms of the prospect of Bournemouth progressing to the quarter-final for only the second time in the club's history.

An official attendance figure of 12,500 was published for the tie, although it is fair to assume this was an estimate. Dorset police mounted a significant operation to guard against the possibility of thousands of ticketless fans descending on Dean Court and attempting to gain entry to the ground. The numbers were not as high as feared, but the constabulary's planning was otherwise prescient. Six hundred frustrated United fans charged a police cordon ten minutes after the kick-off but were eventually repelled by officers on horseback. Earlier in the day, 12 United fans were discovered hiding in the toilets beneath the main stand having broken in the previous evening.

On the field of play, Redknapp's team were holding their own. Richard Cooke, who had been in and out of the side for the past few months, created such havoc amongst the United rearguard that Ferguson deployed no less than four players at left-back through the course of the match in an attempt to contain him. Chances were even during the first half, but the game remained goalless going into the break.

Eight minutes into the second half, United took the lead. Steve Bruce launched a free kick into the Bournemouth half which was headed on by captain Bryan Robson. The ever-alert Mark Hughes pounced between Mark Newson and John Williams to rifle past Gerry Peyton on the half-volley. Three minutes later, Hughes again volleyed past the Bournemouth goalkeeper, but referee Ray Lewis ruled the goal out for a push on John Williams by Steve Bruce.

United had the momentum, but Richard Cooke was still running their defence ragged. On 71 minutes he picked up a precise pass from Mark O'Connor and headed towards Jim Leighton's goal. Teenager Lee Sharpe was able to dispossess Cooke but unable to take control of the ball which ran through to the six-yard box where Trevor Aylott got ahead of Bruce to finish under Leighton's dive.

At 1-1 it was suddenly the Cherries who looked the more likely victors and Ferguson could be seen angrily shouting instructions to his players from the touchline. After a series of corners for Redknapp's team were repelled by the away side, Richard Cooke again took centre stage, picking up a wonderful pass from Ian Bishop and then crossing low into the penalty area. Luther Blissett, who had given Paul McGrath a torrid afternoon, looked certain to score. However, the former AC Milan striker failed to make clean contact and the ball went wide. Blissett's disappointment was clear, but television replays later showed that Steve Bruce had lunged at the striker's trailing foot as he prepared to shoot, relieving him of his left boot, an intervention which did just enough to ensure a replay at Old Trafford.

Blissett rightly retains his hero status at Dean Court to this day, but that late miss has always been seen as a rare low point in his three years at the club. Following a Saturday night in with his video recorder, Redknapp was far more forgiving than some of the Cherries' faithful have been over the ensuing years. 'It was definitely a penalty,' said the Bournemouth manager. 'I didn't think so at the time, but having seen the pictures I know it was for sure. There was no way Luther would miss that and with Bruce fouling him there was nothing he could do with the cross. There are no sour grapes now. It's all over and done with. We have just got to beat United up there.'

United had only lost once at Old Trafford all season, but Alex Ferguson knew his side were not guaranteed their place in the quarter-finals, where the winners would face Brian Clough's Nottingham Forest. 'We deserved to lose,' said the Scot of the encounter at Dean Court. 'They deserved to beat us, and we have got a really tough job on our hands on Wednesday. We certainly cannot underestimate them. We were lucky today and we are relieved to be taking them back to Old Trafford.'

Nearly 4,000 Bournemouth supporters made the journey to Manchester for a replay which attracted a total attendance of 52,422. The Cherries put in another admirable performance at Old Trafford, but were undone by a Sean O'Driscoll error after just 18 minutes. An attempted back-pass to Gerry Peyton ballooned into the path of United striker Brian McClair who half-volleyed past the far post despite Peyton getting his fingertips to the ball. Bournemouth's best period of the game came in the 30 minutes following half-time, with a Jim Leighton point-blank stop from Trevor Aylott being described by Ferguson as the 'save that kept us in the FA Cup'.

'We were so close,' said Redknapp after the game. 'We put on a smashing show and we have shown people what an awful lot we have achieved at our club in the past three or four years. I am proud of every single one of the lads.'

There was to be no negative reaction to the defeat as Bournemouth went on to win three and draw one of their next four games. It was a run of results which included the best away performance of the season at Crystal Palace. Bournemouth roared into a three-goal lead early in the second half, helped on their way by a stunning individual effort from Mark O'Connor. The visitors' advantage looked unassailable when Richard Cooke scored the third goal seven minutes after half-time, but Palace scored twice in three minutes midway through the second period. Gerry Peyton had already saved a penalty from Ian Wright, but the future England striker managed to beat the Cherries' keeper with a hopeful dig to bring the Eagles within one goal of snatching an unlikely point. It was to be Bournemouth's day, however, and Redknapp's side held on to give their travelling supporters genuine belief that a crack at a historic promotion to the First Division was more than a pipe dream.

Such was Harry's delight at the outcome of the match at Selhurst Park that when he learned of Palace manager Steve Coppell's post-match comments about the poor quality of the Dean Court squad, he was able to spin a minor slight into a positive message. 'Yes, we have got born-again players, players that nobody else really wants. They are a bunch of cast-offs from other people, they have been discarded and written off. But by coming into the right atmosphere they respond and play the way we know they can. That team out there was just about the most expensive we can ever field, and it cost little more than £200,000.'

Luther Blissett was also full of glee at the final whistle and heaped praise on his new manager's style. 'The main thing the manager does is tell you the right things,' said the striker. 'He says, "I bought you because I want you to play in my team, so go out there and do it for me and do it for yourself." That means a lot. People are motivated, and they are able to go out there and play.'

It wasn't all smiles, however, as the club's success on the pitch was failing to attract significantly higher attendances. It was a disappointment Redknapp was unable to ignore as a growing band of scouts from other clubs began to turn up at Cherries matches. 'It upsets me and disappoints me that the players look at the terraces and see so many gaps,' he said. 'The last thing in the world I want to do is have a go at our regular supporters. They are greatly appreciated. But where are all the supporters that were clamouring for tickets for the Manchester United FA Cup tie, who hadn't missed a match for 25 years and were complaining how disgraceful it was we didn't have a bigger ground? If we are going to keep our best players like Ian Bishop, we need to fill Dean Court.'

Some Bournemouth supporters took umbrage at Redknapp's outburst and complained about a lack of organisation at the turnstiles leading to long queues which were putting more casual supporters off attending regularly. Tiler was quick to leap to the defence of his friend and colleague. 'Harry is not having a go at those supporters who came to the game. I think a lot of the time Harry can't hear the noise that the crowd is making and for that reason I am going to provide him, and the visiting team, with new dugouts. That way he will hear just how loud the crowd is shouting for the team. It isn't his fault that from where he sits the crowd looks small sometimes and sounds quiet. It is nobody's fault.'

A 2-1 win over Leicester at the end of March put the Cherries back in the play-off positions. With the run-in to the end of the season approaching, Redknapp publicly set a points target for his squad to chase. 'It's not going to be easy but everyone at the top has to play each other so we are all in the same boat,' he said. 'If we get 20 points that should be enough to make it but I won't say we are going to get there for sure.'

The Bournemouth manager's mild note of caution was well placed. Of the ten games that remained to the end of the season, the Cherries would win just one and pick up six points from the 30 on offer to see the dream of promotion to the top tier of English football slip away.

Before a 1-0 defeat to Stoke City on 15 April, David Puckett, who had starred in Redknapp's Third Division title-winning campaign, left Dean Court for Aldershot. Puckett's contribution to Bournemouth's triumph was huge, with 16 goals scored in the first half of the season. However, the prospect of adding to his impressive tally was cut painfully short when his knee ligaments were torn to shreds under a heavy challenge from Bristol Rovers full-back Darren Carr on Boxing Day 1986.

With the successful treatment of such injuries in its infancy, Redknapp probably knew that the 28-year-old striker would never be the same player again. With the likes of Luther Blissett scoring regularly, there was no way back for the former Southampton forward. Regardless of the two and a half years of frustration he had suffered at Dean Court since the injury, the departing Puckett had nothing but kind words for the Bournemouth manager. 'Harry Redknapp has been very good to me. He knew I needed to play league football at this stage in my career, and knowing my chances would be limited at Bournemouth he was happy for me to go on loan a few times. I will forever thank him for that.'

Puckett's sadness at the way misfortune had damaged his career and the Cherries' frustration with the defeat to Stoke, were put into sharp perspective at Dean Court as news began to filter through that something was seriously amiss at the FA Cup semi-final between Liverpool and Nottingham Forest at Hillsborough in Sheffield. Long before the era of smartphones, sketchy information trickled around the ground via a few transistor radios and word of mouth. By the time most supporters arrived home after the final whistle to turn on their televisions, the death toll was well into double figures and mounting.

Raw from watching the scenes at Hillsborough unfold and without the benefit of hindsight, Harry's thoughts on crowd control three days after the tragedy now appear draconian at best. 'No way should we take the fences down here, even after what happened at Sheffield,' he said. 'Do you think because of Hillsborough the hooligans who caused us to put barriers up in the first place are suddenly going to behave? Did they behave after the Bradford fire? Of course not. The blame for the tragedy lies, ultimately, at their door. It is their idiocy that made the fences necessary in the first place. We would never have had them if it wasn't for the nutters. People must not forget, the nutters are still around and we do not want them getting at people in our stadium if they come to watch a game in Bournemouth. The fences, however, much as we all hate them, must remain.'

It is easy to condemn Redknapp's words, but that would be to overlook the era in which they were spoken. Having played and managed through a 20-year period when crowd disorder had all but wrecked the game he loved, it is no surprise that he displayed a less than enlightened approach to resolving the issue.

His opinions may have been forthright and ill-informed, but the Bournemouth manager was under no illusions regarding the suitability of Dean Court as a football stadium. 'It's an embarrassment,' he began. 'The place has just about had it. Even though people like coming here, you only have to look at the facilities to realise they deserve much better. Dean Court is out of date, isn't it? You can repair one thing and suddenly you find something else has to be done.'

Ramifications of the Hillsborough disaster continue to this day, but, as is the way of it for those not directly involved in tragedy, daily life and football at Dean Court continued following a brief period of reflection. Despite the recent run of defeats, Redknapp refused to concede the possibility of a play-off berth as the conclusion of the season came into view. 'Nothing is impossible and we will keep trying to win and finish as high as we can,' he said. 'That is all you can do. No one will admit that promotion is completely out of the question until it is mathematically certain we can't do it.'

Yet even Harry's plentiful supply of optimism had its limits, and a 3-1 defeat at Oxford United in the next match left his team languishing 11 points shy of sixth place with just four fixtures remaining. Redknapp launched an expletive-ridden 45-minute tirade at his players in the away dressing room at the Manor Ground at the final whistle, a tongue-lashing that led his dejected captain Mark Newson to confess, 'The boss has got a point.'

With little but pride to play for in the games that remained, Redknapp sought to use the opportunity to blood youth team prospects. Matty Holmes, a 19-year-old midfielder, had so impressed his manager with his desire to succeed that Redknapp took the unusual step of announcing that he would start the youngster in each of the remaining fixtures.

The undoubted highlight of Holmes's elevation to the first team came in the penultimate match of the season against Manchester City at Maine Road. A win for City would have seen them promoted and celebrations were well under way as a brace from Paul Moulden helped them to a 3-0 lead at the break. So jovial were the City fans in the 30,564 crowd that at this point they even joined in with the cheering from the 300 Bournemouth fans when Peter Shearer scored his first goal for the club from a corner with 20 minutes left. The mood changed somewhat when Holmes also opened his account for the Cherries from another corner and come the 90-minute mark the Maine Road faithful were screaming for the final whistle.

Much to their frustration, seven minutes of injury time were added to the end of the game following a series of stoppages to treat John Smeulders, who was filling in for Gerry Peyton in the Cherries' goal despite a back problem which prevented him from doing any of his own kicking.

With a minute of added time remaining, Luther Blissett burst through the City defence to find himself one on one with Smeulders' opposite number Paul Cooper. The home side's keeper scythed the Cherries' top scorer down and the referee pointed to the spot. Blissett took the penalty himself, keeping his composure amid a cacophony of catcalls from the City fans to snatch an unlikely point for the Cherries.

'We came in at half-time 3-0 down,' recalls Redknapp of a fixture which is still spoken about at Dean Court. 'We got into the dressing room and all the electricity had gone, so we couldn't see a thing. We huddled in this little room while I tried to sort things out. Then we battered them in the second half. If the game had gone on any longer, we would've won. It was an amazing game.'

Another, far less thrilling, draw followed in the Cherries' final game, at home to Plymouth Argyle. For supporters of most other teams in the second tier, the poor run in the final quarter of the season would have been a bitter disappointment, but the Dean Court faithful found huge consolation in reflecting on the club's highest-ever league finish of 12th in the division, a record which stood for a quarter of a century. 'I'll bet the fans are delighted, they have to be,' declared Harry of the season as a whole. 'At the start of the year, I would have been very happy to end up 12th. To be honest, I looked at our fixture list and wondered where the points would come from. Yet we consistently got better. After a sticky patch early on, we were right up there. We can be much more confident going into next season than we were this. The last few months have taught us that we can play in any company and go on to get promotion.'

As it would turn out, nothing could have been further from the truth.

Chapter Fourteen

Riots and Malaise

1989/90

HARRY'S success at Dean Court had not gone unnoticed in the wider football world. Whilst he maintained his commitment to Bournemouth in the light of frequent speculation linking him with moves elsewhere, financial pressure and personal ambition meant he was unable to effectively preach such loyalty to his squad.

Speculation linking Ian Bishop with a move to a First Division club began almost as soon as the Liverpudlian had made his debut in the Bournemouth midfield at the start of the previous campaign. Throughout the season a succession of scouts beat a path to Dean Court to watch him in action, and they rarely left disappointed. Come the summer break, his departure seemed almost inevitable. After orchestrating Bournemouth's remarkable comeback at Manchester City in the penultimate game of the season, an impressed Mel Machin moved swiftly to secure his signature.

Before taking his leave of the south coast, Bishop heaped praise upon the man who had resurrected his career. 'Harry changed my life, it's as simple as that,' he said. 'Without him I might not be the player I am today and might not have got my chance to play in the First Division. Joining his club was the best move I ever made. I just hope one day I can repay him. He deserves so much credit for my career being successful at the moment, because from the day I signed he always kept telling me what a good player I am and made sure I kept trying to do the right things. My confidence shot up. He plays the type of football I like to play and not once did he tell me to stop trying to be creative or to just knuckle down and do the simple thing.

'Harry has done a fabulous job at Bournemouth, something I doubt anybody else could have done. The club is very close to his heart and he is happy with his family and friends in the area. He is ambitious, don't get me wrong, but he wants to do well for Bournemouth. He has got all the credentials to be a top manager and he can't be ignored by the big clubs for ever.'

Although it came as no surprise, disappointment was palpable among the Dean Court faithful upon Bishop's departure. Redknapp does not, however, have a reputation as a canny operator in the transfer market for nothing. As well as the record £625,000 fee for Bishop, City striker Paul Moulden moved in the other direction as a makeweight in the deal. The 20-year-old held a Guinness World Record after scoring a staggering 340 goals in a single season for his under-15s side in Bolton. City fans were bemused at how Moulden, who had netted 21 times in 58 appearances for the Maine Road club, had been let go so easily by Machin. Redknapp, on the other hand, was delighted to add a proven striker to his squad to take some of the goalscoring burden off Luther Blissett.

With Bishop gone, Harry bolstered his midfield with the signing of Gavin Peacock from Gillingham for £250,000 and added striker George Lawrence, defender Paul Miller and goalkeeper Phil Kite to his squad. In total, over half a million pounds was spent on players over the summer, a huge outlay for the club which, alongside the associated hike in the wage bill, meant that the Dean Court board were banking everything on promotion. Redknapp, for one, was not denying it. 'We have to keep going forward, improving and developing. It is the only ambition I have got in the game. I want Bournemouth to take steps in the right direction every season I am here. It's going to be a really competitive league this year, more so than ever before, but we can match the big clubs now, for the first time in our history.'

Despite his apparently profligate spree, perhaps Redknapp's most significant signing of the summer came free of charge in the shape of his son Jamie. The teenage midfielder had been an associate schoolboy with Tottenham Hotspur for the previous two years but remained a regular fixture in and around Dean Court, training with the squad during school holidays and even, as his father would later admit, on many days when he was meant to be at school.

With the prospect of an easier route into the first team at Bournemouth than at White Hart Lane and the obvious pull of working with his father, Jamie completed his final year at Twynham School before spending the summer on loan at Dean Court. Following the conclusion of the loan spell, a deal was agreed between Spurs and the Cherries to allow the 16-year-old to sign for Bournemouth.

At the time, Harry chose to maintain a dignified silence, allowing Brian Tiler to speak on his behalf. 'Jamie has been training with us in the past and he likes it here,' said the Cherries' managing director. 'He knows everyone and it is a good environment. We have agreed to pay Spurs compensation for his release and he will join the club as a trainee. The compensation will take the form of a percentage of any fee we get if Jamie makes the grade and moves on.'

Spurs' manager Terry Venables was not keen to let go of one of the country's brightest youth prospects, but Harry maintains he had every right to sign his son and that he was acting in the best interests of the teenager's fledgling career.

'Jamie never left the club,' says Redknapp. 'He was only at Tottenham on schoolboy forms. He could have signed for Spurs but he left school at 16 and signed for Bournemouth. He could have gone to any club. He had the choice of Arsenal, Chelsea, Tottenham, West Ham, everywhere really. He wanted to play. He said, "I don't want to be 17 or 18 and playing in the youth team at a First Division club." He wanted first-team football right away.'

With his son's immediate future secured, Redknapp braced himself for the season ahead. A stuttering start to the new campaign saw Bournemouth lose at Brighton, draw at home with West Bromwich Albion and narrowly defeat Hull 5-4. In the victory over the Tigers, a first-half hat-trick for Paul Moulden stole the headlines, but Harry remained unimpressed. 'You can't say it wasn't entertaining. We got the win we were absolutely desperate for, but it was hardly the ideal way to do it,' said Redknapp, referring to his side's careless squandering of a 4-1 lead which almost cost them the points.

Prior to the visit of Newcastle United at the end of September, it emerged that no less than 15 professionals at the club were seeking treatment from physio John Dickens for a variety of injuries. 'It is unprecedented,' said Redknapp. 'John couldn't believe how busy he was. It must be a world record. It is by far the worst time for injuries I have ever known.' Perhaps Dickens should have been afforded some assistance, but Redknapp denied there was a crisis. However, it was a portentous sign of things to come as the absence of key personnel would ultimately drag his side into a relegation dogfight.

The lengthy sick list included Paul Moulden, but the diminutive striker was able to shake off a groin strain in time to score a brace against Newcastle, the second of which was an audacious chip over goalkeeper Tommy Wright to claim all the points for the home team.

Defeats to Middlesbrough and Blackburn followed, but Redknapp declared himself happy with his team's performances if not the results. When six points were subsequently collected from Port Vale and Oxford United, all appeared well at Dean Court. Bournemouth's manager declared himself satisfied with his side's progress to date. 'We have made a smashing start to the season,' he said. 'If you had told me beforehand that we would have had 14 points by the start of October and still be in the Littlewoods Cup I would have said, "Thank you very much."'

Redknapp was less thankful regarding the enthusiasm of the Bournemouth public for his team's exploits. When just 6,796 turned up to watch the Cherries see off Oldham Athletic 2-0 in mid-October, he was moved to issue one of his occasional outbursts about the lack of support for his entertaining and largely successful team. 'It is disgusting and it is heartbreaking,' he began. 'How can we be expected to build a team at this club if nobody is prepared to come and watch us? What more do people want? The crowd was a total disgrace; I couldn't believe it.'

The strength of Harry's views did not endear him to all of the Bournemouth fans, with the *Evening Echo* printing letters describing his words as 'pure stupidity' and asking, 'What planet are you from?' in reference to how ill-thought-out membership card and voucher schemes for big games were a significant obstacle to casual fans who did not attend every match. However, with his record at the club providing a kudos few other managers in the Second Division could match, the criticism did little to dampen Redknapp's fury. 'When we were in the Third Division, people said we weren't ambitious. Those idiots drove me mad,' he explained. 'They said if we got in the Second Division people would start coming to watch us. That just hasn't happened. If I wasn't ambitious and I didn't care about the club, then it wouldn't hurt. But I feel we deserve better crowds.'

Perhaps fearful of further repercussions, attendances of 9,353 and 9,970 were recorded for the next two fixtures at Dean Court against Portsmouth and West Ham United respectively. Defeat to Portsmouth saw the Cherries start the day with 13 fit professionals and, after Guy Whittingham's seventh goal of the season had settled the match, end up with just 11 fit players. Somehow Redknapp managed to cobble together a squad for the Littlewoods Cup second-round tie at Sunderland and came away with an impressive 1-1 draw after Peter Shearer scored midway through the first half.

It was the first time Redknapp had faced his old club since leaving Upton Park 18 years earlier. On the morning of the match, Harry's former West Ham manager Ron Greenwood reflected on young Harry's playing days in claret and blue. 'He was very much the east London lad,' began the man who went on to manage England at the 1982 World Cup. 'A great favourite in the club and, eventually, a real hero with the crowd. For the supporters, he was "one of us", a local lad playing for their team. He was an entertainer too and that just served to make him more popular.

'Harry was part of an outstanding youth side that won the FA Youth Cup in 1963. He was one of the better players in that team. He was quick, had speed and the ability to beat people, and he was a good crosser of the ball. He didn't score many goals, but he was a provider. He played to the fans, but he never let us down either.

'Perhaps the signs were already there that Harry would go on to become a manager. He was never any bother and he listened when you spoke to him, and he took advice. He was one of those that learned wherever he was and now I think it shows. I think he is reaping the rewards. Harry was brought up the way we believed the game should be played, and he has kept to those principles ever since. His teams entertain, his teams play enterprising football and his teams do have something of the old West Ham about them. Like many of the men we produced who went into management, his teams show he still believes in the same things as we did all those years ago.'

Harry was desperate that his side perform against his old club, although he was forced to field a scratch eleven as the treatment table continued to groan under the weight of its throng of regular visitors. Those who made it on to the pitch did not disappoint as they battled to a 1-1 draw, providing their manager with a good deal of personal satisfaction. 'I am delighted, I really am,' said Redknapp. 'We played some great football and the defence, which was particularly patched up, was magnificent. I couldn't have asked for any more from any of them tonight, and to perform like that against West Ham, well, it's very gratifying.'

Harry's delight was short-lived, however, when it emerged that Gerry Peyton was ruled out for the upcoming visit to Leeds United and the recently returned Kevin Bond was forced to leave the pitch at Elland Road after just 12 minutes of the match due to a hamstring injury. Bournemouth inevitably lost 3-0 to Howard Wilkinson's Second Division front runners, showing ominous signs of things to come. 'Leeds are a fine side and have a lot of money to spend,' said Redknapp. 'There were 26,000 people there today and the atmosphere was intimidating, just like Leeds of the old days.'

Battling on with a patched-up squad could only go on for so long, and the Cherries soon hit a poor run of form in which they lost four of their next five games. Following the impressive draw at Sunderland in the first leg, Redknapp's team went out of the Littlewoods Cup when a Marco Gabbiadini strike settled the tie at Dean Court. It was a night of some exasperation for the home side who created so many chances during the match that referee David Axcell was moved to take the unusual step of commenting that had he been officiating in a boxing ring he would have stopped the bout in order to prevent Sunderland from taking any more punishment.

Victory over Stoke raised expectations that the Cherries' luck was turning, but events during a 1-0 defeat at Bradford City in the next match demonstrated that the strain of trying to perform with such depleted resources was starting to show. Redknapp's captain, Mark Newson, was making his return to the side following an absence with injury. Trailing since eight minutes before half-time, Harry replaced Newson with winger George Lawrence after 71 minutes with a view to creating a greater attacking threat and protecting Newson's fitness.

What Newson knew of his manager's line of thinking is not clear. As he left the pitch, he exchanged heated words with Redknapp about the decision to replace him. 'I am not happy about what happened and I intend to see Mark about it,' said Harry after the final whistle. 'I won't be able to say what action I will take until I have seen him.'

The meeting clearly did not go well as after the weekend it emerged that Newson had been stripped of the captaincy, fined and transfer-listed. When the Cherries were knocked out of the Zenith Data Systems Cup by Chelsea at Dean Court in midweek, it was Kevin Bond who led the team on to the field, with Newson nowhere to be seen. Although the right-back had served the club with distinction, captaining the 1987 Third Division-winning team, Redknapp had no qualms about enforcing strict measures to maintain discipline in his squad. 'It's up to him now; he has lost the captaincy and won't get it back,' said the Bournemouth manager. 'If Mark changes his mind and decides he wants to play for this club, we will take things from there.'

Fortunately for all concerned, the stand-off between Newson and Redknapp appeared to come to an end when the defender realised he had painted himself into a corner. 'Mark told me he doesn't really want to leave, that he just wants to play for AFC Bournemouth and he apologised for what happened,' said Redknapp, with only a hint of magnanimity. 'That's fine by me. I don't hold grudges and as far as I am concerned, the whole matter is closed. Finished.'

With few other options available, Newson went straight back into the squad for the midweek fixture at Swindon. Coming on as a second-half substitute for the injured Sean O'Driscoll, Newson contributed admirably to a precious 3-2 victory before giving a slightly different version of events over the previous few days than his manager. 'I've apologised and Harry's apologised,' said the right-back. 'Looking back, what happened was a heat of the moment thing. Obviously, we had a difference of opinion, but that was all it was. Harry and I are similar characters with similar temperaments, and we are bound to clash now and again. It's been forgotten in the past and it has been, after a little while, now.'

The heat of the moment was a recurring theme during December as Redknapp was subsequently charged by the Football Association for bringing the game into disrepute for comments he made to referee Ian Henley as the official left the pitch at half-time at the County Ground. Henley had awarded the Robins a penalty in the first half following a challenge by Cherries' winger George Lawrence on Tom Jones which, in the opinion of the Bournemouth manager, did not even constitute a foul. 'It's a shame, but sometimes these things happen on the spur of the moment,' explained Redknapp. 'It is no more than that. It is simply a result of the tension you are under when you are a football manager.'

Redknapp later found himself out of pocket to the tune of £250 after he pleaded guilty to the FA's charge. Having calmed down considerably since the offence was committed, Harry was contrite following the hearing at Lancaster Gate. 'I shouldn't have done it and I hope I never do it again,' he said. 'I tell the players not to protest and then I go and do the self-same thing. It was stupid and it was my own fault. No one regrets the incident more than me.'

That tension would have abated slightly as Redknapp saw his team follow the win at Swindon with a 2-2 draw at West Bromwich Albion and a 2-1 victory over Barnsley at Dean Court. Despite the apparently unending injury crisis, Redknapp sold midfielder Mark O'Connor to Gillingham for £70,000 in the days leading up to the win over the Tykes. What appeared to be a reckless decision to many Bournemouth supporters was taken because Harry knew that in his 16-year-old son Jamie he had a prospect capable of stepping into the first team with consummate ease.

When Jamie was named on the bench for the Barnsley fixture, his proud father was rendered uncharacteristically coy on the subject, leaving it to Jimmy Gabriel to extol the virtues of the Redknapp progeny. 'We have got absolutely no fears about putting Jamie on the bench,' said the Cherries' assistant manager. 'He has got tremendous ability and oozes class. He is a player of great natural talents and I am convinced he will become a magnificent midfielder in the future. He is only 16, but already you can see the quality. He deserves his chance.'

Jamie did not make it on to the field of play against the Yorkshire side, but his prodigious reputation rapidly became a catalyst for the expulsion of the Cherries' youth team from the FA Youth Cup. The youngsters were drawn away at Harry's future employers Tottenham in the second round of the competition, but were forced to pull out of the original fixture due to a flu epidemic which had wreaked havoc in their dressing room. A patched-up squad was able to fulfil a youth league fixture at Northampton, but, following further injuries, again had to postpone the cup tie at White Hart Lane.

It was at this point that Spurs complained to the Football Association and demanded that Bournemouth be thrown out of the competition. Following a hearing in London, the FA found in Tottenham's favour, a decision that left Redknapp senior incandescent. 'It's a disgrace, an absolutely disgusting way to behave,' raged the Bournemouth manager. 'How could Spurs stoop so low? I think Spurs' manager Terry Venables should be called Scrooge for making a decision like that.'

Whilst he was assisting headline writers with their output, Redknapp was also aware that Tottenham's hard stance may have been connected to the return of his youngest son from the London club the previous summer, a move which those at White Hart Lane were less than impressed with. It was a consequence which hurt the Cherries' boss considerably. 'I was so sick I didn't sleep for two nights after I heard the news,' he said of the FA's decision. 'To take away an opportunity like this from kids is so sad.'

There was to be little in the way of festive spirit over Christmas as the Cherries lost 2-1 to Leicester City, who they were facing for the third straight year in a Boxing Day fixture at Filbert Street. Four days later, Bournemouth were beaten 3-1 at Wolverhampton Wanderers. The defeat meant that the eighties, the decade which Harry had begun as a washed-up former footballer unsure of where his next pay packet was coming from and ended as a manager with a burgeoning reputation, would close on a losing streak.

The gloom gathering around Redknapp's team lifted somewhat when what was becoming the traditional avalanche of goals in the fixture with Hull City again fell in the Cherries' favour as they ran out 4-1 winners at Boothferry Park. By now, the Tigers were sick of the sight of Bournemouth, and after pulling back a goal through a penalty, their frustration boiled over as the game drew to a close. With seven minutes remaining, Leigh Jenkinson, who had come on as a substitute at half-time for the home side, launched a volley of such colourful abuse in the direction of a linesman that he was immediately sent off.

A minute later, Hull's fearsome striker Billy Whitehurst lunged his boot towards Gerry Peyton's head whilst ostensibly challenging for the ball, a decision which prompted an angry 'handbags'-style melee in the penalty box.

Somewhat surprisingly, this was the point at which Harry decided he would give his son and brightest youth prospect Jamie his debut in senior football. Coming on for Peter Shearer in the 85th minute, the 16-year-old left the field a few minutes later in little doubt regarding the challenge a player of his ability would face in the lower leagues. 'I hadn't even touched the ball and there was a sending off,' said Redknapp junior after he had watched on in horror when a disgraceful tackle by City's right-back Nicky Brown almost broke Matty Holmes's leg and resulted in the home side going down to nine men. Despite this, Jamie was understandably thrilled to enter the action. 'It was just great to get on,' he continued. 'I was quite nervous during the game, but once I was on it was unbelievable.'

Victory over Hull precipitated a five-game unbeaten run which saw the team consolidate their position in what appeared to be the relative safety of mid-table in the Second Division. Luther Blissett scored a hat-trick in a win over Ipswich, a game in which Jamie Redknapp made his Dean Court debut, coming on for captain Kevin Bond at the ground where he had grown up for just the last minute of the match.

Prior to the triumph over the Suffolk side, Redknapp became the longest-serving manager in AFC Bournemouth's history. His six years and four months at the helm surpassed Jack Bruton's spell in charge from March 1950, although Harry Kinghorn could still claim the record on a technicality, his eight years in charge from 1939 including the six years of the Second World War when the league programme was suspended.

An early exit from the FA Cup meant the Cherries had a free weekend in the middle of February. Rather than give the paper-thin squad the time off, Redknapp and Brian Tiler somehow managed to arrange a friendly with the previous season's losing European Cup finalists, Steaua Bucharest. The Romanian champions were looking to cash in on their status as one of Europe's elite sides, having gained much broader freedom to travel out of the country following the fall of dictator Nicolae Ceaușescu and communism in December 1989.

Arriving in England during the Romanian Liga's winter break, Steaua's officials had received vague promises of friendlies with some of the First Division's biggest names. Upon arrival in the UK, the 1986 European champions found that the only club that were prepared to host them were Redknapp's largely anonymous outfit on the south coast.

Those inside Dean Court hoped the prospect of seeing Romania's greatest ever player, Gheorghe Hagi, who went by the nickname 'Maradona of the Carpathians', would lead to a packed house. With little experience of European football, it was an opportunity the Bournemouth manager looked forward to with some relish. 'It's not every week that players worth around £4 million come to Dean Court,' he said, referring to Hagi and his mercurial team-mate Marius Lacatus.

As it turned out, a somewhat paltry crowd of 4,214 were in attendance, a figure 3,000 lower than the most recent Second Division fixture against Middlesbrough. Those who did turn up were not disappointed, as for just £4.50 they watched Steaua stage a masterclass, with Hagi scoring once and Lacatus twice in a 3-1 victory.

No sooner had the Romanians taken their leave to a standing ovation from the red and black faithful than Redknapp was forced to speak publicly about Jamie for the first time in a professional capacity.

The day after the friendly against Steaua it was reported in a Sunday newspaper that Redknapp junior was attending a two-week trial at Liverpool, a claim his father denied. 'Kenny Dalglish spoke to me and asked what was happening with Jamie,' explained Redknapp. 'I told him he was staying here with me and hoped he would be for some time. He hasn't got to go on trial with anybody. If anybody wants to see how good he is they can come here and watch him. Jamie is here at the ground today and is undergoing treatment on a tweaked back muscle.'

This description of the state of play regarding his youngest son did not raise many questions at the time, but Harry himself, some years later, revealed it to be entirely fabricated. In his autobiography, Redknapp explains that not only did Jamie attend the trial, but Dalglish phoned to tell him after the first day that he wanted to sign the teenager.

Once he was done protecting his prodigious son from the glare of the media, Redknapp himself became the centre of speculation. When Lou Macari failed to attend West Ham's match at Swindon after falling out with his board of directors over a gambling issue, Harry was spotted in the crowd at the County Ground and immediately installed as favourite to take over at Upton Park. Prior to Macari's appointment the previous summer, chairman Jim Nolan twice rebuffed attempts to lure the Bournemouth manager to east London. Yet again, those inside Dean Court were fighting to hold on to their star asset.

Brian Tiler was incensed by media reports. 'It's scandalous that they can say things like this,' he raged. 'Harry is our manager and I am not so sure he wants to leave here anyway.' These were hardly reassuring words for the Cherries' supporters and Redknapp did little to calm their nerves, saying, 'I've not been that involved with goings-on at West Ham, I have been too busy here.'

With the fans left wondering how involved Redknapp had been at West Ham at any point during his tenure at Dean Court, he was given a ringing public endorsement by his old pal Bobby Moore. 'Harry has done a great, great job at Bournemouth,' said the West Ham and England legend. 'He has worked down there successfully for a considerable number of years under a restricted budget and is a great advocate of playing football. He knows everyone on the staff at West Ham and what he has done at Bournemouth he could do even better at Upton Park. I would love him to get the opportunity.'

Those gushing words from the World Cup-winning captain led to speculation that Redknapp had asked his former team-mate to speak up on his behalf, particularly when the Bournemouth manager gave his response to Moore's praise. 'It is very flattering, especially from someone like Bobby, who has been the most influential player in West Ham's history,' said Harry, before issuing the most vague of statements about his future plans. 'We will just have to wait and see what happens.'

Whilst the uncertainty over his future continued, Redknapp was able to steer his side to a sixth game without defeat when Paul Moulden's 13th goal of the season was enough to see off Bradford City. It was a valuable win and one which put the Cherries just six points off a play-off spot with over a third of the season to go. It was also the last time Bournemouth would win for 13 games, and with the benefit of many years' hindsight, represented a turning point in the season which would ultimately condemn the club to two decades of penury.

John Williams' fragile right shoulder was again dislocated in a challenge with the Bantams' Mark Leonard after just 12 minutes, an injury which ended the talismanic central defender's season. Harry knew this was a serious blow and immediately attempted to persuade Mark Newson to remain at Dean Court as his former captain ironed out the minor details of a transfer to Fulham. Newson had the pleasure of turning Redknapp down and made his way to Craven Cottage in a £125,000 deal.

Moulden's strike ten minutes before half-time would turn out to be his last in a Bournemouth shirt. He appeared in the next three matches but failed to score as Bournemouth picked up a solitary point from a possible nine.

Redknapp then dropped Moulden from the side and the next time Cherries fans saw the diminutive striker was in the main stand at Boundary Park before a heavy 4-0 defeat to Oldham Athletic. Asked about his availability for the match by the travelling supporters, Moulden stunned them by revealing that he had just signed for the Lancashire club.

Moulden's sudden exit from Dean Court came about after the former Manchester City player launched a dreadful two-footed challenge at team-mate Shaun Teale at the end of a midweek training session. This reckless lunge put the former Weymouth defender out of action for the rest of the season at a time when Redknapp could ill afford to lose another defender.

At the time, Moulden's moment of madness was covered up, although Redknapp was happy to use the press to push the striker towards the Dean Court exit without revealing the true reason he wanted him out. 'Really and truly Paul has got to do better,' said the Bournemouth manager after Moulden had scored in a reserve team victory over Swansea prior to his sudden departure. 'Certain parts of his game have got to improve for him to become a really good player; his control and the way he holds the ball up, for example. It's up to him now to work at these things.'

Shaun Teale was also persuaded to stay on message, despite the pain and suffering Moulden had caused him. 'I don't blame Paul or feel any animosity towards him. I don't think he has got it in him to hurt anyone,' said the defender, who spent eight days in hospital following the incident. 'We both went for the ball and it bobbled so badly we both missed it. Paul was the one person I would have expected to get out of the way.'

Years later, Teale's version of events is somewhat less vague. 'We went training at Chapel Gate near the airport on a Monday morning,' he remembers. 'For some strange reason, we had a full-size game, and we never did that. During the practice match, I went in for a ball with Paul and he went right over the top of the ball and snapped my medial ligament. It was a horrendous challenge. It wasn't anything to do with me and him. He could have done it to anybody, because he was angry at being left out of the side against Port Vale and he was throwing himself around a bit during the practice match and being a pain. As soon as he hit me, I knew something was badly wrong and that night I was in theatre for ten hours having it fixed. They had to remove a piece of my knee and replace it with a plastic ligament because he had snapped it against the bone. I was five months out of the game. He never apologised, and I'll tell you why. I was in hospital for ten days and by the time I came out he'd been sold. Harry was that annoyed that he literally got rid of him straight away.'

Redknapp knew full well that a 21-year-old striker who could claim 13 goals in 32 Second Division matches was far from surplus to requirements. With a further 13 league games to play it was far from inconceivable that Moulden could have broken Luther Blissett's record of 19 second-tier strikes set the previous season. Harry was also well aware that aside from the former AC Milan forward, Moulden was the only member of his squad that could be relied upon to put the ball in the back of the net.

Unsurprisingly, the sale of Moulden to that season's Littlewoods Cup finalists was not popular with Cherries supporters. As a matter of internal discipline, it was something Redknapp was not prepared to speak about honestly in public. 'All I can say to the supporters is that we sell people when they are no longer of any use to this club,' the Bournemouth manager explained through gritted teeth. 'I have spoken to about ten managers in the last few days and they have all said that it was a good deal. My judgement of a player is as good as anyone else's. Show me a player, with the exception of Colin Clarke and Ian Bishop, who I have let go from here who has done well elsewhere.'

With Teale, Paul Morrell and John Williams unavailable for the remainder of the campaign, Redknapp signed defender Neil Slatter on a month's loan from Oxford United to shore up his ailing defence. Unfortunately, in his first training session Slatter fell on to a stone and acquired a cut on his leg that required three stitches. 'I said, "Welcome to Bournemouth and meet the physio,"' joked Redknapp with gallows-like timing, before remarking in a more serious tone, 'The situation is grim. I'm not sure what I will do, although putting in the reserves seems to be my only option. I got in touch with Billy Bonds at West Ham and asked if he would do me a favour.

'He has got about six players in every position but he won't loan anyone out. It's the same everywhere. This doesn't leave me with a lot of options, to say the least.'

Slatter recovered and was able to play every match during his loan spell, but the Cherries did not record a single win in those five games as the supply of goals dried up and the injury crisis in defence went from bad to worse. Gerry Peyton's persistent thigh injury rendered him unable to run or kick the ball, but Redknapp was forced to play him in the goalless draw against Watford as reserve keeper Phil Kite was unavailable due to the death of his father. Kite, who had also been struck down by a virus, returned for the 2-1 defeat at Portsmouth, but it was the last game captain Kevin Bond would play that season as Redknapp lost the final member of his first-choice back four.

Bond was first struck in the face by the ball and moments later turned his already suspect right ankle after catching his studs in the Fratton Park turf. 'My first thought was that I had broken it,' said Bond. 'My leg and foot went completely numb and I couldn't move my foot at all.'

Presumably Redknapp was also left feeling somewhat numb as he faced the remainder of the campaign without a defence to speak of. 'It's a real pain,' he said after the match. 'There's no experienced central defender on the staff now who can play. It makes things very difficult. I've never known an injury situation like we have had here this season. I have spent more time at the Lansdowne Hospital than I have at home recently.'

Harry still winces at the thought of the misfortune that befell his squad that season. 'We just had a nightmare,' he remembers. 'There was no way we would have gone down that year but for the injuries. We lost all our defenders. We went to Portsmouth and we were winning at half-time and I remember saying to Jimmy Gabriel, "We've lost another two defenders already today. We're going to be in trouble." Jimmy couldn't believe what he was hearing. He said, "Harry, we're still halfway up the league." But we didn't have any players. It was a tough division for us as it was, let alone having half a team missing with injury.'

With eight fixtures remaining, Redknapp set his team a target of 50 points to ensure another season in the second tier. A creditable draw with Wolves brought them to 45 points, but Harry's confidence then took a significant dent as his side suffered four straight defeats to plunge the Cherries well and truly into the relegation mire. The second of these reverses was an Ian Bishop-inspired 4-1 drubbing at Redknapp's old stomping ground of Upton Park. It was the first time the Bournemouth manager had returned to West Ham in an official capacity since he left the east London club 18 years earlier, and to mark the occasion with sentimental poignancy he gave son Jamie his first start in the Football League.

Redknapp junior, who was still on Youth Training Scheme terms with the club, played well despite the scoreline, demonstrating an assured first touch and spraying the ball around with some confidence. This display would have given his father some pleasure alongside the frustrations of a heavy defeat, and afterwards the 16-year-old revealed he received further assistance from an unlikely source. 'I had a chat with Ian Bishop during the game and he was telling me to keep going and just encouraging me all the time,' said the youngster of his opponent in the midfield. 'The two of us get on really well from Ian's time at Bournemouth and when you are out on the field you should enjoy yourself. After all, it is not a war out there.'

Jamie's sagacious ways extended to his expectations of the treatment he would receive on the pitch from those keen to intimidate him. 'You get that all the time, even in youth football,' he said of a few hefty challenges at Upton Park. 'It wasn't a problem. I was nervous before the start and waiting to get my first touch was the worst thing about the game. But once I touched the ball I felt fine.'

With his son now a fully-fledged member of the first-team squad, Harry was faced with the challenge of balancing the twin responsibilities of fatherhood and being his son's boss. It was one that he claims to have sailed through. 'I didn't find it difficult being his manager because Jamie was a good player,' says Redknapp. 'It was easy.'

When the Cherries lost 3-2 at home to Leicester City in mid-April, the tension in and around Dean Court began to rise. After Luther Blissett missed a late penalty, chants of 'Sack the board' rang out from the South End and cushions were hurled on to the pitch. As the game drew to a close, fans continued their vocal protest, singing, 'There's only one Paul Moulden.'

After the final whistle, a group of around 150 fans attempted to gain access to the boardroom to confront Jim Nolan and his directors regarding what they considered to be the misappropriation of profits from player sales. They did not succeed, although Brian Tiler was moved to provide further details of the whereabouts of approximately £500,000 that the club had earned from transfers. 'The money was there to buy before the transfer deadline,' he explained. 'All the £225,000 we received for Paul Moulden was there to spend. But Harry was either not prepared to pay the asking price for the men he wanted or they were just not available. I understand the fans' frustrations. I think it is fair criticism to ask where the money has gone but we cannot expect fans to be accountants and understand the ins and outs of running the club. The cost of running a Second Division side far outweighs the income and we have to balance the books.'

The cacophony of criticism abated temporarily after Bournemouth won a crucial relegation six-pointer at Barnsley thanks to a second-half strike from former Oakwell favourite Trevor Aylott. The result was achieved in nail-biting fashion, with the home side hitting the woodwork in injury time and then seeing what appeared to be a certain goal saved in miraculous fashion by Gerry Peyton.

So overcome with emotion was Redknapp at the final whistle that he made straight for the small knot of travelling fans celebrating on the large away terrace. 'That one was for them,' said Harry. 'I was very emotional at the end and it was for the supporters who came all this way. I thought the game was never going to end and by the time the free kick hit the post I had my eyes shut.'

Redknapp may have wished they had remained shut when he consulted the fixture list to remind himself of his side's two remaining opponents. Fate had dealt the Cherries a cruel blow as they were to meet the top sides in the division, starting with a trip to Bramall Lane to face Sheffield United.

Dave Bassett's Blades proved far too sharp for Bournemouth, taking a two-goal lead within 12 minutes on their way to a 4-2 victory. The final relegation spot was now between the Cherries, Middlesbrough and Barnsley. Bournemouth's rivals for the drop faced each other in midweek at Ayresome Park where Tykes defender Mark Smith struck the only goal of the game in the 39th minute to assure safety for the Oakwell side and put the Cherries' fate back in their own hands.

Boro had 47 points from 45 games and occupied the final relegation spot going into their last fixture at home to Newcastle. Bournemouth had 48 points from 45 games and would face title-chasing Leeds United at Dean Court on the May Day Bank Holiday weekend. In the days leading up to the game, Redknapp sought to take the heat off his side, despite the reality of the situation. 'Our players are relaxed going into this,' he claimed. 'I haven't been able to get all the players together in training this week so possibly that has helped. We certainly haven't been sitting around in a group praying. Who would have thought we would be playing Leeds in this kind of situation? Not long ago they were the Liverpool of the day and no one had ever heard of us.'

Recognition of the peaceful south coast resort and its historically anonymous football club was about to skyrocket for all the wrong reasons. Leeds United had long been tainted by the blight of a notorious hooligan following. Months earlier, both clubs had appealed to the Football League to change the date and kick-off time but this request had been refused on the grounds of fairness to the other Second Division sides.

In an attempt to convince ticketless fans to remain at home, Leeds roped in the services of Yorkshire Television to beam the match live to four venues across the city for up to 4,200 people. With an allocation of just 2,800 for Dean Court, it was an effort not without merits, but with an average attendance of over 25,000 for the season and a weekend by the seaside in prospect, it was never going to be enough.

As the Bank Holiday weekend approached, stories began to emerge of Leeds fans alighting at Bournemouth railway station and immediately offering up to £100 to taxi drivers if they could help them obtain AFC Bournemouth membership cards. By the evening of Friday 4 May, the town was under siege as thousands of Leeds fans arrived, many of whom were intent on running amok.

There were a series of clashes between the somewhat overwhelmed Dorset police and the hooligans, many of whom sported 'Bournemouth Invasion 1990' T-shirts. An estimated 5,000 people had travelled from Yorkshire and the 200-strong force, decked out in full riot gear with dogs, struggled to cope. The majority of the trouble flared around the seafront close to Bournemouth pier. Tables, chairs and windows were smashed up in bars and restaurants and deckchairs and beach huts set alight. Waiters, bar staff, drivers and passers-by were attacked and hospitalised as the weekend descended into an orgy of violence.

'Our worst fears have been realised,' admitted the commander of the police operation, Superintendent Les Burns. 'There are a large number of people without tickets. Police officers were deployed in the town. They then came under attack at various times throughout the night.'

By Saturday morning, Burns had sent for reinforcements in the shape of mounted police from London. By the time they arrived, forged tickets were changing hands at inflated prices as the Leeds mob dragged themselves off the beach where they had spent the night and made their way to Dean Court.

The scene in the dusty Dean Court car park that greeted home fans hoping to see their heroes pull off a surprise win and dodge relegation was reminiscent of the footage of the pitched battles between police and miners during the bitter industrial dispute of 1984. These were scenes the people of Bournemouth had only witnessed on the television news and yet suddenly they found themselves walking to the match through mounted police charging rock-throwing opposition fans whilst a low-flying chopper circled overhead.

Unsurprisingly, many Bournemouth fans walked in the other direction when they saw the violent chaos around Dean Court and others stayed away completely, preferring to stay at home and tune in on the radio rather than risk their safety.

Turning for home was not an option that was available to the Bournemouth players, even those who were unavailable for selection. John Williams, who had not featured since the middle of February after injuring his shoulder, vividly remembers the journey to Dean Court that day. 'As we got nearer to the park, it became impossible for the cabbie to make any progress without the taxi being kicked and shaken by the Leeds fans,' he says. 'The cabbie turned around and said to me, "I'm going to have to let you out here John," which was understandable from his point of view, but I was terrified. I'd made the mistake of wearing my club blazer, and as soon as I got out of the car I was surrounded. Luckily, a couple of the Leeds lads recognised me from the game we had played earlier in the season at their place and for reasons I don't know but will be eternally grateful for, they virtually escorted me to the ground.'

Shaun Teale, who was still recovering from Paul Moulden's moment of madness on the training ground, was another to have a lucky escape. 'I got my Player of the Year award on the pitch after the game,' he recalls. 'I almost got hit by a concrete block on my way in on my crutches. It missed my head by about six inches as they were rioting in the car park. The car park at Dean Court at that time was made up of shale and stone. There was bags of ammunition for the Leeds fans to throw. Anybody walking alongside the main stand was subject to stones flying around their heads. It was horrendous. They'd already burnt out numerous beach huts the night before. They were on the warpath.'

In the present day, it seems to defy belief that the game went ahead at all. However, in the circumstances, kicking off as planned was considered to be the best of a bad bunch of options. Somehow, Redknapp had to find a way to motivate his team and overcome the very real threat to their wellbeing.

Paul Miller, for example, was required to play the entire match in the menacing atmosphere whilst frantically concerned about his family's safety. His wife Patricia was driving to Dean Court when two ticketless Leeds fans leapt into the car, causing a panicking Mrs Miller to narrowly avoid crashing as she attempted to escape.

Ignorant of this attack, some of the national press in attendance criticised Miller for being at fault for the only goal of the game when Lee Chapman rose above the former Tottenham defender to head home in the second half. Bournemouth piled on the pressure for the remainder of the match but could not make the breakthrough and with Middlesbrough winning 4-1 at home to Newcastle, relegation was confirmed.

Like his players, Harry was also unable to block out the off-the-pitch havoc whilst attempting to oversee his team's performance. 'I was so concerned for the safety of our supporters that it was impossible to concentrate on the game,' he revealed. Despite the crushing disappointment of relegation, it was the newly crowned Second Division champions who became the target of Redknapp's anger. 'It is about time Leeds came out and said, "You are not wanted by us, you are scum,"' said the emotional Bournemouth manager. 'Just to let things drift along without saying anything is terrible. The fact that the date of the game was not changed does not excuse their appalling behaviour. The League have not made them behave in this way.'

Harry has had his share of ups and downs in football management over the years, but the match against Leeds remains one of the low points of his career. 'I knew there was going to be trouble,' he says. 'It was the most intimidating match I have ever been part of. It was horrendous. Their fans smashed the town up, they smashed the ground up. Everybody who turned up with a Bournemouth ticket, the Leeds lot would just take their tickets off them. All the cars got smashed up in the car park. The whole thing was just so intimidating. God knows what would have happened if we had won. The ground wouldn't have been there any more. I had friends sitting there, being threatened. They were scared to cheer for Bournemouth. Really afraid. I think there was hardly a Bournemouth supporter in the ground at the end. Leeds had completely taken over the stadium.'

Just three years after the glorious Third Division title triumph, the defeat to Leeds and the abhorrent events surrounding the match represented the low point in Bournemouth's history. Media coverage of the disturbances was widespread, with the club featuring on the national news in print, television and radio for all the wrong reasons. The ramifications would continue for years afterwards as the club struggled to make ends meet in a town that was at best ambivalent to their fortunes.

Amid the highly charged aftermath of the Bank Holiday weekend, there was an unlikely glimmer of hope that, despite finishing in the relegation places, the Cherries could still retain their Second Division status. Swindon Town, who had finished fourth in the division under manager Ossie Ardiles to make the play-off places, were awaiting the outcome of a Football League inquiry into serious financial irregularities at the County Ground.

Swindon promptly beat Blackburn Rovers 2-1 in both legs of the play-off semi-final and then took the spoils at Wembley when Alan McLoughlin's 25th-minute shot took a deflection off Sunderland defender Gary Bennett to secure a 1-0 victory. Celebrations were understandably muted at Wembley as the spectre of severe sanctions hung over the Wiltshire club. On 7 June, Swindon pleaded guilty to all 36 charges levelled against them and admitted a further 20 charges. The League decided that the club would be demoted to the Third Division, a punishment which amounted to two relegations.

More than a month after the anarchic end to the season at Dean Court, the prospect of a silver lining was now closer than ever. With the club and its supporters on the edge of their seats for six long days, hopes were finally dashed when the League announced that Sunderland would be promoted to the First Division whilst Tranmere Rovers, who had lost to Notts County in the Third Division play-off final, would go up to the Second Division. After a High Court appeal the following month, Swindon held on to their Second Division status and Tranmere once again found themselves in the Third Division, none of which mattered to Harry Redknapp and the Cherries who now knew for certain that they would be joining them.

This excruciatingly convoluted finalising of the relegation and promotion spots ended what amounted to Harry's nadir in football management. Yet, cruelly, much worse was soon to come.

Chapter Fifteen

Catastrophe

1990/91

AS the club continued to pick up the pieces, Harry Redknapp spent the early part of the summer break coming to terms with relegation. After a period of reflection, the Bournemouth manager came out swinging. 'I am not going to run away from our problems,' he said two weeks into the close season. 'I don't want to leave this club when it is down. It would be the easiest thing in the world for me to walk away from it all, but I just have to get on with it. I don't intend to see the club slipping back into the kind of position it was in before I arrived. Seven years ago, this club was going nowhere. That won't happen again. I'm still as keen as ever for success and I'll continue to give this club everything I have got.'

Harry then skipped the first week of an end-of-season club tour to the US in order that he could watch Jamie play in an England Under-17s outing against France at Wembley. Redknapp junior had continued to attract attention from the country's biggest clubs, a situation which left his father with mixed feelings. 'It's a hellish position for me,' said Harry. 'I can't keep him here for ever. Plenty of teams want him and the last thing I want to do is impede his progress. I'm torn between what is best for the club and what is best for Jamie.'

Redknapp's angst over mixing his personal and professional life did not get any easier when he was forced to release his eldest son Mark from Bournemouth after the 19-year-old was unable to recover sufficiently from a serious injury to his left ankle.

Upon returning from America, one might reasonably have expected Redknapp to take a break from football after such a torrid end to a long season. However, Harry's appetite for the game was insatiable and he was soon packing his suitcase for Italy to watch the 1990 World Cup.

It was a trip Redknapp had planned with Brian Tiler, who had surprisingly resigned from his post as chief executive at AFC Bournemouth following relegation to the Third Division. With Redknapp describing the situation at Dean Court as 'out of control' in the final months of the season, it was perhaps not such a shock that Tiler decided he had had enough, although no official explanation for his departure was forthcoming from the club.

Harry and Tiler remained firm friends, however, and doubtless welcomed the opportunity to relax away from the pressures of their working lives whilst continuing to indulge their all-consuming passion. They were joined in Italy by York City's chairman Michael Sinclair and Midlands industrialist Eric Whitehouse, a friend of Tiler's from his days at Aston Villa.

After attending matches in the group stage, the party attended the quarter-final between the Republic of Ireland and hosts Italy in Rome's Olympic Stadium. Italy won by a single goal, but the Irish fans continued to celebrate after the defeat, having seen Jack Charlton's side achieve more in the competition than many dreamt possible. Redknapp and friends met many of these buoyant supporters when they ate in a small pizzeria near the Olympic Stadium after the match.

With the group due to make an early start the following day in order to travel to Naples for the quarter-final between England and Cameroon, Tiler and the others were keen to head back to their hotel, the Maga Circe in San Felice Circeo, an hour's drive south of Rome. Always happy to talk, Redknapp kept his friends waiting in the minibus as he chatted to some of the Irish fans about his goalkeeper Gerry Peyton. Although the delay was no more than ten minutes, it would prove to be significant.

Redknapp normally took the aisle seat in the bus, as he did not like to sit by the window. Upon returning to the vehicle, he discovered that Tiler had exacted a modicum of revenge for his tardiness by taking that seat, leaving Harry to sit in the breeze. This discomfort did not prevent Harry from dropping off on the journey, a nap from which he would not wake for two days.

On the SS148 road near the town of Latina, the minibus was involved in a high-speed collision at around 3am. Minutes before the crash, Brian Tiler woke and checked that the driver Paulo, who had been provided by the hotel, was still awake. Typical of many Italian highways, the unlit SS148 had three lanes, the middle of which was reserved for overtaking in either direction. This flagrant disregard for health and safety meant the spot where the collision occurred was notorious for accidents. Travelling the opposite way, a Volkswagen Golf GTI containing three young Italian soldiers exited the overtaking lane for the lane the minibus was in, an extremely dangerous decision which rapidly ended in tragedy.

Reportedly travelling at 90 miles per hour, the soldiers' car collided with the minibus, killing the three Italians instantly. The bus was flipped on to its roof, skidding some 50 yards across the road. Brian Tiler was also killed immediately. Paulo the driver, who was later exonerated of responsibility, had both his legs broken and would go on to spend nine months recovering in hospital. Redknapp was thrown from the vehicle, landing in wreckage with his motionless body soaked in petrol. Michael Sinclair, who was bleeding and in shock but had remained conscious, dragged Harry and Eric Whitehouse away from the minibus, fearing an explosion that would kill them all. 'I could see Brian was dead,' said Sinclair in the days after the accident. 'He took the full impact of the crash.'

Upon arriving at the scene, the Italian paramedics declared Redknapp dead, placing a blanket over his head and body. It was an opinion which was initially shared by the staff at the hospital in Latina when Harry arrived. In the intervening period, an unidentified thief helped themselves to his wallet and valuables, presumably of the opinion that the Bournemouth manager would have no use for them in death.

In fact, Redknapp had narrowly survived but was unconscious for 48 hours. He had a fractured skull, broken ribs and nose and a deep gash on his leg of which he bears the scar to this day. He had also lost his senses of smell and taste. Due to Harry's delicate state, the news of Brian Tiler's death was kept away from him for four days after he regained consciousness. It was left to Eric Whitehouse to break the news. 'Harry took it very hard,' said Whitehouse, who himself was still coming to terms with the death of his good friend.

Shortly afterwards, Harry was sufficiently recovered to speak for the first time about the tragedy. 'Brian was a wonderful, warm bloke,' he said. 'I am devastated and my heart goes out to his wife Hazel and daughter Michelle.'

Tiler's death had a far greater impact on Redknapp than the accident itself. 'The thing for me is, I was asleep at the time and I never woke up,' he explains. 'I was unconscious so I never saw any of it, I don't remember anything at all about it. I've got no recollection of anything. Brian was a great character, larger than life. It was a massive blow to lose him.'

Redknapp's head injury meant the atmospheric pressure inside a regular aeroplane would have been too much for his skull to bear. Consequently, he was unable to return to the UK in time to accompany Sandra to Tiler's funeral at Moordown Baptist Church.

Mark and Jamie flew out to see their father in Italy soon after the accident, with Jamie fainting upon seeing Harry's injuries. Two weeks later, the Cherries paid £10,000 to charter a low-flying jet from the airline Euro Assist to bring their manager back to Bournemouth Hurn Airport. Upon arrival, Harry was taken to the Lansdowne Nuffield Hospital, where he was reunited with Sandra for the first time since the accident.

It had been a terrible summer for Redknapp and AFC Bournemouth. With no manager to take charge of team affairs after relegation and the whole of Dean Court in shock over Brian Tiler's passing, the directors had to summon the will to ready the club for the return to the Third Division.

With Harry absent for an indefinite period, assistant manager Terry Shanahan and chief scout Stuart Morgan were handed control of the first-team squad on a caretaker basis. Harry was unable to hand over the reins completely, however, and from his hospital bed oversaw protracted negotiations to bring Tony Pulis back from Gillingham to act as player-coach at Dean Court.

Redknapp also maintained his involvement in team affairs through the ongoing speculation about Jamie's future. As the new season approached, Redknapp junior, who had signed a one-year professional contract upon turning 17 in June, was being linked with a move to Chelsea, Everton and Liverpool. Jimmy Gabriel, now assistant manager at Everton, had known Jamie since birth and was not averse to using this connection to tempt the midfielder to Goodison Park. 'I regard him almost as a nephew,' he said. 'I am very close to the Redknapp family. I am sure he can handle all this attention. He is a terrific kid. Of course we would be interested; we are always interested in skilful players. Obviously I have spoken to our manager Colin Harvey about him and he knows I rate him highly, but we have not made a bid for him.'

Bournemouth chairman Jim Nolan claimed the youngster was not for sale. 'The big clubs can look all they want, but he is not leaving and that is final,' he said. 'We think he is priceless. He is the best young midfielder in the country. We have just signed him and we are not in the business of selling our best players before the start of the season.'

Nolan's words appeared somewhat flimsy to supporters in the weeks leading up to the new campaign as goalkeeper Phil Kite left for Sheffield United and star midfielder Gavin Peacock was transfer-listed in an attempt to reduce the Dean Court wage bill. Revenue had been hit hard by the drop into the Third Division, but in the days before relegation clauses in players' contracts, the club continued to pay Second Division wages to many of Redknapp's squad.

With no cover for Gerry Peyton following Phil Kite's departure, Redknapp entered into negotiations with his old sparring partner Barry Fry for Barnet goalkeeper Peter Guthrie. A fee of £15,000 was agreed between the two clubs, but not before Fry and Redknapp had reopened hostilities that had previously seen the Barnet manager threaten to have Harry shot following the transfer of Mark Newson. 'As far as I was concerned, a deal was agreed with Bournemouth for £20,000 for Peter,' claimed Fry. 'Then I had a call from Harry Redknapp. He offered £10,000, take it or leave it. He was adamant. It's really not on. I've known Harry a long time and it's a bit naughty of him to behave in this way.'

In the week leading up to the opening fixture of the season at Brentford, Redknapp paid a brief visit to Chapel Gate to see his squad training in an attempt to provide them with the motivation to begin the season with a win. 'At the end of the day, they must do it for themselves, the supporters, the club and Brian Tiler,' said Harry. 'Come 3pm on Saturday, I'll be a nervous wreck and very tense. There's no way I can go to the match. I will just make myself ill and I can't afford to take that chance. I just hope the lads can get the kind of result I'm looking for.'

Harry was presumably content when his side recorded a 0-0 draw, but would have been less than pleased when it became the first in a disappointing sequence of results at the start of the Third Division season. Bournemouth's only win in their opening five fixtures came in the Rumbelows Cup against Birmingham City. Terry Shanahan and Stuart Morgan hoped a change in fortunes was imminent when victory in the league was finally recorded against big-spending Bradford City, but the Cherries won only once more in the subsequent five fixtures, leaving Redknapp's side just above the relegation zone.

The squad had been promised a £200,000 bonus to split among themselves if an immediate return to the Second Division was secured, but without Redknapp to guide them and the hangover from the worst few months in the club's history still evident, this end-of-season windfall appeared a remote possibility.

A 3-0 win over Fulham at the end of September proved to be a false dawn as the Cherries went on to lose their next two Third Division fixtures and exit the Rumbelows Cup at the hands of Millwall. One of the few bright spots in the defeat at The Den was the performance of Jamie Redknapp, who on his return from a groin injury drew praise from Terry Shanahan. 'Jamie did very well,' said the Cherries' caretaker manager. 'He is only 17 but he has plenty of talent and can be a great player.'

Jamie's return to the side could not have been more timely. The Millwall defeat proved to be the last game at the helm for Shanahan, Morgan and Tony Pulis as Harry Redknapp declared himself fit and returned to his day job 14 weeks after almost losing his life in Rome. It was an emotional return for Redknapp and one which was warmly welcomed by players, staff and supporters alike. 'I never realised how much the club meant to me,' said Redknapp. 'I care so much about it and I'm desperate to return. Football is my life and when I get up in the morning I am anxious to get to the ground. I have been overwhelmed by the reaction to my return and I thank them all. I'm back now and I want to be a winner again. I want us to get back up that Third Division table. But I won't be putting in as many hours as I used to. Leaving early and driving like a maniac to matches at night will no longer be a feature.'

The lengthy period of convalescence had provided Redknapp with ample opportunity to reflect on his circumstances. Although he made some adjustments to his approach to his work, his love of the game never dimmed. 'It was a horrendous time after the accident,' he says. 'My motivation really was to come back to work, to get back into football. I did that as soon as it was possible. I came back and got on with it again. I had no intention of not coming back. Bournemouth was my club. Terry Shanahan and Stuart Morgan took over and I think they found it very difficult. Going from a coach to a manager is very different, a lot of pressure. They found it hard to cope with. So I think they were pleased to get me back.'

Redknapp's absence certainly took its toll on both himself and those who stepped into his shoes. 'It didn't go too successfully, I must admit,' says Stuart Morgan. 'There was a lot of doom and gloom. It wasn't a good period for myself and Terry; we were struggling. We lost a lot of momentum. When Harry did come back we weren't exactly in the best of shape. The accident was a massive blow and obviously knocked him back a bit. He wasn't the fittest around the training ground for the rest of his time at the club.'

Harry's resolution to achieve a better work-life balance weakened even before he officially returned to Dean Court. After a short break in Majorca, he spent the weekend prior to his return scouting at Portsmouth and Brentford. 'I was the only Football League manager at Brentford,' he said. 'That's why I have been successful.'

With the Cherries languishing in the lower reaches of the Third Division, Redknapp had some stern words for his squad. 'It's going to take a lot of work to get back up this league,' he said. 'No one thinks as much of this club as I do and if the players don't feel the same way they can go. I could easily spend the next four months at home with my feet up and keep my specialist happy but I want to get back into the job. I'm feeling positive and determined. I remember a time when no one cared about this club. That is not going to happen again. I only want people who are totally committed to this club. I want to be a winner. If you want to be part of that, get your act together. If you don't, get on your bike.'

Harry's tough talking and managerial acumen had a remarkable impact as Bournemouth went on a 12-match unbeaten run immediately following his return. In his first match back in the dugout, a 1-1 draw with Crewe Alexandra at Dean Court, Redknapp received a rousing ovation from the 5,548 fans in attendance. 'They gave me a fantastic reception,' he said of his adoring public. 'I couldn't have stayed out there for too long. It was very emotional for me. It made me realise the fans think a lot of me. The people of Bournemouth have always been like that and I can't thank them enough for all their support.'

Despite the significance of the occasion, Harry was disappointed in the result and continued to publicly criticise his squad's attitude and lack of leadership. His hard-line stance since his return was soon paying dividends as the Cherries won 3-1 at Huddersfield in the following fixture to record their first away victory of the season.

Liverpool manager Kenny Dalglish and Everton boss Colin Harvey were both in the stands at Leeds Road scouting Jamie Redknapp. Dalglish had phoned Harry on the morning of the match to enquire as to whether Jamie would be playing, and although he was told the midfielder would be on the bench, he still chose to travel from Merseyside. The journey proved to be in vain as an impressive display from Shaun Brooks meant that Harry saw no need to introduce his son to the field of play.

With Efan Ekoku yet to secure a first-team spot, Luther Blissett was shouldering the majority of the goalscoring responsibility at Dean Court. Redknapp sought to rectify this, signing Charlton striker Andy Jones for £80,000 prior to a 0-0 draw at Preston. Whilst the Dean Court faithful were speculating where the money to fund the deal had come from, Jones rapidly paid a portion of the fee back when he scored the only goal of the game against promotion-chasing Tranmere Rovers just 74 seconds into his home debut.

It was a strike that inspired a three-match winning run in the league which saw Bournemouth rise to fifth place in the Third Division table, having been 19th when Redknapp returned from his convalescence. Among this sequence, the Cherries played out a 0-0 draw against Gillingham in the Leyland DAF Trophy, a game which saw Jamie Redknapp establish himself in the Bournemouth midfield. His mature performance ensured selection for the league game against Rotherham a few days later, where he played a key role in a 4-2 victory, with Luther Blissett claiming a hat-trick.

Less than 24 hours after the victory over the Millers, Jamie was again heavily linked in a Sunday newspaper with a move to Liverpool. The report claimed he had signed for the Anfield club following the Rotherham match for what was described as 'next to nothing'. It was a development that rendered Harry apoplectic. 'What a joke!' he raged. 'I can't believe it. I have no idea where the story came from. It is complete and utter rubbish. Jamie has been playing well and as far as I am concerned he is perfectly happy with us. I am determined to find out who wrote it and will be making several phone calls to get to the bottom of it.'

The Bournemouth manager's mood did not improve when chairman Jim Nolan suddenly resigned amid rumours that local businessman Derek Block was seeking to buy AFC Bournemouth and move the club to Poole, some seven miles from Dean Court. Block, who counted Poole Stadium among his portfolio, saw an opportunity to seize control of a club in an almost perpetual state of financial turmoil. Nolan's replacement Peter Hayward described Block's interest as 'wild and woolly talk', although he knew the Cherries' precarious position meant they were vulnerable to a hostile takeover. Redknapp, who had seen the opportunities created by the 1987 Third Division title triumph wither during a summer of boardroom upheaval at Dean Court, did not react well to the possibility of further off-the-field disruption. 'It's a load of rubbish; we don't want to move to Poole,' he began. 'Peter Hayward and Jim Nolan put their money up when no one else did to bring this football club back into the town. They brought the club back to the people who care about it, which is the most important thing to me. If the club moves to Poole, the first thing they can do is find themselves a new manager. I stayed here a year ago when I could have walked out and now I want some stability.'

Redknapp eased the club's money problems slightly when he sold midfielder Gavin Peacock to Newcastle United in exchange for £150,000 and utility player Wayne Fereday. Peacock had only missed two games all season prior to his departure and had regularly drawn praise from Redknapp for his performances and attitude, despite having made it clear that he was ready to move on. The midfield struggled following Peacock's departure, and in an attempt to kick-start their performances, Redknapp dropped his son Jamie to the substitutes' bench during a run of disappointing results. The decision did not have the desired effect, with Harry even saying, 'I don't know why I left my son Jamie out of the team. When he came on he showed he was a different class to anyone else on the pitch,' after a 5-0 drubbing at league leaders Grimsby Town.

Jamie was restored to the starting line-up for the trip to Chester City in the third round of the FA Cup and responded with a dominant display in a thrilling 3-2 win. It proved to be the young midfielder's final appearance in red and black. Five days later, on 10 January, it was confirmed that he was about to sign for Liverpool after months of speculation.

His father had hoped Jamie would at least see the season out at Dean Court, but the situation at the club demanded the player be sold. 'It will be a sad day for me to see him leave home and AFC Bournemouth,' said Harry, 'but it represents a smashing move for the kid. I am having to sell him because of the desperate financial plight of this club.'

'It was a good deal for Bournemouth,' recalls Redknapp. 'He was going to Tottenham as a schoolboy, but I brought him back because he wanted to play league football rather than play in the youth team with one of the other clubs. It all worked out well for everyone. It was a record price for a teenager at the time and it was good business for Bournemouth, so I think they were pleased.'

Jamie's transfer made headlines in the sports pages of the national newspapers. Speculation was rife about the size of the fee, with some reports going as high as £1 million. Understandably, this did little to calm his already emotional father. 'I am angry at some of the figures I have heard,' said Harry. 'It is the last thing Jamie needs at this point. Liverpool will pay us a straight fee of £350,000. There will be no instalments. People forget the kid is only 17; there is enough pressure on him.'

Harry joked in television interviews that his wife Sandra had refused to cook him dinner for a week after he revealed he was selling her son to a club over 250 miles away, although in truth the deal was not a surprise to Mrs Redknapp. 'Sandra knew what was going on,' says Harry. 'Kenny was ringing our house all the time. As soon as Jamie broke into the first team, Liverpool came in for him, but he didn't want to go. He didn't want to play in Liverpool's youth team or reserves. But I had Kenny Dalglish ringing me every single day wanting to buy him. In the end, Kenny said, "He will play." I said, "Kenny, he's only just 17; he's not going to get in Liverpool's first team." Kenny said, "He will. He will play." So Jamie signed.'

The strain of breaking up the family unit was also uppermost in Jamie's mind as he packed his bags for Anfield. 'We are very close and I will greatly miss my dad, mum and brother Mark,' he said. 'In the past I have been able to put all the speculation about my future to one side. But it suddenly got to me after Saturday's match against Chester and my decision to leave was made then.'

'I rate my dad Harry as the biggest influence on my career. Unfortunately, there were always going to be people who would say that whatever I achieved at Bournemouth happened simply because my dad was boss. Nothing could be further from the truth. The players always accepted me as one of the lads and allowed me to think only of football. At no point was there any talk of favouritism. I will miss everyone at the club and my friends in the area but they can feel sure that AFC Bournemouth will always be in my thoughts.'

Harry had stated that Jamie would play his last game for the Cherries against Bury that weekend, but it was no surprise to anyone when he was not even named as a substitute. Jamie did travel to Gigg Lane on his way to Anfield and found himself besieged by autograph hunters and press the moment he stepped off the coach.

After watching his now former team-mates see off the Shakers in an impressive 4-2 win, Jamie aired his mild disappointment at not being able to participate in the victory. 'It would have been nice to have played at Bury but I understand my dad's decision,' he said. 'I will work hard at Liverpool. It is a great opportunity for me.'

With the deal done, his father was somewhat more verbose, and he began by slamming press reports that deliberately misquoted Jamie's opinion of Merseyside as an undesirable place to live. 'I was disgusted by some of the things that were printed,' said Harry. 'Jamie is thrilled to be going to Liverpool. The fanatical support the club has and the incredible football knowledge of their supporters played a large part in his decision to sign. Jamie has the ability and character to succeed at Liverpool. I am just glad the speculation and rumours are now over and he can get back to playing football. Kenny Dalglish anticipates great things from him and I am confident Jamie won't let him down.'

When he finally secured Jamie's signature, Dalglish was keen to praise Harry's efforts in guiding his son to the top. 'Jamie is a credit to his mum and dad,' he said. 'We have the interests of everyone at heart at Anfield. We will do our best for him and hope he is as successful as he wants to be. He is a credit to Bournemouth.'

With her son moving so far away, Sandra Redknapp was understandably concerned for his wellbeing. 'It was very emotional when Jamie left,' she said. 'We are a very close family. You think part of your life is gone and things will never be the same again. But I feel a lot better now I have seen where he is staying. His digs are like a home from home. If Jamie's happy, I'm happy.'

With Kenny Dalglish demonstrating such warmth towards the Cherries in general and the Redknapps in particular, Harry took full advantage and signed Liverpool's reserve centre-half Alex Watson immediately after Jamie had gone in the other direction. The fee for Watson was quoted as £100,000, although it was made clear that Redknapp had gained permission from Bournemouth chairman Peter Hayward to dip into the £350,000 the club had received for his son.

With six-figure fees suddenly becoming part of the conversation around the club, the Dean Court faithful awaited the inevitable news of further financial difficulties. They did not have to wait long, as the ink was barely dry on Watson's contract when Hayward revealed that Bournemouth had recorded an annual loss of over £840,000. Hayward was quoting from the club's annual accounts, a document which also showed that the highest paid employee at Dean Court, presumably Redknapp himself, was taking home an annual salary of around £70,000. Despite this figure, Hayward declared himself very satisfied with his manager's performance. 'I can't think of a better manager for the club at a time like this than Harry Redknapp. His record on transfer dealings is remarkable and he is very important to us. Harry will continue to wheel and deal like he always does.'

Bournemouth's recent run of impressive league form continued after Jamie's departure, with the Cherries beating Brentford 2-0 in their next league game. With the team pushing up the table and an FA Cup fourth round tie against south coast neighbours Portsmouth to look forward to, Redknapp took time out of his schedule to discuss his success as a manager. 'It's difficult to put your finger on it,' he began. 'You have to be a good judge of a player. We have all made mistakes in this area, but I like to think I have more often made the right choice. You can be the best coach in the world, but if you sign bad players you will never get success. You have to know a lot of people in the game. I get on well with 99% of managers and they know if they are fair with me I will be fair with them. But I don't forget the ones who take liberties.'

Within the dressing room, Redknapp sought to set a light but professional tone. 'I believe there should be a good atmosphere in the club,' he said. 'I want my players coming into the ground with a smile and to enjoy training. I ask them to call me Harry and not boss. But while essentially there is a relaxed atmosphere, they know if they take a liberty, I will hammer them. I have a wicked tongue and a fierce temper. I've been fortunate in that since I became manager I've never really had a serious problem with a player. There might have been the odd minor problem, but on the whole the players here have been a real credit. They generally behave themselves.'

Although he had a lifestyle and income that were beyond the vast majority of the Cherries' supporters, Harry was keen to remain a man of the people. 'I've never tried to put myself above anybody,' he said. 'There's no airs and graces with me. The fans are just as important to this club as me or anyone else.'

Despite his desire to create an informal environment around Dean Court, Redknapp drew the line at socialising with his squad. 'Things could be said that could cause aggro,' he said, presumably referring to the loosening of tongues that can occur after a few cold drinks. 'If I am not at work, I spend my time at home.'

When he was at work, he maintained total control over team affairs, with the prospect of interference from directors an anathema. 'If that happened I'd pack the job in,' he said. 'No director has second-guessed me or questioned any of my team selections. In the best way they can, they are very supportive.'

Following a 5-1 defeat at Portsmouth in the FA Cup fourth round, Harry became increasingly frustrated with the inability of his squad to sustain a run of positive results. He elected to point the finger at the standard of refereeing in the league as a reason for this patchy form. 'Referees are not interpreting the rules properly,' he said as the winter months drew to a close. 'Some care, some don't. I have the greatest respect for the man in the middle as he has the hardest job in the world. But at the end of the day we are out to entertain supporters, not ruin the game. You go into their dressing room before a match and some refs come across as dictators. In no uncertain terms they lay down the law and remind you they are in charge. What's going on just now is diabolical. Players are frightened to tackle. And you can't talk back to the majority of referees. In my playing days referees had much more common sense.'

When Bournemouth backed up a 3-1 victory at Stoke with a 1-0 win over Chester on Redknapp's 44th birthday at the beginning of March, supporters hoped that springtime would see the Cherries back in the battle for the play-off places. But a calamitous 3-0 reverse at home to Wigan followed, leading Harry to redirect his ire from the match officials to the club's own fans. In the 42nd minute of the match, with Bournemouth already 2-0 down, Luther Blissett missed a penalty he had won after a clumsy challenge by Latics midfielder Kevin Langley. It was an error that saw the home side booed from the field of play at half-time, a chorus of disapproval that did not impress Redknapp. 'They were well out of order,' he said. 'The players came off after giving their all in the first half, yet they were getting stick. What they needed was encouragement, not abuse.'

There should be no real surprise that following the horrendous few months he had endured since the end of the previous season and the difficult working conditions he was striving to build another successful team within, that the pressure would start to show with Redknapp. Kenny Dalglish, who had relentlessly pursued Jamie's signature, stunned football followers when he resigned as Liverpool manager less than six weeks after he had secured the transfer of the young midfielder, citing stress as the reason for his surprise departure. Dalglish had dealt with even greater trauma than Redknapp, with the Heysel and Hillsborough disasters fresh in his memory, and the Bournemouth manager did not find it difficult to empathise with his counterpart. 'Management certainly doesn't do anything for your health,' admitted Harry. 'After the recent defeat to Birmingham, I suffered for days. It was as if someone close in my family had died. I didn't want to talk to anyone. I felt awful. To go through what you do in management can be sheer torture. I very rarely have a lunch break and I've known days when all I've had to eat is a slice of toast because I have been on the go so much.'

Redknapp had had little trouble overcoming the lack of transfer funds throughout his years as Bournemouth manager, and again made light of the club's plight when he re-signed winger Richard Cooke on a free transfer in the days leading up to transfer deadline day. It was a signing which immediately paid off, with Cooke terrorising top-of-the-table Grimsby Town in his first match back in the side, inspiring the Cherries to a surprise 2-1 victory. It was to be the end of Bournemouth's run of positive results, with a frustrating 2-0 reverse at Leyton Orient following four days later.

Soon after the defeat at Brisbane Road, the Football Association announced plans to form a new top division in English football, which would be known as the Premier League. This sea change in the game, which would break up the Football League after 104 years, was sold to the public as a boost for the England team, with the potential financial windfall for all those involved presented as a secondary benefit. Still somewhat giddy from England's run to the semi-finals of the World Cup a year earlier, resistance from supporters to the change was insignificant. Redknapp was not so easily fooled. 'I can't accept all this talk about the Premier League being planned to benefit players and the England international scene,' he said. 'It is solely about money.'

With seven games remaining until the end of the season, Redknapp remained optimistic his side would be in contention for promotion. 'I believe 14 points will be at least enough for a play-off place. Four victories from our remaining home games and a win or two draws from our three away matches should clinch it.' This sequence of games began brightly, with Richard Cooke again starring as the Cherries beat Bolton Wanderers 1-0. Three days later, the plan to record three points in each home game was in tatters as Cambridge brought their direct approach to Dean Court and left with a 1-0 win. The U's were managed by former Redknapp favourite John Beck, but that did not prevent the Bournemouth manager from laying into the visiting team's style of play. 'The Cambridge style is sad for the game and I detest it,' he said. 'They are killing the skill factor in football. My fear is that their success will encourage a lot more sides to adopt a high-ball system. That would be disastrous for football in this country. Skill will always win in the end.'

Having got the play-off push somewhat back on track after a Luther Blissett brace gave the Cherries a win at Crewe in their next fixture, Redknapp had an almost immediate opportunity to prove that his favoured brand of passing football held the moral high ground when a visit to Cambridge's Abbey Stadium followed just eight days after the defeat to John Beck's side at Dean Court. However, in a fixture rearranged after a postponement earlier in the season, former Cherries striker Steve Claridge scored twice as United overpowered Bournemouth to cruise to a 4-0 triumph. After such a thumping defeat, Harry knew better than to add to his tirade regarding the U's style of play, limiting his comments to,

'Cambridge were superb and if they continue to play like that they will be promoted as champions.'

Bournemouth looked unlikely to be promoted through any of the available avenues. However, a win and a draw in their final two home games against Huddersfield and Preston respectively meant that, with other results going their way, the Cherries were still in with a shout of the play-offs going into the final game of the season at Shrewsbury. A 3-1 defeat followed, confirming the Cherries would be spending at least another season in the Third Division. After praising the support shown by the 2,000 travelling fans, Redknapp took his squad to task. 'Our players have got to realise what it takes to win things,' he said. 'And some of them have got to learn what this game is about.'

Days after the season had come to an end, chairman Peter Hayward spelled out the reality of another year in the third tier. 'It is now inevitable we will have to sell players,' said Hayward. 'Harry is also going to have to offload highly paid players. I have been speaking to him about this problem since the day I became chairman. He understands the position. I am tied by contracts negotiated in the past. The wage bill is my prime target in my efforts to reduce our debt.'

Gerry Peyton and Luther Blissett, perhaps the two most important players in Redknapp's side, were soon on their way out of Dean Court. Harry himself could have followed them through the exit, as he was offered the manager's job at Stoke City and heavily linked with a move to Bournemouth's neighbours Southampton. Despite saying, 'Whoever gets the Southampton job will be one of the luckiest men in football,' Redknapp reiterated his commitment to AFC Bournemouth, repeating his position that only a 'special offer' would tempt him to move on.

Chapter Sixteen

All Played Out

1991/92

WITH the Cherries' financial situation in a seemingly perpetual state of disarray, it was business as usual in the transfer market, with the club forced to sell its best players during the close season. As well as the departures of Luther Blissett and Gerry Peyton, Shaun Teale signed for First Division Aston Villa in a deal worth up to £500,000. Harry, however, was not overjoyed at losing his best defender. 'We only sold Shaun because the bank manager insisted we had to sell and Shaun was our most valuable player,' the Bournemouth manager told a pre-season fans' forum held at the Dean Court supporters' club.

Some of the money raised from the departures was used to lure Jimmy Case from Southampton and West Ham striker Jimmy Quinn to Bournemouth. Peyton was replaced by Vince Bartram from Wolves and defender Mark Morris arrived from Sheffield United for £95,000.

The signing of three-time European Cup winner Case remains particularly fresh in Harry's memory. 'Jimmy Case was a great lad,' he says. 'I met him at the services. I was sitting watching the local news when it came on: "Newsflash, Southampton have just released Jimmy Case." They had not offered him a new contract. I got straight on the phone, found Jimmy's number, rang him up, met him at Rownhams Services on the M27 and had a cup of tea. I said, "I'd love you to come to Bournemouth, Jim." He said, "Well, I'm interested Harry. What's your best offer?" I told him and it wasn't particularly big money or anything, and he said, "That's your best offer?" I said, "Yeah Jimmy, it is." He said, "All right, I'll sign." So I said, "Brilliant, Jim. Can you come to the ground now so we can get it done? In case somebody else comes in, as you're going to get plenty of offers." He said, "No. I've given you my word, I don't care who comes in. If Arsenal comes in, I ain't going." So we shook hands and that was it. Jimmy was just a great guy.'

After taking charge of his first pre-season for two years, Redknapp was characteristically optimistic on the eve of the new campaign's opening fixture at home to Darlington. 'There is a buzz about the place and hopefully we can get off to a good start,' he said. 'The ground has been given a new look and so has the team. I have a squad full of winners who know what it is like to taste success and believe me, they want to celebrate again.'

Celebrations seemed some way off when Darlington staged a smash and grab raid to win 2-1, scoring with their only two shots on goal. 'At half-time,' said a bewildered Redknapp, 'we were convinced they would never score.'

Defeat at Cardiff in the first leg of the opening round of the Rumbelows Cup was followed by a creditable draw at Stoke. Before the match at the Victoria Ground, it emerged that Redknapp had resisted the overtures of the Potteries club during the close season. 'Their chairman made me a very good offer,' he revealed. 'But although I was impressed with what he said, I decided my future was at Dean Court.'

Whilst endeavouring to unlock the potential he seemed sure his squad possessed, Harry was also required to defend his family in public. Jamie, who had begun his first full season with Liverpool, was reported to be unhappy at Anfield due to a lack of first-team opportunities. 'It's a diabolical report and totally untrue,' raged his father. 'Everyone seems to be jumping to conclusions because he isn't featuring in the team news. He loves Liverpool and is happy there.'

In fact, Jamie was struggling with life under Graeme Souness who had yet to grant the 18-year-old his first-team debut. Harry may have vehemently denied it at the time to protect his son, but in his autobiography he describes in some detail how, upon visiting Jamie at his digs in Liverpool, the young midfielder broke down in despair at being ignored by Souness.

Prior to the trip to Ayresome Park to face Middlesbrough in the second round of the Rumbelows Cup, further details emerged of the growing financial crisis at Dean Court. The overdraft with Lloyds Bank had reportedly risen to £2.4 million, with interest payments of £5,000 per week. With the future of the Cherries appearing to be once again on the line, the Bournemouth manager was prepared to go to extreme lengths to keep the club afloat. 'I would beg, borrow or steal to keep AFC Bournemouth going,' he said. 'This club means too much to me. I have been thinking for a while about becoming financially involved in the club. I am not prepared to let this club go under.'

This was fighting talk from a man who was still some way short of the millions he would go on to accrue when managing in the Premier League. As part of their reporting of the economic chaos at Dean Court, the *Evening Echo* revealed that Redknapp was earning £65,000 a year, an unusual step at the time and one which drew an apology from the paper after Redknapp had registered a complaint about the invasion of his privacy.

Whatever he was earning, Harry had long since learnt to build a squad with little or no transfer kitty and was under no illusions about the almost non-existent possibility of hanging on to his best players. 'I honestly don't think our present financial situation is any worse than it has been in recent seasons,' he said. 'I have always had to buy cheaply and sell big. It will always be like that. I don't think the fans are interested in who owns the club. It is the team and the results they are interested in. I supported Arsenal as a boy, home and away, and I couldn't tell you who owned the club but I could tell you who was playing inside-left or up front.'

At the 11th hour, board member Norman Hayward, who had once been a member of the Cherries' reserve team, purchased Peter Hayward's majority shareholding for a reported £500,000. The immediate future of the club was secure, but debts of almost £2 million remained. 'We have got a target we must reach by the end of the season,' said Norman Hayward, 'and we have got to hit it before we can continue the road to recovery.'

The new owner and chairman did not elaborate any further on how much money the club needed to raise, but exiting the Rumbelows Cup following defeat in the second leg to Middlesbrough cannot have added to his confidence that the necessary finance would be forthcoming. Bournemouth lost 2-1 after extra time at Dean Court, with young defender Keith Rowland conceding the decisive penalty in the 118th minute.

A 2-0 win over Hartlepool the following weekend saw Redknapp's side keep a fifth clean sheet in a row in the Third Division, an impressive record made more so by the fact that Redknapp had been without injured defensive stalwarts Paul Morrell and John Williams throughout. Unfortunately, solidity at the back appeared to be taking its toll on goalscoring. When Bournemouth drew 1-1 with Leyton Orient in their next match, it was a seventh draw in 12 league games. The appearance of Andy Jones on the O's team sheet provided one explanation for the lack of punch in attack. Jones had been sold to the Brisbane Road club a fortnight earlier for £80,000 amid the financial chaos and rumours of a falling-out with Redknapp. The Bournemouth manager denied the rift, although Jones stated in the match programme with regard to leaving Dean Court that 'nothing was further from my mind'.

On 23 October, Jamie Redknapp finally made his debut for Liverpool in the second round of the UEFA Cup at Auxerre in the Burgundy region of France. Graeme Souness was forced to call upon the 18-year-old due to injuries and the UEFA stipulation that only four non-English players could feature in the 16-man squad.

Jamie's progress at Anfield had been hampered by a hernia operation, but that did not prevent newspapers from speculating on his future at Liverpool in the 18 months since his arrival. 'I was furious with some of the reports,' said his father. 'There was talk of him being out of favour with the new management and even going to West Ham United. Jamie was off the scene only because of injury. I was extremely concerned how the rumours would affect him. He has since returned to fitness and played well for the reserves. I would be bursting with pride if Jamie played tonight, but I am just happy he is in the squad.'

Emotional scenes may have ensued in the Redknapp household as Jamie started in midfield in a game broadcast live on television. Liverpool lost 2-0, with Jamie featuring for 79 minutes until cramp saw him replaced by Mike Marsh. It was a steady but unspectacular debut for Redknapp junior, but that was more than enough for Harry. 'I felt nervous watching him,' he said. 'He's only 18 but there he was playing in Europe. I would have been the first to say if he hadn't played well, but his general play was excellent.'

After beating Stockport at Dean Court, Redknapp may have thought things were looking up in his day job, but consecutive defeats to relegation candidates Torquay and Swansea in the space of two days in early November rendered the enraged Bournemouth manager unable to speak to the press after the games.

In both of these confidence-crushing matches, Redknapp was able to field new signing Paul Wood. After a successful loan spell at Dean Court and a protracted transfer saga which stalled more than once over the winger's personal terms, Harry eventually sealed a deal with Sheffield United for £40,000. Soon after Wood signed permanently, supporters' questions about where the money to buy him had come from were answered when it was revealed that wealthy Cherries fan Ken Gardiner had paid the entire fee from his own pocket.

This extremely generous donation saw Redknapp heap praise on Gardiner. 'It was an unbelievable gesture from Ken,' he said. 'It is the first time anything like that has happened in my time at the club. I've known Ken as a friend for the best part of 15 years. He has been a tremendous supporter of this club.' This friendship, which appears to have solely revolved around AFC Bournemouth, was not destined to last much longer. By the season's end, Redknapp and Gardiner would have fallen out in dramatic fashion.

Victory over non-league Bromsgrove Rovers in the FA Cup and a 0-0 draw at home to Brentford proved to be the start of a mini-revival on the pitch as the Cherries won four of their next five games in all competitions.

Although Redknapp was prioritising the league in public, he knew that a decent run in the FA Cup could provide a potentially lifesaving boost to income. In the second round, the Cherries again hosted Third Division leaders Brentford. A last-gasp goal from Jimmy Quinn handed Bournemouth a 2-1 victory and set up a potentially lucrative home tie against Newcastle United in the third round. 'It is a massive boost for our morale and our finances,' said owner Norman Hayward. 'I was very proud of the players. They worked so hard.'

Harry's day became even sweeter when he learnt that Jamie had scored Liverpool's equaliser in a 1-1 draw at Southampton on his First Division debut. 'My family deserted me to watch Jamie at The Dell,' said the proud father. 'My wife Sandra never goes to games but she went along to watch. My dad also decided to desert me for Southampton. Obviously Jamie is more important to him than I am. My elder son Mark had the day off work so he went along to The Dell as well. It must have been wonderful to see Jamie score.'

With most of the headlines coming out of Dean Court focusing on money problems, Harry had increasingly come under criticism by some fans for the alleged size of his pay packet. Before the Cherries faced Birmingham in mid-December, another story emerged regarding the Bournemouth manager's remuneration which may have given his critics cause to reconsider. Redknapp had refused to draw his salary since the start of the season, forgoing an estimated £20,000 in wages in order to ease the strain on the club's threadbare purse strings.

'I don't want to make a big thing out of this,' said the Bournemouth manager. 'It's true that I've decided to work without pay, but I'm doing it because I want this club to survive. Everyone at AFC Bournemouth must do something to help the club survive and this is my way of doing so. I have an understanding with the club that when the situation improves I will get the money that I am owed. I love this football club and will do just about anything to keep it alive.'

After not making a big thing of his wage sacrifice, Harry had words of reassurance for his legion of supporters at Dean Court following numerous approaches from other clubs for his services. 'I can't see myself leaving this club,' he said. 'The fans have been too good to me.'

The breakaway of First Division sides to form what would become the Premier League loomed large over clubs like Bournemouth with the very real possibility that the income they would receive from broadcast rights would drop significantly. However, a lifetime in the Football League blinkered Redknapp's view of what the new top tier would mean for the English game. 'I don't for a minute believe this new Super League will change anything. I can't see any difference between it and the First Division,' he said before railing against the appointment of management consultant Rick Parry and Barclays

Bank chairman Sir John Quinton to head up the new division. 'Who are these people? What do they know about the game?' raged Redknapp before recommending a few appointments of his own. 'Instead of people like Bobby Moore and Bobby Charlton, two of the greatest names in world football, we have got a nobody like Parry who has played hockey most of his life.'

Subsequent events did not suggest that Redknapp's pessimism over the establishment of the Premier League was entirely justified, although he did see through the proffered rationale that it would provide a boost for the national side for the fallacy it turned out to be. 'Frankly, this Super League is all about money and nothing else,' he said. 'Forget any talk about it helping to improve England's international chances or improving facilities for the fans.'

Not content with giving the concept of the Premier League short shrift, Harry went on to share his dim view of the role club chairmen played in the game he loved. 'There are some chairmen who have been in the game two, three years who know nothing about football,' he began. 'They have probably never kicked a ball or been to a game and yet they are involved in the running of football. Most chairmen see results, they don't see football. They don't understand how in the long term they are doing damage to the greatest game in the world.'

When it came to matters on the pitch, Redknapp was more than happy to outline the roots of his philosophy. 'Certain teams might be successful with their long-ball tactics, but I hate their use of the game,' he said. 'I will believe it should be a game of skill until the day I die. The way I look at it, players have got all day to work on their skills. They should be able to pass the ball from A to B no problem. In every player there is a footballer waiting to come out. A man working for Ford knows how to change spark plugs. Why shouldn't footballers know the basics of their job too?'

Harry was also ready to air his views on the work of the judiciary. Just before the festive fixtures kicked off, ten Leeds fans were convicted of offences committed during the May Day Bank Holiday riots during the previous year. The maximum sentence handed out by Judge Maclaren Webster QC was 16 months in prison, but most of the convicts were released on probation or given community service orders. Redknapp, who had hitherto given no indication of familiarity with criminal law, would have gone much further. 'We need stiffer sentences all round for people who commit crimes. I've got no time for people who do things like that,' said the Cherries' boss, who gave little consideration to criticism of the Football League for not rescheduling the match. 'It was a bad fixture but it wasn't the Football League who were throwing bricks and beating up police. Those people involved in the trouble are animals, morons and the scum of the earth. There is no place for them in our society. I pray it will never happen again.'

The FA Cup third-round tie against Newcastle attracted 10,651 fans to Dean Court, providing a timely boost for the club's finances which were now on life support. Between Christmas and New Year, further revelations came to light that had chairman Norman Hayward pleading with the supporters to dig deep into their pockets to keep the club alive. 'We need your help or this club will go down,' he said. 'We need £50,000 now to keep the club going. I cannot imagine this town without a Football League club. AFC Bournemouth has inspired and entertained so many people. For the sake of our special supporters we must save the club. If the worst happens I don't want people wishing six months or a year from now that they had done something to help.'

Redknapp, whose acumen in the transfer market had kept the Dean Court coffers topped up time and again during his tenure, was faced with the distinct possibility of having to sell more of his squad. 'As the chairman says, if we don't get some money in the club will fold,' he said. 'It's always a fear having to sell your top players, but I have got to get some money in – it's obvious.'

Desperate times called for desperate measures and as well as player sales, the fundraising lottery Cherry Aid was launched and car boot sales and sponsored walks organised. Prior to kick-off in the Newcastle tie, doubtless at the behest of Hayward and his fellow directors, Redknapp took to the microphone to plead with fans for further donations. 'If we can all pull together we can save this club,' he said to applause from the terraces. 'Please fill in the Cherry Aid forms being handed out. Things are tough, but with your support, we can turn it around.'

Duty done, Harry returned to the dugout to watch his side have the better of a goalless draw against Ossie Ardiles's team. Bournemouth claimed they should have been awarded a penalty after Paul Wood was fouled in the second half, but Hayward and Lloyds Bank would have been delighted with the prospect of a further cash injection from the replay to sustain the club in the short term.

The replay at St James' Park offered a potential £60,000 windfall for the club to add to the £50,000 made from the original tie. Chief executive Brian Wells also saw the chance to raise more funds by chartering a 94-seat aeroplane for the team to fly to the north-east and then charging willing supporters to join them. Among those snapping up the £144 return flight tickets were three 15-year-old boys from Bournemouth, who paid their fares with the proceeds from their paper rounds.

Sadly for them, the countless early mornings proved in vain when thick fog from the River Tyne saw referee Vic Callow postpone the replay just 17 minutes after the kick-off. This was a bitter blow for all of the travelling fans, some of whom were making an 18-hour trip by car, but it was the answer to the club's financial prayers as far as Norman Hayward was concerned. Another £30,000 was banked from the postponed fixture and the rearranged replay offered a sizeable sum which would go some distance to seeing the Cherries through to the end of the season.

Following a thumping 3-0 win over Wigan Athletic at Dean Court, the plane was chartered for a second time, with tickets costing £90 on this occasion. One of the passengers on the plane was BBC commentator Tony Gubba, who along with his camera crew accompanied the Cherries to the north-east in preparation for a highlights package to be shown later the same night.

Gubba and his colleagues were not the only additions to the travelling party. As Redknapp recalls, the intervention of one of the biggest names in British sport saw one of the young supporters boarding the plane with his heroes. 'Ian Botham was training with us at that time,' explains Harry. 'He was in pantomime in Bournemouth and he came and trained with us for about 12 weeks. He was fantastic. There was this young lad and he had saved all his paper round money up so he could go up to the Newcastle game, but it got called off in the first half, so Ian paid for him to fly up with the team to the rearranged tie. I thought that was great of him.'

Gavin Peacock, who had been in Redknapp's starting eleven when Bournemouth beat the Magpies two years earlier, gave Newcastle an early lead on the night, but Paul Wood drew the Cherries level in the dying minutes of normal time. Newcastle scored a second goal almost as soon as extra time kicked off but Kevin Bond calmly equalised to send the tie to penalties. For over 100 years, FA Cup ties had been played to a finish with multiple replays not unusual. Security concerns, fixture congestion and player fatigue saw that tradition end in 1991 and the shoot-out at St James' Park was only the second in the competition's entire history.

Jimmy Quinn, Denny Mundee, Richard Cooke and Shaun Brooks all scored from the spot, but the hero on the night was goalkeeper Vince Bartram who, after Liam O'Brien had sent his effort over the bar, saved from Kevin Brock to send the Cherries through to the fourth round. 'It is easily the greatest moment of my career,' said the 23-year-old goalkeeper. 'I practised penalties in training before the match and I didn't save one.'

Redknapp, who was interviewed wearing nothing but a towel after the match, was equally delighted, although he had some sympathy for the home team. 'What an exciting game and what a way to finish,' he said. 'But penalties are a bad way to finish a game. There has to be a better method. If there is the need for another replay then so be it. Naturally it's great to win a shoot-out, but it's a horrible feeling for the other team.'

As well as their share of the gate receipts from the crowd of 26,954, the Cherries also garnered welcome payments from the BBC and Sky, although the figures would only make a small dent in the club's debt. However, coupled with the money the club would receive from a fourth-round tie at Ipswich, it was the lifeline the club so desperately needed. 'A club like ours in deep trouble needs every payday it can get,' said Norman Hayward as he poured the champagne in the away dressing room at St James' Park. 'This is just the boost we need. The money should see us through the season.'

The tie at Portman Road was scheduled to be played on the Saturday following the win against Newcastle, but a frozen pitch brought another postponement, this time before Bournemouth fans had set off from Dean Court. An extra week's rest to recover from the extra time did not do Redknapp's side any favours as they went down 3-0 at Portman Road after Denny Mundee was sent off for a professional foul on future Arsenal striker Chris Kiwomya.

The defeat was a double disappointment for Harry, as going into the contest he knew that a win for his side would set up a meeting with son Jamie's Liverpool and another valuable payday. 'It's disappointing to go out of the cup,' he said before finding the silver lining. 'But we enjoyed great support and the club has done very well financially out of the competition.'

Bournemouth missed out on another chance to boost the coffers when they were knocked out of the Autoglass Trophy by Wrexham, but three straight wins in the league has Cherries supporters on the terraces singing 'Going up' as their team climbed the table. Striker

Efan Ekoku rediscovering his scoring touch after a year without a goal was another welcome development on the field of play, but it came at a price. Bournemouth had agreed to pay his former club Sutton United another £20,000 upon the forward making 40 appearances for the Cherries, although this was ultimately renegotiated to a 'take it or leave it' £10,000.

Prior to a 3-0 victory at Exeter, club stalwart John Kirk announced his intention to retire at the end of the season. Kirk was 63 at the time and had served under a succession of Bournemouth managers as trainer and physio for 30 years and had known Redknapp since the 24-year-old winger first arrived at the club from West Ham in 1972. 'When he was a player, I must admit I didn't see managerial quality in him,' said the former Bolton goalkeeper. 'I changed my mind after I saw him coach. Harry is a very deep thinker and is his own man. He has always been a jovial character to me. I had great days when John Bond was manager, but to be honest, I have only ever felt real elation with Harry as boss.'

A run of positive results saw the Cherries go into April in fifth place in the Third Division table. Unfortunately, with a prize of promotion that could potentially secure the club's future at stake, Bournemouth's form began to stutter during the run-in to the end of the season.

After a win at Shrewsbury followed a 2-0 defeat at Peterborough, Bournemouth were in sixth place and faced seventh-placed Huddersfield Town in the next match at Dean Court. The Terriers had won each of their last four games to race up the table and gave the Cherries a tough examination in a 1-1 draw on a rain-drenched night in Dorset.

Top scorer Jimmy Quinn was absent from the game against the Leeds Road side, but returned to face Fulham at Craven Cottage the following week. His presence did not have the required effect, however, as Bournemouth went down 2-0, a result that dealt a severe blow to their play-off hopes. Redknapp knew his team couldn't afford to slip up again, but refused to throw in the towel. 'Nothing is settled yet,' he said. 'We still have two games left and there is everything to play for. I don't think we are dead yet.'

Automatic promotion had fallen by the wayside some weeks previously. Although Harry would have preferred to go straight up rather than battle it out in the play-offs, he supported the introduction of the end-of-season knockout format. 'They do nothing for my heart,' he said, 'but I think the play-offs are brilliant. They keep the season alive until the last day. If it hadn't been for them our season would be over.'

The final home game of the season saw long-time rivals Reading provide the opposition at Dean Court. Despite the relatively close proximity of the two clubs, the attendance was almost 1,200 short of the previous home game due to local non-league side Wimborne Town appearing in the FA Vase Final on the same day. Wimborne went on to win the trophy with a 5-3 victory over Guiseley Town, but those who chose to remain on the south coast to watch the Cherries were not to regret their decision.

In a thrilling match which saw the Royals equalise in the 86th minute, Bournemouth saw their play-off hopes continue into the final week of the season after Jimmy Quinn slotted home a penalty with the very last kick of the game to claim a 3-2 victory. It was a goal that induced an immediate pitch invasion, with referee Colin Trussell blowing for full time as he ran towards the tunnel. However, the joy of the home fans was not reflected backstage at Dean Court after the match.

After emerging from the dressing room to report back to the directors in the boardroom, Redknapp had to be pulled off Ken Gardiner when he took his 'friend' by the throat. In his autobiography Harry claims that the catalyst for this moment of rage was a derogatory comment Gardiner made about the late Brian Tiler. Commenting on the skirmish, Redknapp makes it clear his praise for Gardiner following the Paul Wood transfer was not entirely sincere. 'Ken said something stupid about Brian and we had a fall-out,' says Harry. 'He was a bit of a snob. Called people by their surnames; wasn't for me really.'

Harry identifies this confrontation as the point at which he decided his future lay elsewhere. There is no excuse for attempting to strangle one's colleagues, but it is easy to imagine that upon returning home that evening, Redknapp's emotional state would have been such that leaving Dean Court would have appeared a genuine option.

The mood of the Bournemouth manager and that around the club did not improve when the Cherries and several hundred hardy supporters made the journey to the north-east to face Hartlepool on the final day of the season. A win for Bournemouth, coupled with favourable results elsewhere in the Third Division, would see them sneak into the play-offs.

With the game remaining goalless as the second half wore on, Harry instructed his side to go into all-out attack for the win. It was to no avail as Hartlepool, with an 18-year-old Steve Fletcher up front, won the game in injury time with a goal from Lenny Johnrose. With the very existence of the club still in significant doubt, it was another low point for the Cherries and Redknapp after the glory years of the late 1980s.

As he made the long journey south after seeing his team finish the season in eighth place, Redknapp knew if he remained at Dean Court, management was unlikely to get any easier. The financial malaise showed no signs of abating, with even the board's prudent decision to take out insurance against paying promotion bonuses to the playing squad almost backfiring to the tune of £100,000 when London-based Continental Assurance went into liquidation.

'The hardest part is still to come for me,' said Harry, in reference to the decisions he had to make on 12 out-of-contract players, including Jimmy Case, Kevin Bond and Sean O'Driscoll. 'There are tough decisions to be made. We are in a desperate position.'

As well as this dilemma, Redknapp said he had 'a million and one' other problems to deal with at the club, but took umbrage at the suggestion that he might not have the stomach for another season in the hot seat. 'Lack of motivation?' he railed. 'Let me tell you, there is no one more motivated, desperate even, to bring success to this club than me. In fact, my desire is so strong that it almost ruins my life at times. I am like a zombie on a Saturday night if the team has not won. Even my wife Sandra can't lift me. I feel so disappointed. It hurts me too much. I take things too personally. But that is the way I am. I can't do much about it. This football club is my life. No other club interests me and that is the truth.'

In passionate mood, Redknapp went on to praise the club and its supporters. 'The fans have been absolutely magnificent,' he gushed. 'No manager has a better relationship with the supporters. The club has got to survive. It's bigger than me or any player. I have had to sell some good players in the past to help the club stay alive. I didn't want to lose Gavin Peacock, Ian Bishop, Shaun Teale or my own son Jamie. It has always been the case that we have had to sell to survive. This summer will be no different.'

Sean O'Driscoll had made 437 appearances for Bournemouth since Redknapp had signed him from Fulham for just £5,000 in 1984. The prospect of handing the energetic midfielder a free transfer did not fill the Bournemouth manager with joy. 'I felt sick at the thought of letting Sean go,' said Redknapp. 'I have been dreading for the last week having to give him the news. These are very difficult times for the club. I have got to make decisions I don't like. I have no choice.'

Jimmy Case and Player of the Year Kevin Bond followed O'Driscoll out of the Dean Court exit. Both were keen to stay but understood the situation at the club was grave. As he departed, Case, who had played under both Bill Shankly and Bob Paisley at Liverpool, heaped praise on Redknapp. 'It was a delight to work with Harry,' said the three-time European Cup winner. 'You always know where you stand with him. He never holds a grudge and he has a superb footballing brain. I learnt a lot from him.'

By the end of May, Bournemouth had just 16 senior professionals on their books and no funds available to bolster this paper-thin squad. Despite his determination to continue to manage the club, whispers continued to be heard around Dean Court that Redknapp had had enough of the constant struggle to make ends meet and of his fractious relationship with some on the board of directors.

On Tuesday 9 June, Cherries' supporters woke to the news that Harry Redknapp had resigned as Bournemouth manager. It was a decision that left many shocked and surprised, although considering the turmoil the club had been in since relegation two years previously, and the impact of the tragic car accident in Italy, perhaps the biggest surprise was that it had not come sooner.

Majority shareholder Norman Hayward and vice-chairman Brian Willis pleaded with Harry to change his mind, but he was not for turning. 'I believe my decision is the right one,' said the 45-year-old Redknapp. 'After nine years in charge, that is a long time by anyone's standards. I feel I need a change and a new challenge. I am also convinced that the club will benefit from having a fresh face. This is purely a personal decision and I must stress there is no question of any other issue forcing me into this situation.'

The entire Redknapp family gathered at Harry's side, with Mark still living at home and Jamie visiting the family at Whitfield Park in Ashley Heath. As he has consistently done throughout his career in management, Redknapp was able to draw on his rock-solid marriage to sustain him in challenging times. 'Sandra told me if it made me happy to quit then she would be happy too,' he said, before describing the emotional wrench of leaving Dean Court. 'Although I believe a change will do everyone good, it goes without saying that it is still a sad day for me. This club will always have a special place in my heart and I will always have a keen interest in what happens here. I have no immediate plans to leave the area. I don't know what the future holds, but if the club needs me then all they have to do is lift the phone.'

Redknapp received unqualified public support from Sandra. 'It was Harry's decision,' she said. 'I would never stand in his way or interfere.'

Aside from his family, football was Redknapp's happiness. He was rapidly linked with management roles in Turkey and South Africa but immediately ruled them out, saying, 'I couldn't see myself going out there. I've got my sons Mark and Jamie here and it would have been too far away. We are too close as a family.'

Sean O'Driscoll, who had been one of Redknapp's first signings upon taking the reins at Dean Court, could see that his manager was struggling to maintain his enthusiasm for the job as the season wore on. 'I spoke to Harry at the end of the season and he was down then. I was not stunned by the news. For the first time he has put health and happiness before football.'

The clamour for specific reasons for Redknapp's departure did not produce any results, leaving many supporters bewildered as to what had led to his decision to resign. Despite this lack of clarity, it is fair to suggest that stress and fatigue were significant factors. Upon breaking the story of his decision, the *Bournemouth Evening Echo* ran a photo of a disconsolate Redknapp taken after the 2-0 defeat to Fulham at Craven Cottage in April, an image that led the now ex-Bournemouth manager to consider his position. 'I couldn't believe how I looked,' he said. 'It did make me wonder. I have no idea what the future holds for me. The important thing for me just now is to have a complete break from football, but who can tell what is likely to happen in the near future?'

The news of Redknapp's departure drew comment from many of his associates in the game and they were overwhelmingly positive. Jimmy Gabriel, who had played and coached with Harry at Dean Court, said, 'Harry did a superb job at AFC Bournemouth and I had some marvellous times with him while I was his assistant.

The club had no real direction or purpose before Harry arrived as manager. Harry turned things around completely. He used his wits and natural talent to talk people round and get them interested in the club. He could be abrasive at times, but that was because he was so desperate for the club to be successful. Harry put Bournemouth on the map.'

Upon informing the board of directors of his desire to leave, Redknapp recommended Tony Pulis as the man to replace him, a move which launched the Welshman's long career in football management. 'Harry told me he was resigning and then said he was recommending I should take over,' said Pulis. 'I wasn't so sure at first, but he was adamant. Harry is without doubt the biggest character I have met in football and I have met a few. Technically, he is the best football coach I have ever worked with. His knowledge of the game and of players through every division is fantastic. Harry has been a great influence on me and I've learned so much from him.'

Harry then refuted rumours that he was soon to be returning to the Boleyn Ground as Billy Bonds' assistant at West Ham United. 'I saw a few of the stories, but, as things stand, there is nothing in them,' he said. 'I am very flattered to be linked with the club where I began my career as a player. But I have not spoken to anyone there about a job. Since I resigned I have certainly had a chat with Billy Bonds, but he was only asking my opinion on certain players. Who knows what will happen? Maybe Billy will call me with an offer. Who knows? It could be a week before I'm back, or it could be four years.'

It turned out to be a week. Redknapp joined Bonds at West Ham in mid-June, a move which resulted in a sense of disappointment in and around Dean Court. 'I am surprised he has ended up at another club so quickly,' said Norman Hayward. 'When he left he told me he was exhausted and wanted a break.' It is not clear whether Redknapp had discussed this position with Bonds prior to resigning from his job as manager of Bournemouth, although Harry insisted the appointment was not prearranged.

For the time being, the now former manager remained popular with the Cherries' fans, receiving a standing ovation when he made a swift return to Dean Court as the Hammers faced Bournemouth in a pre-season friendly. Norman Hayward presented Redknapp with a statuette of a racehorse to commemorate his services to the club and it appeared that despite his 'break' only lasting a matter of weeks, Redknapp was still held in high esteem by most in and around the club.

Looking back on his decision to resign many years later, it is clear that Harry had been offered a position at West Ham before resigning and his role as Tony Pulis's kingmaker was exaggerated. 'I needed a break from managing,' he says. 'Managing and coaching are completely different. When you're the coach there's no pressure; you go home at night, you sleep whether you win or lose. The players all like you because you're out there coaching. When you are the manager, it's a completely different world. If you don't pick the players, the players hate you, their wives hate you, their kids hate you, their mums and dads hate you. Everything stops with you. The fans hate you when you lose. It was non-stop and I'd had enough after a long, long spell and suddenly I got a chance to go and work as a coach and I fancied it; thought it would do me good to go and work with some players and coach every day which I enjoy doing.

'There'd been changes at Bournemouth. Norman Hayward had come in as chairman and I always felt Norman wanted Tony Pulis. He had a close relationship with Tony and they are still big friends. I think Norman was quite happy to give Tony the job. My relationship with Norman wasn't as good as it was with other people like Peter Hayward or Jim Nolan or people like that over the years, so I decided it was time to move on. You can't stay for ever, can you? I had a great time at Bournemouth. I loved every minute of it there. Absolutely fantastic.'

Stuart Morgan, Redknapp's trusted lieutenant, had seen his friend's departure coming for some time. 'Things changed with the death of Brian Tiler,' he says. 'The club went through about four or five chairmen and I think it got Harry down a little bit to be honest. Norman Hayward wanted to see the back of him. They never really got on. Hayward didn't exactly stand in his way.'

The supporters who had sung Harry's name long and loud at the friendly and throughout the previous nine seasons were in for a shock when Bournemouth's annual accounts were published at the end of 1992. They showed that Redknapp, who had a three-year rolling contract at the time of his departure, had negotiated a £100,000 golden handshake.

This revelation led to a furious reaction from the fans, many of whom have yet to forgive Redknapp to this day. It felt like a slap in the face to many of the supporters that had been making contributions to Cherry Aid in the belief that the club was short of money. Bournemouth Council, who, in a rare act of goodwill, had promised £15,000 to resurface the potholed car park around the ground, withdrew the offer upon learning of the payout.

Norman Hayward tried to quell the widespread anger by claiming that he had funded the payment out of his own pocket. Redknapp, meanwhile, looked to retain his dignity whilst defending his record in boosting the club's finances time and again. The likes of Shaun Teale, Gavin Peacock and Colin Clarke had all been sold on for a sizeable profit during Harry's tenure, and he was keen to remind people of the key role he had played in Jamie's development and subsequent transfer.

'If those cynical fans believe I shouldn't have been paid that £100,000,' he said, 'then I give you the name of Jamie Redknapp. Signed for nothing and then sold for £350,000, with another £350,000 eventually reaching the club after Jamie had made so many appearances for Liverpool. A man is entitled to £100,000 if a club gets £700,000 for his own kid.'

Even today, Harry makes no apology for accepting the payment. 'Norman Hayward was looking to make a change,' he says. 'I had money that I was owed, and some of it was wages I hadn't been paid. Everything I got I was entitled to; it was my money. Every manager who leaves a football club, I don't care who they are, gets paid off. What I was due was what I was due.

'My conscience is completely and utterly clear.'

Epilogue

HARRY Redknapp took his leave from Dean Court in June 1992, but his association with the club continues to this day.

Of the eight permanent Cherries managers that have succeeded him, seven either played with or under Redknapp.

Tony Pulis took the reins between 1992 and 1994 and, despite this first foray into management leading to calls from fans for his sacking, went on to carve out a successful career as a Premier League manager. Pulis's management style draws comparison with his presence on the pitch as a hard-tackling midfielder. Harry says, 'Tony couldn't really play, but he knew how to stop those that could.'

Former team-mate Mel Machin managed the Cherries for six years between 1994 and 2000, at a time when Harry threatened to become financially involved to save the club when liquidation appeared imminent. Machin was succeeded by long-serving Redknapp midfielder Sean O'Driscoll, who occupied the manager's office at Dean Court for a further six years to 2006. Both men are fondly remembered by the Cherries' supporters, which is significantly more than can be said for former striker Jimmy Quinn. Quinn scored 24 goals in 54 appearances in his one and only season as a Bournemouth player, but lasted only half as long as the club's manager. The Ulsterman took over from Kevin Bond in September of 2008 but, after just eight wins in 25 games, he departed on New Year's Eve four months later.

Lee Bradbury, who managed the club for 14 months between 2011 and 2012, played for Portsmouth during Harry's initial tenure at Fratton Park, although the striker did not feature prominently under Redknapp, spending much of this period on loan elsewhere.

The most significant of the Redknapp diaspora is Eddie Howe, who went on to replace Harry as the club's greatest-ever manager upon guiding the club to the Premier League in 2015. The teenage Howe was already part of the youth system at Dean Court in the latter days of Redknapp's tenure at the club, although Harry admits he has no recollection of the youngster.

Ten years later, Redknapp had become well aware of the defender and, impressed by a series of solid seasons in the Bournemouth rearguard, he made Howe his first signing two days after assuming the reins at south coast neighbours Portsmouth in March 2002. Howe's two years at Fratton Park proved ill-fated, however, as he suffered a season-ending injury on his debut at Preston North End two days after signing and then broke down with the same injury on the first match of his return in the opening game of the following campaign against Nottingham Forest.

That was to be the sum total of Howe's appearances for Portsmouth. He was loaned out by Redknapp to Swindon in 2004 but did not play a single minute for the Robins. Desperate to extend his playing career, Howe returned to Bournemouth on loan at the start of the 2004/05 season, an arrangement that was made permanent three months later when the fan-funded 'Eddieshare' appeal and Redknapp's goodwill brought him back to Dean Court.

When Howe's playing days came to an early conclusion at just 29 after his injuries caught up with him two years later, long-time Redknapp associate Kevin Bond gave the now retired defender his first role in coaching. Bond had followed his father in managing Bournemouth from 2006 to 2008, a period of intense turmoil for the club during which the Cherries were relegated to League Two after a ten-point deduction for financial irregularities in 2007/08 and then suffered a further 17-point penalty for additional offences before they had even kicked a ball in the 2008/09 season.

Bond was replaced by Jimmy Quinn after only a handful of games that season. With Quinn's management style failing to galvanise his squad or supporters, the club was staring relegation from the Football League and almost inevitable extinction in the face.

The former striker was duly relieved of his duties and with next to no money to fund a replacement, the Cherries turned to the 31-year-old Howe. Appointing such a youthful figure with no management experience whatsoever appeared almost suicidal for a club in its darkest hour. However, Howe defied all expectations, keeping the Cherries in the League before masterminding a series of promotions which, despite him spending almost two years at Burnley in the intervening period, saw Bournemouth promoted to the top tier of English football for the first time in their history in 2015.

This fairytale ascent did not go unnoticed by Redknapp who, with his own career in management winding down as he approached 70, found himself back in the stands at Dean Court more and more often. 'I think they are the best team to come out of the Championship in the past ten years,' he said at the start of 2016. 'I just love watching them play. It is how I enjoy the game being played. They have been absolutely fantastic, a real breath of fresh air. They play as well as anyone in the division and, while they may not win every week, when I watch other games it just doesn't compare with Bournemouth. Everything about the team is so good and the players have made so much progress. The whole group has been amazing. Eddie has done such a wonderful job; it is just incredible. Maxim Demin and Eddie Howe are the two key players in the success of the club. Eddie has been fantastic; the job he has done there has been unbelievable.'

Although he trumped Redknapp's 1987 Third Division title triumph by winning the Football League Championship in 2015, the self-effacing Howe maintains that Redknapp tops the list of Cherries managers. 'Personally, I don't believe that our title is superior because Harry was at the club a long time and he was the one who led the club into the Championship for the first time,' says Howe. 'What he has done with his career after those moments with Bournemouth are incredible achievements so I always regard Harry as Bournemouth's iconic manager and that will not change.'

Bournemouth's only manager not to have played with or under Harry since he resigned as the Cherries' manager in 1992 was Paul Groves. He was, however, on Redknapp's coaching staff at Portsmouth between 2006 and 2008.

Groves, who had captained Grimsby to the Auto Windscreens Trophy when the Mariners beat Bournemouth at Wembley in 1998, succeeded Lee Bradbury at Dean Court in March 2012. His tenure was not a success, recording just three victories from 20 games in charge. With Groves struggling at the beginning of the 2012/13 season, despite significant investment in the playing squad, Bournemouth's owners Maxim Demin and Eddie Mitchell drafted in Redknapp as an advisor to their manager.

'I met Harry for a chat this morning and he offered to come in on a voluntary basis,' said Mitchell at the time. 'He still has a passion for the club and for football and he's got too much to offer for us to let him slip through our fingers. I have said in the past we have got on our doorstep one of the best managers in the country. I have spoken to Paul about bringing Harry closer. We are all trying to gain knowledge from Harry and, hopefully, we will. It would be great to be able to have that knowledge around the club and I would like to be able to bring it closer, and that is what I am going to try to do.'

Whilst Redknapp's presence cannot have been very reassuring for Groves, Harry was keen to play down his new role. 'They have got a good manager and a good coaching staff,' he said. 'If I can just weigh in with little bits here and there, and if they want to ask my opinion, I am only too pleased. It is not a financial thing in any shape or form. If they give me a cup of tea at half-time in the boardroom, I would be delighted. That is all I want out of it. It is not a case of me coming in for any reason other than Eddie Mitchell asked me if I could just give them a little bit of a hand if I can, where I can. I will do that. If I can help in any way, I will, because I have got a lot of time for the football club. This is home for me, this is where I live. I spent nearly ten years here as manager, so I love the club.'

With Groves losing the support of Cherries' supporters, Eddie Mitchell's desire to see Redknapp around the club bore the hallmarks of seduction. This appeared to be all but confirmed at the end of September 2012 when, with Groves unable to turn results around, several newspapers claimed that Redknapp had rejected the chance to retake the reins at Dean Court as he awaited offers from bigger clubs.

Harry held out for two months before becoming the new manager of Queens Park Rangers, by which time Groves had been replaced by the returning Eddie Howe. Howe did not, it appears, require any direct assistance from his old manager.

Despite rumours about the nature of his involvement with team affairs whilst Groves was in charge at Dean Court, Redknapp maintains that it was little more than superficial. 'I never went in the dressing room or got involved.' he says. 'I went to a game at Yeovil where they won and played ever so well. I thought Paul Groves and his assistant Shaun Brooks were so unlucky it was unbelievable. I thought the football they played was fantastic. Every bit of bad luck that could have been had, they were getting.'

As well as having a hand in producing an apparently endless string of graduates to perform his old job, Harry has frequently helped his successors at Bournemouth to improve their playing squads. Whilst he was manager of West Ham, Dean Court became something of a finishing school for the likes of Rio Ferdinand and Jermain Defoe. Both men played for Bournemouth in the embryonic stages of their careers, with Defoe's ten goals in as many games seeing Bournemouth narrowly miss out on a play-off berth in 2001.

As well as frequently supplying the Cherries with loan players whilst at Upton Park, Redknapp often offloaded surplus squad members on a permanent basis. The most notable names to make this journey from east London to the south coast were midfielder Matt Holland and centre-forward Steve Jones.

Holland became team captain at just 22 years of age. He soon found himself acting as a figurehead in the appeal to save the Cherries from liquidation in January of 1997, before the club sold him for £800,000 to Charlton in July of that year to do just that.

Redknapp sold Steve Jones to Bournemouth for £150,000 in November 1994 and was so impressed by the striker's performances at Dean Court that he brought him back to the Boleyn Ground in May 1996. Between those transfers, Jones scored 26 goals in 74 games and played a key role in saving Bournemouth from relegation to the Fourth Division in the 1994/95 season.

Despite going on to manage various clubs for 25 years after he left Dean Court, Redknapp has found himself facing the Cherries just four times in competitive games over that lengthy period. Harry managed exclusively in the Premier League and the Championship of English football during that time, whereas Bournemouth spent the vast majority of those years in Leagues One and Two.

The first meeting between Redknapp and Bournemouth occurred in October 1999 in the third round of the Worthington League Cup. With Eddie Howe in defence, Bournemouth, who were mid-table in League One at the time, kept Premier League West Ham at bay for an hour before Marc Keller and a young Frank Lampard gave Harry victory over his former club.

Another 14 years would go by before Redknapp would lead a team into a fixture against the Cherries. With Bournemouth finding their feet in the Championship after an absence of 23 years, a Joey Barton-inspired QPR ran out 3-0 winners at Loftus Road. The return fixture the following April saw Bournemouth gain revenge in a 2-1 victory that saw Harry sit in the away dugout at Dean Court in a competitive match for the only time in his career to date.

In August of 2017, with Bournemouth implausibly kicking off their third Premier League season, the Cherries faced Birmingham City in the Carabao League Cup during Redknapp's brief spell at the helm. Bournemouth had never lost at St Andrew's, and this trend continued as Eddie Howe's team saw off the Blues and Redknapp in a 2-1 victory.

Where official fixtures between Harry and the Cherries have been minimal, Redknapp ensured that the teams he was managing played a pre-season friendly at Dean Court on an almost annual basis. The visits of the likes of Spurs, West Ham and Portsmouth brought a much-needed financial boost to the cash-strapped club. 'I came here every year and played a pre-season game, whichever club I was at,' says Redknapp. 'That was always the first game on the list. And we always let them keep the gate money; I always insisted with the chairman. They just paid for the coach or something, instead of splitting the gate like normal.'

Harry's altruism went further more than once as Bournemouth teetered on the brink of liquidation. In 1997 he made a significant donation to the fan-led appeal to buy the club after an avalanche of winding-up orders had almost plunged the Cherries into the abyss. 'I was involved with Bournemouth at that time,' Harry recalls, without going into detail. 'I did make a loan or whatever. Any way I could've helped, I would've helped.'

The fan buyout succeeded and Bournemouth became the Football League's first supporter-owned community club. This arrangement proved less than ideal, however, as new investment became difficult to attract due to the fact that the fans would always retain a 51% controlling interest in the Cherries under the auspices of their constitution.

By November 2004, Bournemouth were looking for an injection of £5 million to end their financial woes once and for all. The ideal of the community-owned club had faltered and the Cherries were permanently up for sale. Redknapp was days from resigning his post as manager of Portsmouth for the first time, and this pending departure led him to speculate about the possibility of owning his former employer. 'Bournemouth have always looked for someone to come in and buy the club and I think I would enjoy coming in and getting involved,' he said at the time. 'One day in the future it is certainly something I would be interested in doing. I'd look to bring in one or two friends who also care about the club. It would definitely interest me at some point, but it is a way down the line for me at this moment. They are terrific people at Bournemouth and if I could get involved and help out in some way and make an investment into the club, I would do that. But it is not like it will happen today or tomorrow. Who knows when?'

The answer turned out to be never, as Redknapp continued in management for another 13 years. By then, the Cherries had struck gold under Eddie Howe and they no longer required investment from their former manager.

Following the unprecedented success of the club in recent years, it looks likely that Harry will never return to Bournemouth in an official capacity. However, the chance of Redknapp once again appearing on the team sheet at Dean Court remains a possibility. In May 2014, Redknapp's seven-year-old grandson, also called Harry, signed for the Cherries' academy. Described as 'direct, strong and a good little goalscorer' by Bournemouth's technical development officer Matt Holmes, Redknapp junior could yet continue his family's legacy at AFC Bournemouth.